SUPERMAN™

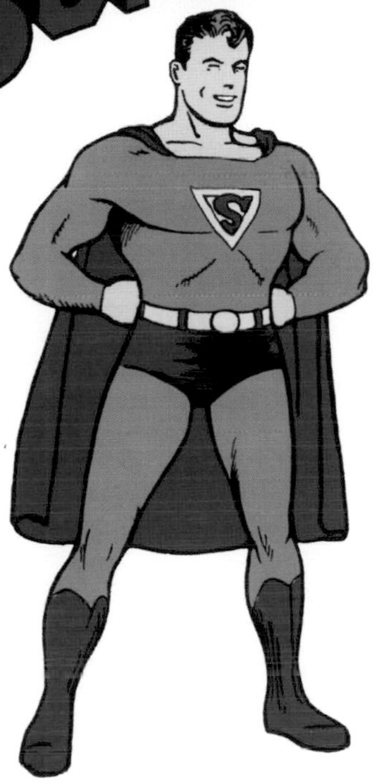

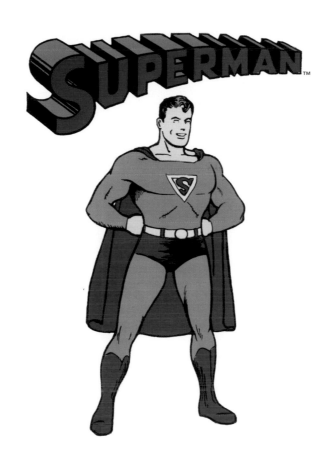

**LONDON, NEW YORK, MELBOURNE,
MUNICH, AND DELHI**

Senior Editor Alastair Dougall
Senior Designer and Brand Manager Robert Perry
Designers Owen Bennett, Nick Avery
Design Manager Maxine Pedliham
Publishing Manager Julie Ferris
Managing Editor Laura Gilbert
Art Director Ron Stobbart
Publishing Director Simon Beecroft
Senior Pre-Production Producer Jennifer Murray
Senior Producer Shabana Shakir

Superman created by Jerry Siegel and Joe Shuster

First published in the United States in 2013 by
DK Publishing. 375 Hudson Street, New York, New York 10014.

10 9 8 7 6 5 4 3 2 1

001-184083-May/13

DORL29338

A catalog record for this book is available from the Library of Congress.

ISBN: 978-1-4654-0875-4

Color reproduction by Altaimage, UK
Printed and bound in China by Hung Hing

Discover more at
www.dk.com

SUPERMAN™

THE ULTIMATE GUIDE TO THE MAN OF STEEL

WRITTEN BY

DANIEL WALLACE

CONTENTS

"I'm here to help
out and make
things better
any way I can.
I'm here to stay."
Superman

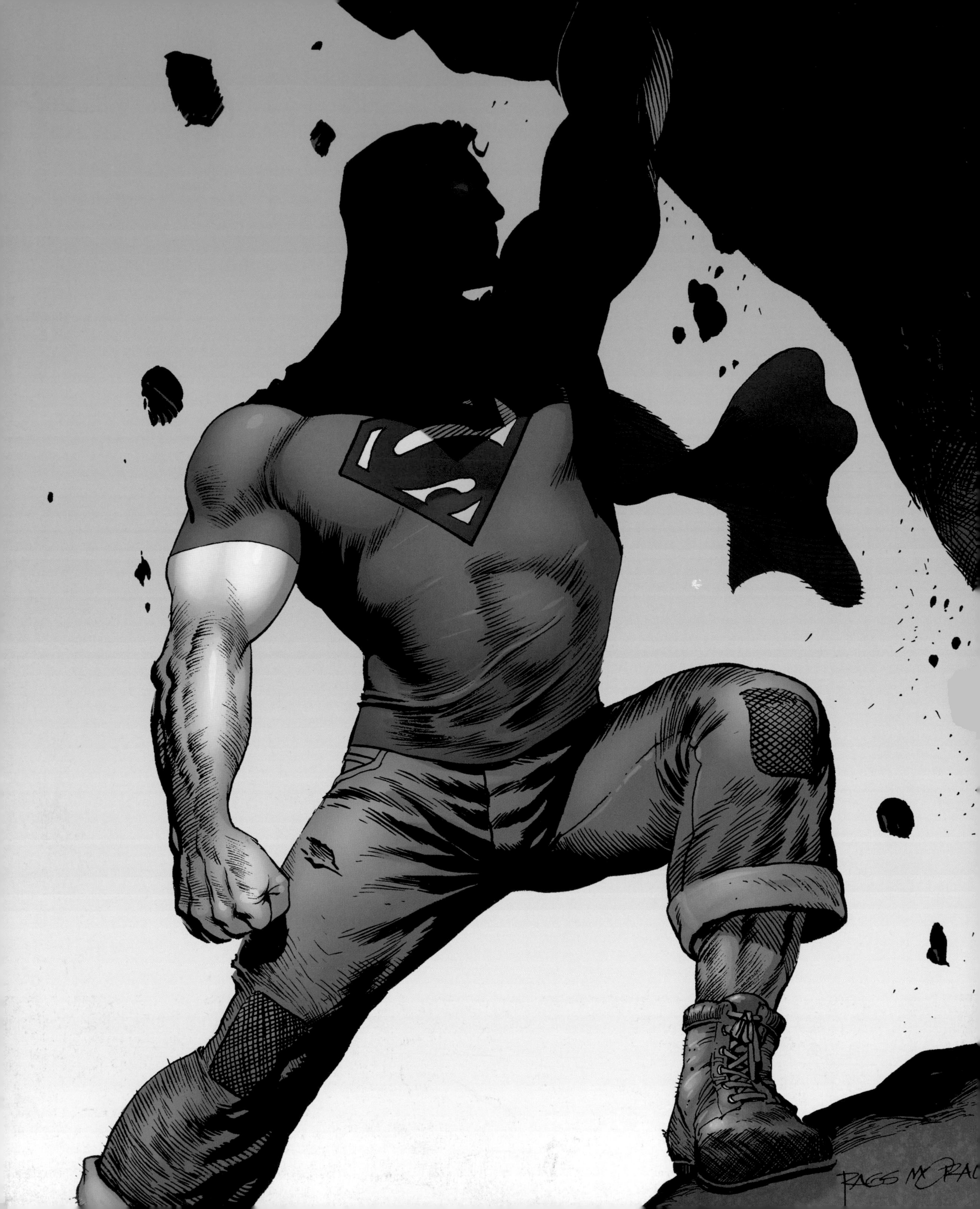

FOREWORD

SUPERMAN'S FIRST ADVENTURE, in *Action Comics* #1 June 1938, opens in mid-leap, with the story already underway. The narrative, edited to simulate Superman's pace and velocity, drags us into its slipstream and, with a cocky grin of encouragement, leaves us no option but to accelerate to keep up.

From the opening hallucinatory flash of that red cape blurring through the night, via 75 years of regular appearances in an array of comic book titles, radio shows, movies, novels, games, and even musicals, Superman's tireless race to reach the next emergency, save the next life, thwart the next criminal masterplan, has never let up and shows no signs of stopping. That's how it is with Superman; he was created to be unstoppable.

Of all his great powers (over the years Superman has acquired an enviable list, including heat vision, freeze breath, X-ray vision, and more) it may well turn out to be the special talents of longevity and adaptability that count for most. In his time, and without losing any of the basics of his enduring appeal, Superman has been a vigilante champion of the oppressed, a true-blue American patriot, a suburban patriarch, a troubled cosmic seeker, a go-getting yuppie, an alien Messiah, a romantic lead, and an opinionated radical.

For three-quarters of a century, this ultimate immigrant hero, welcomed to Earth from a doomed world, has dramatized, on an epic stage of distant worlds, cosmic destinies and far-flung futures, all the familiar conflicts, battles and triumphs of everyday life. As you'll see, the best Superman stories dress in the gaudy trappings of pulp science fiction; however, they also wrestle with big, universal emotions of grief and triumph, jealousy, selfless love and, most of all, hope. The Man of Tomorrow, born on a distant planet, first and greatest of the super heroes is, ironically, among the most human.

Somewhere, right now, Superman is in mid-leap. Somewhere, he's already on his way to save the world, or stop a bully. Somewhere, the clock is already ticking, the story has already begun.

Here's your chance to get caught up.

Grant Morrison
Scotland, October 2012

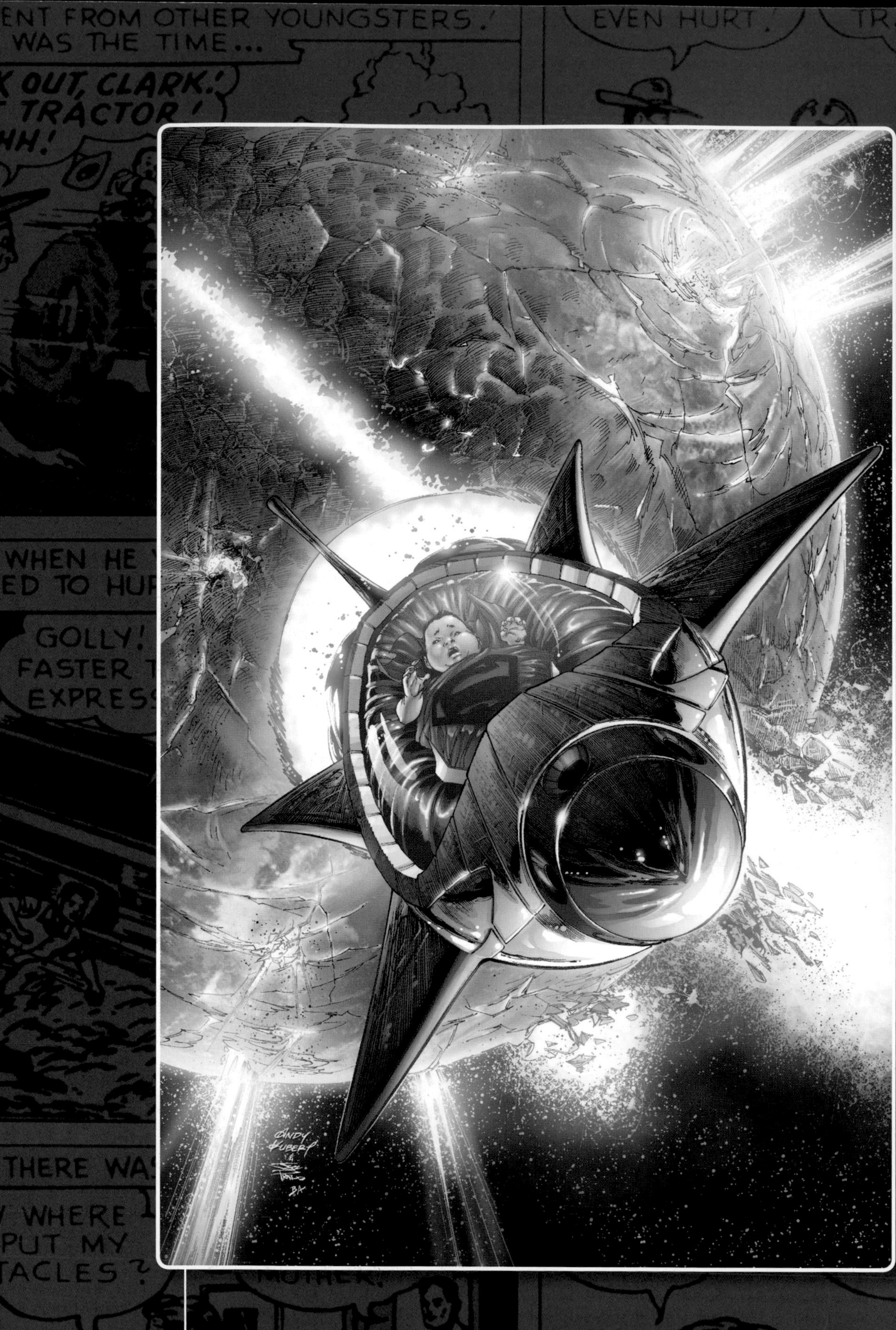

ENT FROM OTHER YOUNGSTERS.
WAS THE TIME...
EVEN HURT.
K OUT, CLARK.
T TRACTOR!
WHEN HE
ED TO HU
GOLLY!
FASTER T
EXPRESS
THERE WAS
WHERE
PUT MY
TACLES?
MOTHER.

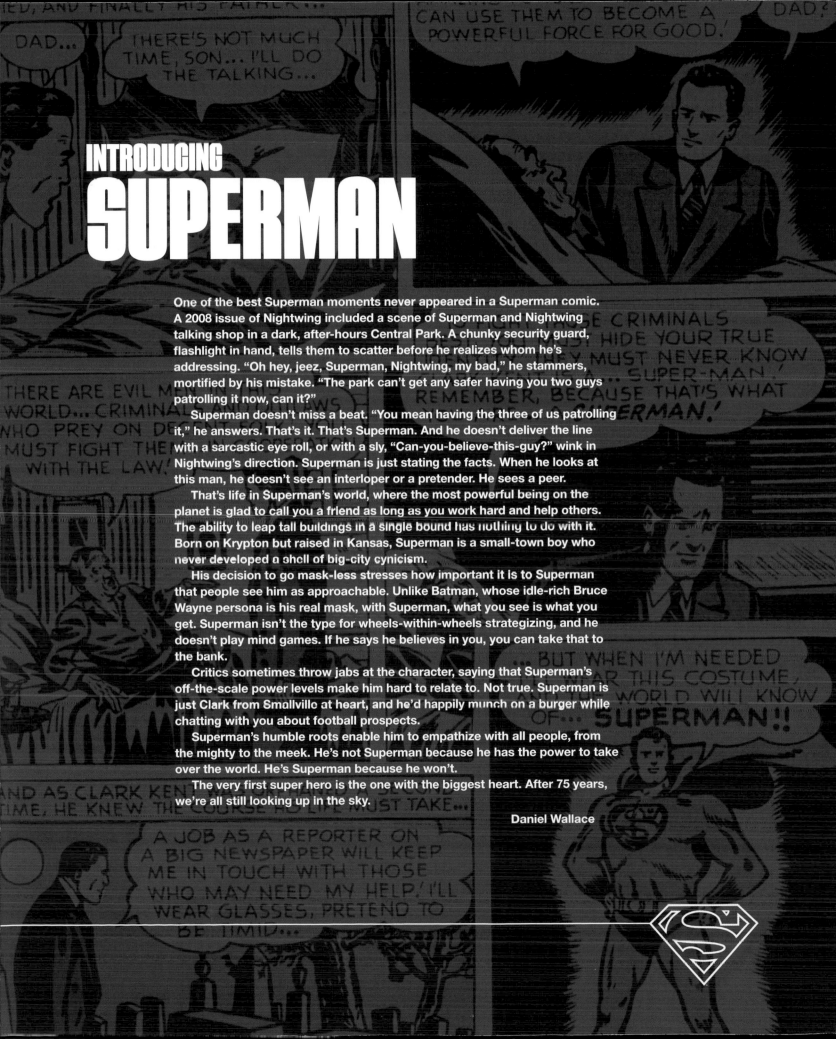

INTRODUCING
SUPERMAN

One of the best Superman moments never appeared in a Superman comic. A 2008 issue of Nightwing included a scene of Superman and Nightwing talking shop in a dark, after-hours Central Park. A chunky security guard, flashlight in hand, tells them to scatter before he realizes whom he's addressing. "Oh hey, jeez, Superman, Nightwing, my bad," he stammers, mortified by his mistake. "The park can't get any safer having you two guys patrolling it now, can it?"

Superman doesn't miss a beat. "You mean having the three of us patrolling it," he answers. That's it. That's Superman. And he doesn't deliver the line with a sarcastic eye roll, or with a sly, "Can-you-believe-this-guy?" wink in Nightwing's direction. Superman is just stating the facts. When he looks at this man, he doesn't see an interloper or a pretender. He sees a peer.

That's life in Superman's world, where the most powerful being on the planet is glad to call you a friend as long as you work hard and help others. The ability to leap tall buildings in a single bound has nothing to do with it. Born on Krypton but raised in Kansas, Superman is a small-town boy who never developed a shell of big-city cynicism.

His decision to go mask-less stresses how important it is to Superman that people see him as approachable. Unlike Batman, whose idle-rich Bruce Wayne persona is his real mask, with Superman, what you see is what you get. Superman isn't the type for wheels-within-wheels strategizing, and he doesn't play mind games. If he says he believes in you, you can take that to the bank.

Critics sometimes throw jabs at the character, saying that Superman's off-the-scale power levels make him hard to relate to. Not true. Superman is just Clark from Smallville at heart, and he'd happily munch on a burger while chatting with you about football prospects.

Superman's humble roots enable him to empathize with all people, from the mighty to the meek. He's not Superman because he has the power to take over the world. He's Superman because he won't.

The very first super hero is the one with the biggest heart. After 75 years, we're all still looking up in the sky.

Daniel Wallace

LOOK!

UP IN THE SKY... IT'S A BIRD... IT'S A PLANE... NO, ITS...

SUPERMAN!

64 PAGES OF ACTION!

ALL IN FULL COLOR

THE COMPLETE STORY OF THE DARING EXPLOITS OF THE ONE AND ONLY SUPERMAN

The first issue of the self-titled *Superman* series appeared in May 1939. Having spun off from *Action Comics*, the series marked the first time a comic book character had ever gone on to headline his own title. The first issue reprinted some *Action Comics* material for the benefit of new readers, but introduced Superman's adoptive parents, the Kents.

When two teenage sci-fi fans got together, their brainstorming led to the creation of a new heroic archetype. Jerry Siegel had a writer's ear for storytelling, while Joe Shuster drew square-jawed protagonists who looked like they could move mountains. The high school classmates collaborated on a mimeographed fan publication titled *Science Fiction*, in which they published a story entitled "The Reign of the Superman." This tale starred an average man who became an evil genius. The character didn't bear much resemblance to the future Man of Steel, but Siegel and Shuster recycled the name for a muscular champion of the oppressed who had come to Earth from a far-off, alien planet.

Siegel and Shuster pitched their Superman character to newspaper syndicates and to publishers just getting started in the growing field of comic books. The only thing they got in return was a stack of rejection letters. Shuster burned the original pages of their Superman submission. Only the cover survived the flames.

But their Superman idea wouldn't die, and the two reworked the concept while they lined up paying gigs as comics professionals. DC published Siegel and Shuster in the pages of *New Fun Comics*, where their characters Henri Duval and Dr. Occult appealed to those with a taste for military adventure and weird mysticism. Comic books had begun to show signs of becoming the next big thing, and DC hired Siegel and Shuster to supply regular doses of fresh content. They supplied the features "Federal Men" and "Radio Squad," and in the all-new title *Detective Comics* they had minor hits with "Slam Bradley" and "Bart Regan, Spy."

Superman remained their dream project, and they finally saw their chance with DC's launch of *Action Comics* in 1938. The new hero got cover billing and immediately struck a chord with readers. This Superman, who could "hurdle a twenty-story building," soon had DC flying high, and the world's first true super hero changed the course of the American comics industry.

"All this time we really felt that we had something that was very different, something that the public would really take to its heart."

Jerry Siegel

JERRY SIEGEL

The son of Jewish immigrants who settled in Cleveland, Ohio, Jerry Siegel was the youngest of six children and had a passion for tales of the fantastic. Not finding enough outlets for his imagination, Siegel decided to make his own stories, starting one of the first science-fiction fan magazines and collaborating with classmate Joe Shuster on parody comic strips appearing in their high-school newspaper. Siegel and Shuster decided to break into comics together, but it took years before their Superman concept finally found a home.

JOE SHUSTER

Joe Shuster grew up in a Jewish family in Toronto, the son of a tailor who couldn't afford expensive drawing materials. The artistically-minded Shuster earned cash as a newspaper delivery boy for Toronto's *Daily Star* and scrounged drawing paper from discarded rolls of wallpaper. In 1924, his family moved to Cleveland, where Shuster met Jerry Siegel. Their mutual interest in science fiction led to a professional partnership, and their work became a frequent sight in the earliest titles published by DC. When *Superman* #1 appeared in 1939, it included this from Shuster: "I hope the boys and girls of America enjoy reading Superman as much as Jerry and I enjoy writing and drawing it."

No. 1   JUNE, 1938

Action Comics

10¢

Publication Date
June 1938

Editor
Vincent Sullivan

Cover Artist
Joe Shuster

Writer
Jerry Siegel

Penciller
Joe Shuster

Inker
Joe Shuster

ACTION COMICS
Vol. 1   # 1

> "I still can't believe my senses! He's not human! Thank heaven he's apparently on the side of law and order!"
>
> **Governor of Metropolis**

Main Characters: Superman, Lois Lane
Main Supporting Characters: George Taylor, Butch Matson, Senator Barrows, Alex Greer
Main Locations: Metropolis

BACKGROUND

With the first issue of *Action Comics*, DC inaugurated the age of the super hero. Other DC titles on the newsstand in 1938, including *Detective Comics* and *More Fun Comics,* drew on familiar humor and private-eye genres. *Action Comics* #1 contained straightforward adventure tales from the likes of boxer Pep Morgan and Scoop Scanlon, Five-Star Reporter. No one expected the Superman feature to become the issue's breakout hit.

Yet the cover promised something no one had never seen before: a man in a brightly colored costume with a billowing cape, holding a Sedan above his head and smashing it into a barricade while stunned observers fled the scene. Everything that would define the super hero archetype—the costume, the powers, the fight for justice—was present on that cover.

The interior pages of *Action Comics* #1 added more elements crucial to the super hero mythos, such as the hero's secret identity and his often uneasy relationship with the public.

Of course, readers of that first issue had no idea that they'd just witnessed the birth of a major American genre. But they did know that they wanted more. *Action Comics* became DC's first runaway success; within a year *Detective Comics* had followed *Action*'s template by introducing DC's second super hero star, the Batman.

THE STORY

Saving an innocent woman from execution and putting a bully in his place are all in a day's work for Superman. His debut adventure also sets up the dynamic between Clark Kent and Lois Lane. Superman isn't yet able to fly, but he has enough strength, speed, and toughness to fight injustice.

A short overview of Superman's origin and his otherworldly abilities opens the issue, explaining that a scientist from a doomed planet sent his son to Earth as a baby. A passing motorist found the rocket and its passenger, and delivered the infant to an orphanage. The boy's incredible abilities soon became obvious **[1]**.

By the time the alien reached adulthood, he could leap as high as a 20-story building and outrun an express train **[2]**. The visitor resolved to use his powers to help the powerless as Superman **[3]**.

As the adventure opens, Superman races through the night, a bound woman in his arms. His destination is the governor's mansion. When the butler refuses to let him see the governor, Superman tears the solid steel door of the governor's bedchamber off its hinges **[4]**.

Superman hands over a confession by the murderess he's just deposited on the mansion's lawn, proving the innocence of another woman who is scheduled to die in the electric chair in less than ten minutes **[5]**. Moments before the switch is thrown, the governor phones the prison and halts the execution.

The next day, *Daily Star* reporter Clark Kent meets with his editor, who assigns him to cover the Superman beat **[6]**. Clark promises, "If I can't find out anything about this Superman, no one can!"

After saving a woman from being beaten by her husband, Clark asks his fellow reporter Lois Lane on a date. As they share a dance, he asks her why she normally avoids him at the office **[7]**. Suddenly gangster Butch Matson muscles in. Clark, not wanting to blow his cover in front of Lois, plays the part of a meek pushover **[8]**, but Lois pluckily slaps Matson's face. She leaves the club, accusing Clark of being a spineless coward. Matson and his hoodlums follow, run her cab off the road, and kidnap her **[9]**. Meanwhile, Clark—as Superman—prepares for another round with Butch Matson.

Superman pursues Matson's Sedan at high speed, picks it up with his bare hands, shakes its passengers loose **[10]**, and smashes it beyond repair. He then hefts Matson with one hand and hangs him from a telephone pole **[11]**.

Lois doesn't have a way back into town, but that's not a problem for Superman. He cradles her in his arms and carries her home with a series of tremendous leaps **[12]**.

The next morning, Clark Kent takes the train to Washington DC to investigate government corruption. As Superman, he hangs outside the apartment window of Senator Barrows, eavesdropping on an incriminating conversation between the senator and slick lobbyist Alex Greer.

Superman decides to frighten Greer into a confession by taking him on a high-wire tour of the city's telephone lines. In a cliffhanger ending, Superman—not yet possessing the ability to fly—misjudges a jump and appears to be headed for a fall **[13]**…

SUPERMAN SPEAKS

Superman is a hero who can often do more good with his words than with his fists. Though he might doubt himself in private moments, Superman is a source of inspiration for millions.

"I'll wear glasses, pretend to be timid… but when I'm needed I'll wear this costume and the world will know of… Superman!"
(Superman #53, 1948)

"That's the American Way. Life, liberty, and the pursuit of happiness —and second chances. That's the idea that America was founded on, but it's not just for people born here. It's for everyone."
(Superman #711, 2011)

"I worry because everyone seems to look up to me and it's making me a little uncomfortable. I can try but I can't solve every problem. I don't know if I can live up to this… myth they want me to be."
(JLA #6, 1997)

"From now on, whenever there are people who need my very special kind of help, it won't be a job for plain, ordinary Clark Kent. It'll be a job for Superman."
(The Man of Steel, 1986)

"It's never as bad as it seems. You're much stronger than you think you are. Trust me."
(All-Star Superman #10, 2006)

"For years I've been playing big brother to the human race. Have I been wrong? Are they depending on me too much... too often?"
(Superman #247, 1972)

"You have no idea what It means to be Superman. It's not about where you were born. Or what powers you have. Or what you wear on your chest. It's about what you do... it's about action."
(Infinite Crisis, 2006)

"All I know is that we have to try. That's what life is. We try. We push back against the darkness, just a little."
(Superman #701, 2010)

"In this world, there is right and there is wrong, and that distinction is not difficult to make."
(Kingdom Come #3, 1996)

"I'm here to stand up for people when they can't stand up for themselves, and I'm here to help out and make things better any way I can. I'm here to stay."
(Action Comics #8, 2012)

"Dreams save us. Dreams lift us up and transform us. And on my soul, I swear, until my dream of a world where dignity, honor and justice becomes the reality we all share, I'll never stop fighting."
(Action Comics #775, 2001)

"The Batman works as well as he does in Gotham City because the people there tend to fear him. But I gotta say... It sure is great to be loved."
(Action Comics #594, 1987)

The suit is woven from exotic alien fibers that have a tensile strength far beyond any substance known to Earth science. Kryptonian biotech allows the suit to appear instantly at its wearer's command, and to disappear just as quickly.

Superman's cape accompanied him to Earth inside his escape rocket and is indestructible. It had originally been worn by Jor-El's father, and was the only item of Kryptonian clothing that Superman possessed during his early career.

The S-shield insignia is the symbol of Krypton's House of El, the family to which Superman—Kal-El—belongs. The symbol appeared on the suit after it sensed its wearer's bloodline. When the suit is in its colorless, inert state, the symbol completely disappears.

KRYPTONIAN TECH

In his early adventures in Metropolis, Superman wore his cape with his regular street clothes, including a t-shirt printed with the S insignia. During a fight aboard Brainiac's world-collector ship, Superman retrieved a suit made of a pure white material, which reacted to his touch and displayed the red, yellow, and blue colors of the House of El. Explaining to the people of Metropolis that his new look represented Kryptonian formal wear, Superman joked that he'd keep the outfit since "it matches the cape."

The belt is ceremonial, though Superman can use its hidden compartments to carry small, flat items while keeping his hands free.

Superman's boots are nearly indestructible and are able to stand up to the friction of running at super speed. Before he obtained his suit, Superman used to wear out multiple pairs of work boots every week.

THE SUIT

It's the unmistakable uniform of the world's most famous super hero. Bold primary colors, a swirling cape, and a Kryptonian crest resembling the letter S announce the arrival of the Man of Steel.

1939 The original costume established the look; only the S-shield would undergo significant revision.

1942 During wartime, Superman's costume featured an elegant S-shield.

1955 The S-shield incorporated blocky elements as Superman entered the Silver Age.

1993 Following his death and return, Superman wore an all-black suit without a cape.

1997 A containment suit maintained his shape when Superman became a being of pure energy.

2002 Black replaced yellow as the backgro of the S-shield after the Imperiex war.

STYLE EVOLUTION

1961 Superman's S-shield settled into a consistent form during this period.

1978 The S-shield grew more substantial as Superman faced the challenges of the Bronze Age.

1987 Superman's Crisis on Infinite Earths' suit was sewn by Martha Kent.

2004 The suit's yellow highlights returned around the time of the Vanishing incident.

2006 The Secret Origin retelling placed him in a classic, traditional version of the costume.

2011 The New 52 costume has a high collar, solid blue pants, and a raised S-shield.

The costume is universally famous, and the combination of primary colors with a flared-cape silhouette has changed very little over the years. In any era, it's always clear when Superman is on the scene.

SUPERPOWERS

On Krypton he would have been an ordinary person, but Earth's yellow sun fueled an array of incredible abilities. With more raw power than just about any other hero on the planet, it's no wonder the people of Metropolis gave him the name Superman!

EARTH'S YELLOW SUN —THE SOURCE OF ALL SUPERMAN'S POWER

SOLAR BATTERIES

The red sun of Krypton kept the latent superpowers of Kryptonians in check. But Earth's yellow sun charges the cells of Superman's body and makes his amazing abilities possible, including his super-hearing and his near-photographic memory. Superman weakens when his body is deprived of solar radiation.

INVULNERABILITY Almost nothing on Earth can harm Superman. Bullets bounce off his skin; he can enter a volcano without an environmental suit. Superman has been slammed by a high-speed train and exposed himself to the vacuum of space without suffering any lasting damage. Even his fingernails are invulnerable.

SUPER-SPEED His running speed and reaction time almost put Superman in the same class as The Flash. Superman has caught bullets in mid-air and read entire medical texts in seconds.

X-RAY VISION Superman's Kryptonian eyes can detect radiation beyond the visible light spectrum, and his X-ray vision can penetrate any substance except lead. His eyes also enable him to scan his surroundings at microscopic level or spot an object hundreds of miles away.

HEAT VISION
Superman's eyes can emit beams of microwave radiation capable of melting rock. Because he can fire his heat beams at anything he sees through his crystal-clear, telescopic vision, Superman rarely misses his target.

COMBAT MASTER Superman has trained with some of the world's greatest warriors. His knowledge helps him to use his skills with precision and avoid unnecessary damage.

FLIGHT Superman can fly, controlling direction and speed with unconscious mental commands. He combines flying abilities with super-strength to accomplish astonishing feats. Superman's maximum flight speed is unknown; in space, he accelerates to incredible velocities.

SUPER-STRENGTH

Superman can bend steel and swing telephone poles like baseball bats. When trading blows with a super-powered enemy, the concussive force of his punches can shatter every window for a city block. Superman rarely cuts loose with the full power of his super-strength, for fear that he may accidentally hurt someone more than he intends.

HOW STRONG IS SUPERMAN?

FREEZE BREATH By inhaling and pressurizing a lungful of air, Superman can exhale at sub-zero temperatures and freeze foes in their tracks. He has also used his breath as a hurricane-force deterrent against crowds of enemies. With a single breath, Superman can survive for hours in space or underwater.

INTELLIGENCE Superman can remember anything he has ever read or seen. He has a gift for logic puzzles and games of strategy.

21

HOW STRONG IS SUPERMAN?

The Man of Steel's strength levels have varied over the years, but he can easily crush stone with his fists and carry tanks on his back. At his upper limits, Superman has moved planets.

GOLDEN AGE BEGINNINGS

When Superman debuted in the 1930s, he couldn't fly—at least not at first—but he had no trouble leaping 20-story buildings. Superman could run faster than an express train and heft cars above his head. When it came to invulnerability, only a bursting shell could break his skin. Superman's powers were said to be the result of the lower gravity of Earth as compared to Krypton.

SILVER AGE POWERHOUSE

As the character moved through the sci-fi-obsessed 1950s and beyond, he acquired new powers and increased his existing abilities to almost unimaginable extremes. Superman could now not only fly faster than the speed of light, he could break the "time barrier" and visit both the past and the future. In addition to possessing heat vision, X-ray vision, and freeze breath, Superman exhibited a few, rarely-used skills, including the power of super-ventriloquism. Sunlight took over from gravity as the explanation for Superman's superpowers.

THE MODERN AGE

A reboot in the mid-1980s limited Superman's powers. Superman didn't gain the ability to fly until his late teens. An invisible, telekinetic aura became the explanation for Superman's invulnerability; this aura also protected his costume from damage. Superman could no longer fly at light speed, and he initially needed to breathe through an oxygen mask when traveling through outer space.

THE NEW 52

Superman's fresh beginning incorporated elements from every era. As the Man of Steel, he was younger, less experienced, and had not yet discovered the limits of his abilities. He realized he could read books at super-speed and retain the information.
As Superman, he had his familiar powers and also exhibited new ones, including firing radiation bursts from his eyes to scramble electronics.

10 FEATS OF SUPER-STRENGTH

After time-traveling to ancient Atlantis, Superman builds a huge metal crane to prevent the fabled city from sinking beneath the waves. (*Superman* #146)

When Superman learns that Lex Luthor has won the US presidency, he takes out his anger by splitting one of the moons of Saturn in half. (*Superman: Lex 2000*)

Superman, with help from Wonder Woman and Green Lantern, moves Earth's moon out of its orbit. (*JLA* #58)

To protect his Justice League teammates from a legion of fallen angels, Superman endures the burning fires of Heaven while wrestling the supernatural entity Azmodel. (*JLA* #7)

As a charity stunt during a World Series game, Superman hits a baseball into space. One month later, the ball hits a painted target on the moon. (*Superman* #671)

Green Lantern is convinced that no one can break through the energy constructs created by his power ring, but Superman easily shatters them. (*Justice League* #2)

While investigating a shady pawn dealer, Superman turns a lump of coal into a glittering diamond with a squeeze of his hand. (*Action Comics* #115)

Superman carves an iceberg into a gigantic paddlewheel and spins it at an incredible rate to temporarily redirect ocean currents. (*World's Finest Comics* #68)

Supercharged after a plunge into Earth's sun, the Man of Steel pushes the artificial planet Warworld through a dimensional rift all the way to the dawn of time. (*Action Comics* #782)

During tests conducted by Dr. Veritas, Superman exercises in a machine that replicates the weight of the Earth (5.972 sextillion metric tons) for five days straight. (*Superman* #13)

WHAT ARE SUPERMAN'S WEAKNESSES?

KRYPTONITE

Superman's biggest weakness is Kryptonite, a radioactive crystal formed within Krypton's core and blasted into space during the world's explosive death. Each color of Kryptonite has a different effect on Kryptonian physiology. When Superman is exposed to Green K, the most common variety, he immediately feels weak and nauseated. Extended contact will kill him. Some of Superman's deadliest enemies have learned to weaponize Green K, including Metallo—the man with the Kryptonite heart—and the Kryptonite Man, whose body is infused with Kryptonite energy. When Superman worried that he could become a danger under the influence of a mind-controlling super-villain, he gave a piece of Kryptonite to his friend Batman to use against him if all other methods failed.

KRYPTON EXPLODES

"HE'S FASTER THAN A BOLT OF LIGHTNING. HE CAN STOP A MISSILE WITH TWO FINGERS. HE CAN MOULD TITANIUM BETWEEN HIS MOLARS LIKE GUM. BUT THERE IS ONE SUBSTANCE THAT CAN TEAR HIM APART FROM THE INSIDE OUT. ONE SUBSTANCE THAT CAN KILL HIM..."

GREEN KRYPTONITE
The radiation from Green K can weaken and kill any Kryptonian, including animals that originated on the planet such as the dog Krypto.

RED KRYPTONITE
Red K is completely unpredictable. It has temporarily removed Superman's powers, changed his personality, even transformed him into an ant-creature.

BLUE KRYPTONITE
This variant only affects Bizarro beings. Sometimes it gives Bizarros an intellectual boost, sometimes it kills.

BLACK KRYPTONITE
First discovered by Darkseid, Black K has the power to split a Kryptonian into two beings, one good and one evil.

WHITE KRYPTONITE
White K is a rare variant that is harmless to Kryptonians but deadly to all forms of Krypton plant life.

JEWEL KRYPTONITE
Formed from the remains of Krypton's Jewel Mountains, this substance amplifies the mental powers of Phantom Zone criminals.

GOLD KRYPTONITE
With a single exposure, Gold K removes a Kryptonian's superpowers forever.

Mr. Mxyzptlk used his magic to put Superman through embarrassing changes.

MAGIC AND MIND CONTROL

The universe operates under predictable scientific laws, except where magic is concerned. Enemies like Mr. Mxyzptlk and allies like Zatanna both wield mystical energies that can be mastered by memorizing spells or brewing potions. Magic usually bypasses Superman's defenses but, fortunately, occurrences are rare.

More common are telepathic or psionic attacks that get inside Superman's head. Foes such as Manchester Black have read Superman's mind to uncover his secret identity, and Maxwell Lord once turned Superman into a brainwashed puppet and forced him to do battle with Wonder Woman.

PSYCHOLOGICAL DISTRESS

Superman is not immune to the pain of loss. His secret identity of Clark Kent is a vital buffer for keeping friends and family safe from his enemies. But no secret stays buried forever, and foes such as Conduit and the Secret Society of Super-Villains have attacked his loved ones, paralyzing Superman with guilt over his failure to keep them safe. Superman respects all human life, so a threat made against an innocent hostage may distract Superman long enough for a crook to make a clean getaway.

RED SUN

The red rays of Krypton's sun kept the natural abilities of the planet's inhabitants in check. Superman's enemies have sometimes used this fact to strip the Man of Steel of his powers. They turned Earth's yellow, empowering sun red during the Pokolistan crisis and again during the war against New Krypton. When Lois and Clark cared for the young Kryptonian Christopher Kent (I or-Zod), they gave him a wristwatch that emitted red sun radiation and thus suppressed his superpowers.

LEAD

Superman can see through any substance except lead. The metal has no effects on Superman, but it is deadly to Daxamites such as Superman's friend Mon-El. Lois Lane once hid her head inside a lead box, believing that a sorceress, claiming to be the legendary Circe, had given her the face of a cat.

PHYSICAL LIMITATIONS

Superman's strength levels have fluctuated throughout his career, but he has never had the unlimited power of the Spectre or other magical beings. There are always weights he can't lift, enemies he can't outrun, or puzzles he can't solve. Superman's support bench for academic or scientific challenges includes Batman and Dr. Emil Hamilton. And if a threat is too powerful —or too numerous—to fight solo, Superman can always call in the help of the Justice League.

BREATH CONTROL

Superman can operate for hours on a single lungful of air. Before he had perfected this superpower, he wore an oxygen mask when traveling in space or underwater.

EXTREME TRAUMA

Extreme trauma will kill Superman, just as it would any normal human. Doomsday inflicted fatal injuries on the Man of Steel.

KRYPTON

The world of Krypton housed an enlightened populace and a host of scientific wonders, but it exploded when a radiation buildup in its core could no longer be contained. Only a few of its people survived, with the most famous of them, Superman, becoming known as the "Last Son of Krypton."

A BRIEF HISTORY OF KRYPTON

Before its destruction, Krypton orbited a red dwarf star in the constellation of Corvus, 27 light years from Earth. Though Krypton's leaders valued the benefits of science, many advances came without any sense of moral direction. One scientist created the unstoppable killer Doomsday through a cruel experiment in forced evolution. Genetic advances soon allowed the Kryptonians to breed clones as menial laborers, a period that ended when one clone, Kon, rebelled against his overseers. Kon's uprising led to hundreds of thousands of deaths and caused all clones to be viewed as abominations. Damage to Krypton's weather-control towers in the uprising unbalanced the planet's ecosystem, giving rise to a cult that hoped to obliterate all life in a coming "cosmicide." As Krypton's people withdrew further from their natural origins, they came to prize cold sterility and a rigid adherence to tradition. Jor-El, Superman's scientist father, discovered proof of the planet's impending destruction, but Krypton's Council refused to heed his warnings.

ANCIENT KRYPTONIAN ARCHITECTURE

KANDOR

Brainiac, the Collector of Worlds, came upon Krypton prior to its destruction to seize a souvenir. His force fields isolated the city of Kandor and miniaturized it within a bottle, much to the horror of the remaining Kryptonians, including the Military Guild's commander, General Zod. For years Kandor sat on a trophy shelf in Brainiac's interstellar ship, until Superman came to the rescue.

BRAINIAC CAPTURES KANDOR

KRYPTON'S ECOSYSTEM

Krypton was more massive than Earth, giving it a higher gravitational pull. Kryptonians controlled the planet's climate via special towers. Notable attractions included the Fire Falls, the Scarlet Jungle, Meteor Valley, and the Jewel Mountains. Plant and animal life included herds of horned Rondor beasts and thickets of moving trees.

GREAT RAO

Kryptonian mythology claimed Rao to be the god of light, and the planet's ancient inhabitants named their sun after the object of their worship. The red rays of Rao emitted a radiation that kept the natural superpowers of all Kryptonians in check. Krypton had several moons, though the rogue scientist Jax-Ur destroyed the moon of Wegthor in a failed experiment to develop an interstellar star drive. The Ruling Council outlawed further research into space travel following the Wegthor incident.

RAO'S SOLAR SYSYTEM

THE KRYPTONIANS

Within their sterile cities, the Kryptonians grew isolated from the natural world and relied on robots for their needs. Technological innovation became a rarity, although a few brave scientists, like Jor-El, spoke out against the cultural stagnation encouraged by the Council. Jor-El's brother, Zor-El, even invented a force-field generator, which later allowed Argo City to survive Krypton's total destruction. Most Kryptonians had little interest in exploring their own solar system and beyond, and so they never learned of the incredible powers that could have been theirs under the rays of a yellow sun.

KRYPTONIAN CITIES

The Kryptonians lived clustered together in several high-tech megalopolises. Kryptonopolis was the planetary capital and the seat of the Ruling Council. Kandor was a cosmopolitan center of culture, while Argo City was a center for genetic research.

THE HOUSE OF EL

Centuries of prestige allowed the House of El to earn both wealth and political power. Jor-El became the youngest-ever Kryptonian inducted into the Science Council, and his wife Lara graduated from the prestigious Kryptonian Military Academy. The House of El's symbol is a Kryptonian glyph meaning hope, one that Superman adopted for his costume's insignia.

JOR-EL AND LARA

THE PHANTOM ZONE

Jor-El discovered the existence of an extradimensional white void which he called the Phantom Zone. Within its endless expanse, living beings could exist indefinitely in an intangible, bodiless state. Krypton's worst criminals received sentences of exile in the Phantom Zone. All of them—especially General Zod—hated Jor-El for becoming their jailer.

THE JOURNEY BEGINS

Krypton had days to live and only Jor-El of the Science
Guild could see the signs. An 8th-level genius, Jor-El
had constructed an enviro-pod to venture deep beneath
Krypton's crust and verify the truth of the planet's
impending core collapse. His wife, Lara, a fellow
scientist and graduate of Krypton's military academy,
gave birth to their child Kal-El as Krypton entered its
death throes. Jor-El had no time to complete an escape
ark, but the prototype could carry a single, very small
passenger. Wrapping their infant son in a red cloak that
bore the symbol of the House of El, Jor-El and Lara sent
Kal-El into the void. They died along with their world.

Kal-El's rocket crashed near Smallville, Kansas,
and was discovered by Jonathan and Martha Kent.
The Kents had failed to conceive a child of their own,
and felt responsible for safeguarding the strange but
helpless arrival.

Passing motorists
Jonathan and
Martha Kent found
the crashed rocket
in a cornfield.
They didn't know
the baby's origin,
but they knew that
he needed a family
to care for him.

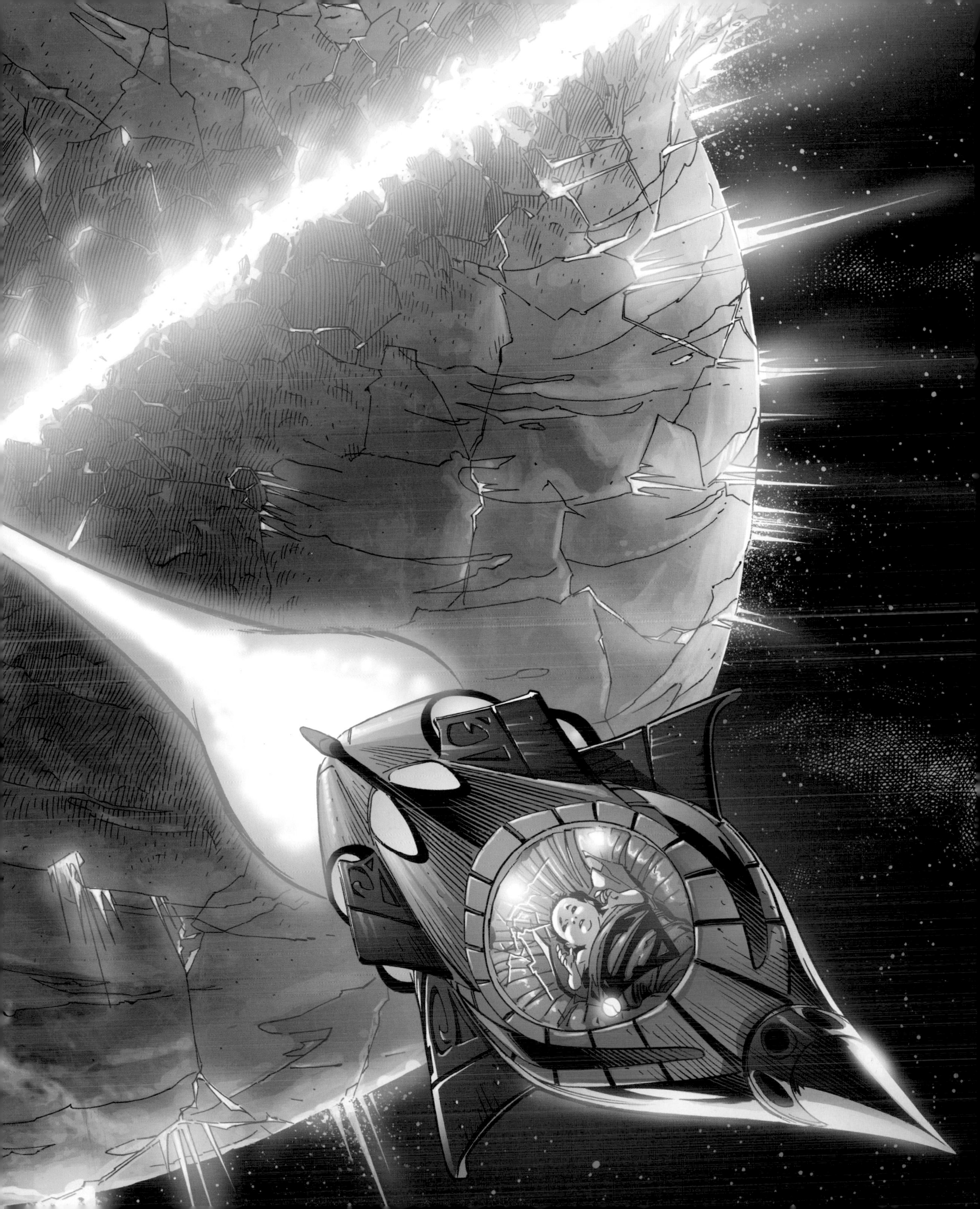

THE KENTS

When Jonathan and Martha Kent found a rocket from another world, they knew they had a responsibility to raise its tiny passenger the right way.

After Jonathan and Martha married, they tried several times to conceive a child. The arrival of Kal-El's rocket seemed like a miracle and spoke of a greater destiny for them both.

Jonathan and Martha Kent lived on a farm in Smallville, Kansas which had been in the Kent family for generations. They desperately wanted a child, but couldn't afford the cost of fertility treatments or the paperwork needed for adoption. When they came upon a crashed spacecraft while driving along a rural road, they decided to protect the baby inside from the government's agents. Jonathan Kent tricked military investigators by passing off a deformed calf as the "alien pilot" he had found inside the rocket.

The Kents named the boy Clark, and a sudden blizzard isolated them from their neighbors long enough for Martha plausibly to claim the boy as her biological son. Clark received moral guidance and a strong work ethic from his parents. As he grew, his superpowers began to appear. Clark discovered that he could wrestle a bull to the ground and hoist farm machinery with one hand. Jonathan warned him to use his abilities with care, for his own protection as well as the safety of others.

Clark's developing superpowers were a puzzle for Jonathan and Martha, who didn't know if his true parents might one day come looking for him. They urged Clark to be discreet when applying his super-strength and his heat vision.

"Go use that strength of yours to help and inspire folks. Maybe that 'S' can be something that reminds us of the best we can be."
Jonathan Kent

FAMILY HISTORY

The Kents have Kansas roots that date back to 1854, when Silas and Abigail Kent moved to there from Boston to start a newspaper and promote the cause of abolition. After pro-slavery activists murdered Silas, his sons Nathaniel and Jeb ended up on opposite sides of the American Civil War. Nathaniel, who fought for the North, married a Native American woman and later became the sheriff of Smallville.

Clark bid goodbye to the home he grew up in, filled with memories of his parents, but could not bear to sell it. Instead, he leased the farm to a neighbor.

THE NEW 52

In the new reality established after the Flashpoint event, Jonathan and Martha Kent died after Clark finished high school, forcing Clark to make his own way in the world. After Clark left Smallville for college, he eventually settled in Metropolis to become a crusading journalist at the *Daily Star*. Whenever he could, Clark returned to Smallville to visit his parents' graves.

SMALLVILLE

Smallville is a tiny town located in the plains of Kansas. Smallville taught Clark Kent to see through superficial flashiness and perceive the true character within. The town's history dates back to the 1800s, and its primary industries have always been corn, wheat, and dairy farming. Many families, including the Kents, operate historic homesteads on the city's outskirts, while the tightly-packed downtown district contains City Hall and a shopping district. Most businesses in Smallville are locally owned and have operated out of the same storefronts for decades, including a barber shop, a soda fountain, and a movie theater. Clark Kent and his friends Pete Ross and Lana Lang graduated from Smallville High School, and every year the town plays host to the Smallville County Fair.

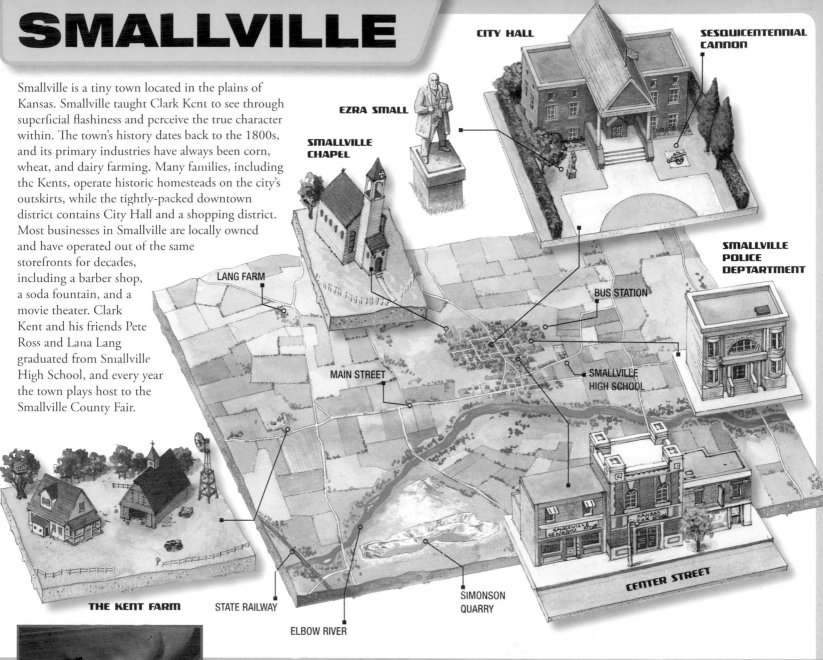

CITY HALL
SESQUICENTENNIAL CANNON
EZRA SMALL
SMALLVILLE CHAPEL
SMALLVILLE POLICE DEPTARTMENT
LANG FARM
BUS STATION
MAIN STREET
SMALLVILLE HIGH SCHOOL
THE KENT FARM
STATE RAILWAY
ELBOW RIVER
SIMONSON QUARRY
CENTER STREET

Smallville is situated in a stretch of the Midwest known as "Tornado Alley." During one twister, Clark used his newly discovered power of flight to save the life of his teenage sweetheart, Lana Lang.

SMALLTOWN LIFE...

The simple pleasures of Smallville aren't much when compared to the big-city sights and sounds of Metropolis, but its residents wouldn't have it any other way. Throughout Clark's childhood and teenage years, Smallville's sleepy familiarity kept him grounded and gave him an appreciation for friendly smiles and neighborly handshakes—qualities that helped make Superman one of the world's best-loved heroes. Lex Luthor briefly attended Smallville High School, but he constantly mocked those whom he perceived as his intellectual inferiors.

THE FORTRESS OF
SOLITUDE

It is the one place on Earth where he can truly be himself. Through many incarnations, Superman's Fortress of Solitude has stored both Kryptonian relics and treasured memories.

Superman built the first Fortress above the Arctic Circle. It held souvenirs of his adventures and animal specimens for his interplanetary zoo. Rooms celebrated Lois Lane, Jimmy Olsen, and others. There was also a huge diary with writing etched by heat vision on its metallic pages.

A colossal key pointed the way toward the imposing front door of the Fortress. Only Superman had the strength to lift this key and turn it in the massive lock.

PIECES OF KRYPTON

After stealing a shard of Kryptonian sunstone, Lex Luthor built alien war machines and tried to conquer Metropolis. Superman defeated his enemy and found a better use for the powerful artifact from his homeworld. The sunstone erected a crystalline Fortress of Solitude, and its interfaces contained a complete history of Kryptonian culture and an interactive, artificial-intelligence projection of his father, Jor-El.

Superman threw his Kryptonian sunstone into the arctic ice, triggering a chain reaction that built the Fortress in minutes.

Statues of his parents Jor-El and Lara have stood proudly inside almost all versions of Superman's Fortress.

MOBILE BASE

With a little extradimensional engineering, John Henry Irons built the first truly mobile Fortress. A glowing puzzle globe, when solved, gave Superman access to a vast chamber in a parallel reality. Superman usually hid the globe-entrance to this Fortress in an inaccessible crevasse in the Andes. Inside this Fortress, newsfeeds alerted Superman to worldwide catastrophes and a science lab allowed him to experiment on alien technology.

PERUVIAN FORTRESS

After Superman saved a million people from the effects of the Vanishing, he felt a new connection to life in all its forms. For a time, he operated from a stone structure deep in the South American rainforest.

52 The new embodiment of Superman's Fortress of Solitude lies hidden in the Arctic. It contains the bottle city of Kandor, a Phantom Zone projector, and other wonders retrieved from Brainiac's world-collector ship. Early in his career, Superman used Brainiac's captured ship as an orbital retreat.

METROPOLIS

It is called the City of Tomorrow, but most know it best as the home of Superman. Metropolis, which holds more than 11 million people, has become one of the world's greatest cities under the Man of Steel's protection.

"EVERYONE IN METROPOLIS LOOKS UP IN THE SKY. SOMETIMES WE SEE HIM, SOMETIMES WE DON'T. BUT WE ALWAYS KNOW HE'S AROUND."

METROPOLIS CITIZEN

BEGINNINGS

In 1634, Dutch settlers founded the settlement that would become Metropolis, establishing a port on the Eastern seaboard. The mid-19th century saw the Hob's Bay section of the city grow as a mercantile center, leading to violence between the second-generation residents of Metropolis and immigrants arriving from Ireland. By the turn of the century, Metropolis' influential Luthor family fostered the Industrial Revolution by constructing Luthor Steel Works.

Today, the six boroughs of Metropolis are split by the West River and Hob's River. The central borough of New Troy is home to corporate skyscrapers and tourist attractions. The city's other boroughs include Bakerline, Park Ridge, Queensland Park, Hob's Bay, and Southside (known as Suicide Slum).

Metropolis, nicknamed the "Big Apricot," has a reputation for optimism and technological progress that contrasts with the gloomier image of nearby Gotham City. Metropolis' transit systems are state of the art, and it is home to important companies including S.T.A.R. Labs and Galaxy Communications. Lex Luthor was once Metropolis' most famous citizen—until Superman came to town.

DUTCH SETTLERS

HOB'S BAY RIOTS

THE STEEL WORKS

HIGH-TECH UPGRADE

The 64th century villain Brainiac 13 gave Metropolis' infrastructure a boost by uploading a computer virus that transformed materials and machinery into something out of a science fiction story. The people quickly adapted to their futuristic surroundings. The effects didn't last, however. A time-quake undid Brainiac 13's work and restored the city to something resembling its former appearance.

MAJOR METROPOLIS LOCATIONS

The *Daily Planet*: The city's iconic newspaper and a leading worldwide media outlet. The building's roof is crowned with a famous golden globe.

Centennial Park: A relaxing stretch of greenery in midtown, Centennial Park houses a bronze Superman statue erected to commemorate the hero's sacrifice against Doomsday.

S.T.A.R. Labs: Metropolis' Scientific and Technological Advanced Research facility is responsible for some of the world's greatest genetic breakthroughs, and also for its most horrifying mutations.

LexCorp Tower: A symbol of Lex Luthor's ambition and ego, the LexCorp Tower houses corporate workplaces, secret storehouses and Lex Luthor's well-defended penthouse office.

WayneTech: Bruce Wayne placed a branch of his research-and-development company on Metropolis' Avenue of Tomorrow so he could take advantage of the latest breakthroughs from the city's scientists.

Steelworks: A foundry and high-tech laboratory operated by John Henry Irons (also known as the super hero Steel), this sprawling complex has also been called the Ironworks.

City Hall: The hub of Metropolis' city government and the site of the mayor's offices, City Hall is a frequent target for super-villains.

Stryker's Island: Located on an island in the West River, this maximum-security prison is specifically designed to contain superpowered criminals.

Suicide Slum: The nickname for Metropolis' Southside district, Suicide Slum is a high-crime, poverty-stricken area. Its streets were patrolled by the Guardian.

University of Metropolis: Clark Kent's *alma mater*, Met-U is located in Queensland Park and is considered one of the nation's top learning institutions.

Shuster Sports Arena: A major entertainment and exhibition space that also hosts home games for Metropolis' professional hockey and basketball teams.

Glenmorgan Square: A bustling retail and entertainment center, Glenmorgan Square is named after the city's wealthy Glenmorgan family and is popular with tourists.

Metropolis PD: The headquarters of the Metropolis Police Department also houses the offices of the Special Crimes Unit, which deals with superpowered threats.

Metro District: A nucleus for many businesses and research facilities, the Metro District is located in midtown and is bisected by the Avenue of Tomorrow.

Ace O'Clubs: A pub on the seedy side of Metropolis, the Ace O'Clubs is run by Superman's friend Bibbo Bibbowski.

Frank Berkowitz Memorial Stadium: Named after the city's former mayor, the Berkowitz stadium plays host to the Metropolis Monarchs of professional baseball.

Valhalla Cemetery: Located on Metropolis' outskirts, this private cemetery is dedicated to the memory of super heroes who have fallen in battle.

36-37

THE DAILY PLANET

HISTORY

The *Daily Planet* newspaper is recognized worldwide for its journalistic ideals. The *Daily Planet*'s origins date back to the Revolutionary War; some of America's Founding Fathers wrote for the newspaper, urging the public to back the new independence movement.

The newspaper's most recent successes came under the tenure of Editor-in-Chief Perry White. Reporters, including Lois Lane, Clark Kent, and Ron Troupe, racked up a trophy shelf of Pulitzer Prizes. The *Planet* has also expanded into digital and social media. Some, including Clark Kent, feel the *Daily Planet*'s high standards have fallen in the process.

Located in the heart of the New Troy borough, the Daily Planet Building is a Metropolis landmark, formerly famous for the spinning globe atop its roof. Marking the *Daily Planet*'s sale to Galaxy Communications' Morgan Edge, the old globe was demolished and replaced by an illuminated tower. The *Daily Planet* is now an arm of Galaxy's news outlets; it still has a local rival in the *Daily Star* newspaper.

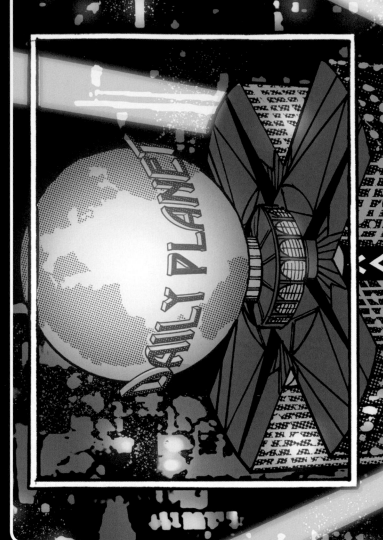

STOP PRESS

The corridors of the *Daily Planet* offices are lined with framed newspapers, each headline a key historical moment. Shortly after Superman arrived in Metropolis, reporter Lois Lane convinced the super hero to agree to an exclusive interview.

The *Daily Planet* became linked to Superman in the public eye, which certainly boosted sales of the paper.

The razing of the former Daily Planet Building brought an end to a great chapter of Metropolis journalism. A new, gleaming tower soon rose in its place.

Morgan Edge is the billionaire CEO of Galaxy Communications, whose acquisitions of rival news outlets has given him a near-monopoly over the mainstream media.

CLARK KENT

RON TROUPE

PERRY WHITE

JIMMY OLSEN

LOIS LANE

THE BULLPEN

Day or night, the *Planet* is always buzzing. Investigative reporters such as Clark Kent and Lois Lane aren't expected to stay at their desks—which enables Clark to leap into action as Superman. Other familiar faces include Editor-in-Chief Perry White, photographer Jimmy Olsen, entertainment columnist Cat Grant, political reporter Ron Troupe, and sports editor Steve Lombard.

CLARK KENT

"I had more hard knocks growing up on the farm in Smallville than anything the big city can throw at me."

The world's greatest super hero hides in plain sight behind a pair of glasses. Clark Kent isn't just a prominent Metropolis journalist, he represents the real Superman. Shaped by small-town values, Clark never forgets the moral principles instilled in him by his parents during his boyhood in Smallville.

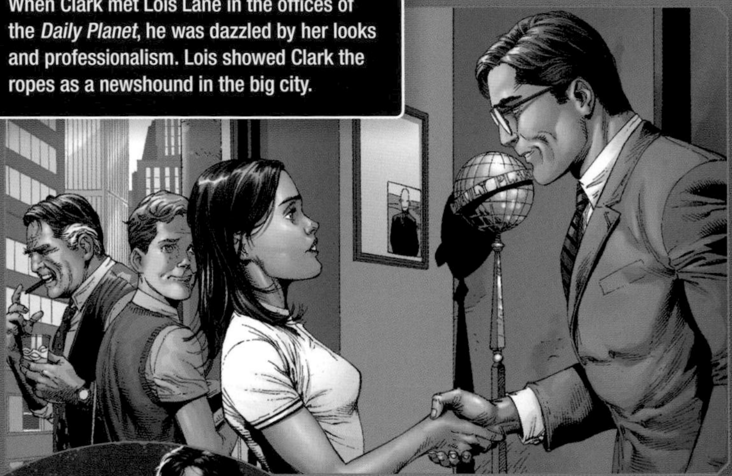

When Clark met Lois Lane in the offices of the *Daily Planet*, he was dazzled by her looks and professionalism. Lois showed Clark the ropes as a newshound in the big city.

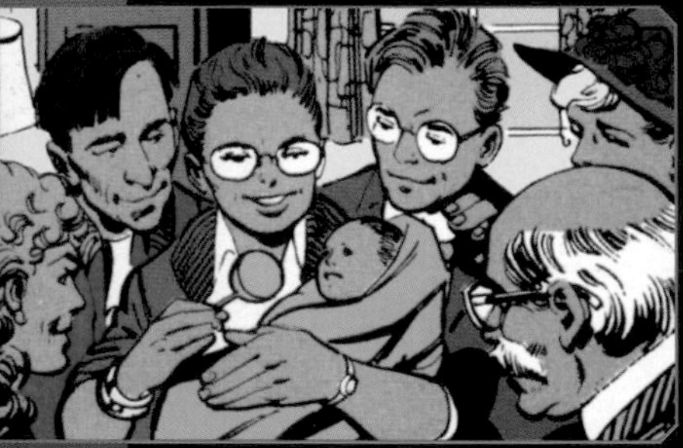

Martha Kent showed off her "new arrival" to visitors. She could never have guessed what the future held.

ORIGINS

Crash-landing in a field in Kansas, Kryptonian child Kal-El was taken in by Jonathan and Martha Kent who raised him as their son Clark on their farm near the town of Smallville. His best friends there were Pete Ross and Lana Lang.

As an adult, Clark moved to the city of Metropolis and found work as a journalist, largely for the famed *Daily Planet* newspaper, where his colleagues included reporter Lois Lane and photographer Jimmy Olsen. As Clark forged ties with his new home, he carefully covered his tracks concerning his alternate identity as Superman. He knew that if his secret was discovered, everyone he cared for would be in danger.

Clark and Lois Lane have always been attracted to each other; in a previous timeline they were even married. In the current reality, they have so far remained strictly colleagues, despite Clark's hopes for something more. Clark has also briefly dated Lois' younger sister, Lucy.

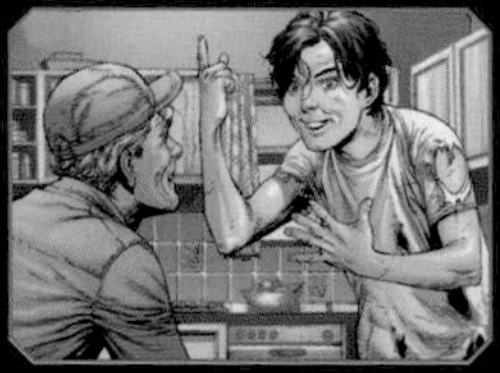

Clark raced home to tell his parents when he discovered he had superpowers.

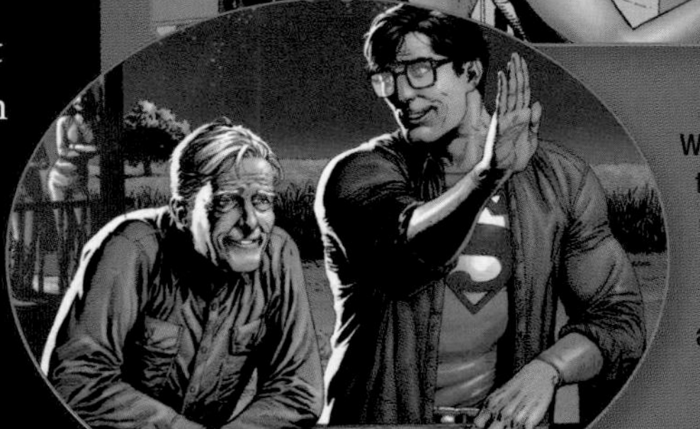

Whenever time allowed, Clark returned to Smallville, Kansas, to share stories of his adventures with his parents. In the current timeline, Jonathan and Martha Kent died before Clark arrived in Metropolis.

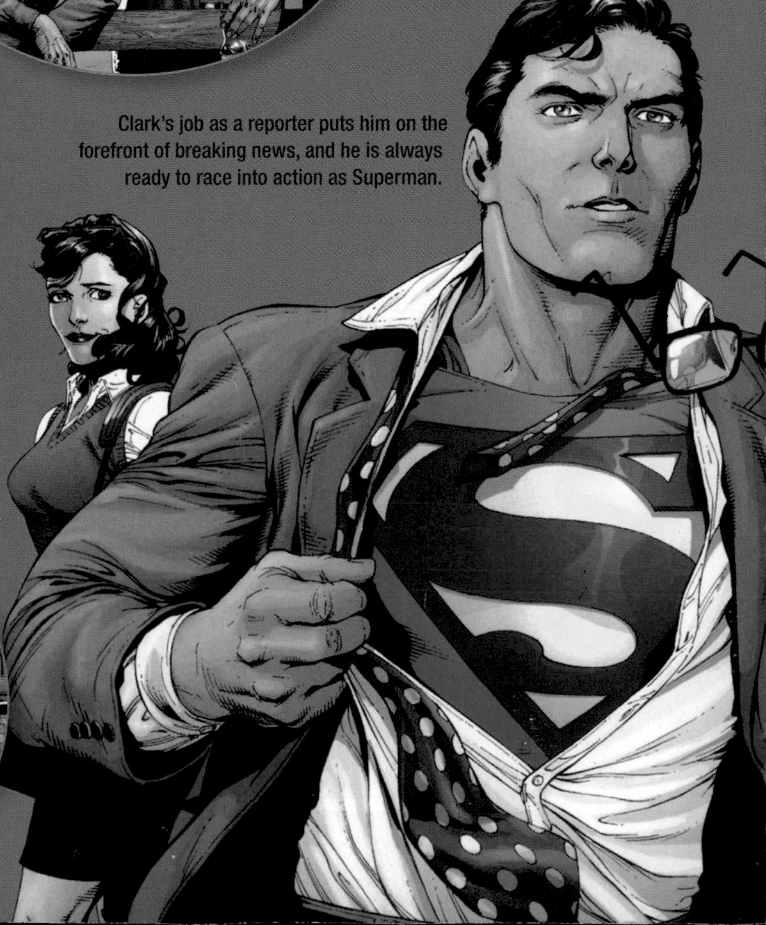

Clark's job as a reporter puts him on the forefront of breaking news, and he is always ready to race into action as Superman.

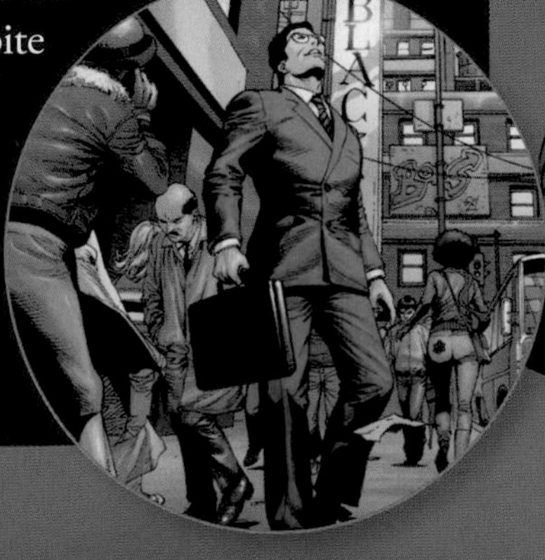

Arriving in Metropolis, Clark found the city's towering skyscrapers a huge change from the open spaces of Kansas.

FIGHTING FOR TRUTH

As the news business shifted from hard-hitting reportage to showbiz gossip and superficial fluff, the *Daily Planet* changed ownership. Clark rejected the dumbed-down new regime of media mogul Morgan Edge. Remaining true to his ideals of making the world a better place, Clark resigned from the *Daily Planet*. As a freelancer, Clark returned to his investigative-journalist roots, determined to uncover and expose corruption in sleaze-ridden Metropolis.

Frustrated with the *Daily Planet*'s shrinking news budget and growing focus on celebrity gossip, Clark left the paper and started his own news-gathering organization.

Clark's clothing is selected to look as inconspicuous as possible. He was once fond of suits, but now prefers loose-fitting street clothes that help hide the musculature underneath.

KEY DATA

REAL/FULL NAME Clark Kent (formerly Kal-El)

FIRST APPEARANCE *Action Comics* #1 (June 1938)

OCCUPATION Investigative journalist

AFFILIATIONS *Daily Planet*

POWERS/WEAPONS Clark is a trained news investigator. He has all of Superman's powers but has to keep them hidden. He can learn languages or assimilate information in minutes and with perfect recall. He is also a super-fast typist. X-ray vision has also proved useful in his career.

LOIS LANE

"Metropolis is definitely not a 'slow news day' kind of city. Especially lately."

Lois Lane, star reporter for the *Daily Planet*, is feared by Metropolis's most powerful figures for her ability to expose the truth. Although Lois has at times been romantically linked to Superman, she rarely needs to rely on him to pull her out of trouble.

ORIGINS

The daughter of General Sam Lane, Lois grew up on military bases with her younger sister Lucy before moving to Metropolis as an adult. There she found work at the *Daily Planet*, impressing editor Perry White with her reporter's instincts and her never-quit spirit. Lois took Clark Kent under her wing when he started at the *Planet*, beginning a professional relationship with a hint of romance. At the same time, she pursued Superman as a news story and soon had the Man of Steel plastered across the front page.

In one version of events, Clark eventually proposed marriage to Lois. He revealed his secret identity as Superman and, after their wedding, the two journalists settled into married life in their Metropolis apartment. Lois and Clark even became the adoptive parents of a Kryptonian boy.

The current timeline erased the marriage and placed the first meeting between the two during a period when Clark worked for a rival newspaper, the *Daily Star*, although Lois soon brought him over to the *Daily Planet*. Five years later she had risen to the post of Executive Vice President of New Media under the *Daily Planet's* new owner, mogul Morgan Edge.

Lois Lane's nose for news soon landed her in hot water with tycoon Lex Luthor.

Accompanied by photographer Jimmy Olsen, Lois often relies on the *Daily Planet's* news helicopter to get an aerial view of breaking events in Metropolis.

During one of their first encounters, Superman saved Lois from what would have been a fatal fall. She was grateful for the rescue, but her first thought was to get an exclusive interview with the mysterious Man of Steel.

Lois teamed up with Batman to infiltrate the White House and retrieve a Kryptonite ring from President Lex Luthor. The Dark Knight was impressed with her coolness under pressure and ability to think on her feet.

Lois feels she can never live up to her father's impossible standards.

Sent by the *Daily Planet* to cover the conflict in Umec in the Middle East, Lois soon found herself in the front line of the action. Shot by a sniper, she hovered between life and death. Superman, her husband in this timeline, vowed to stay by her side.

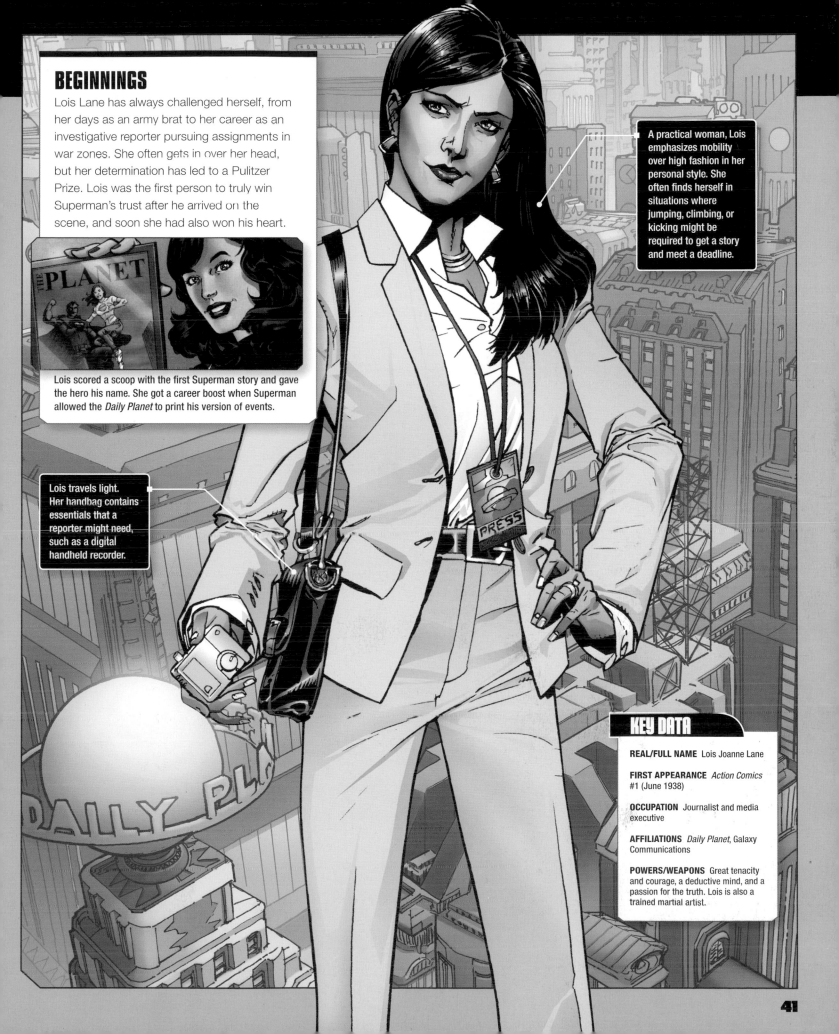

BEGINNINGS

Lois Lane has always challenged herself, from her days as an army brat to her career as an investigative reporter pursuing assignments in war zones. She often gets in over her head, but her determination has led to a Pulitzer Prize. Lois was the first person to truly win Superman's trust after he arrived on the scene, and soon she had also won his heart.

Lois scored a scoop with the first Superman story and gave the hero his name. She got a career boost when Superman allowed the *Daily Planet* to print his version of events.

A practical woman, Lois emphasizes mobility over high fashion in her personal style. She often finds herself in situations where jumping, climbing, or kicking might be required to get a story and meet a deadline.

Lois travels light. Her handbag contains essentials that a reporter might need, such as a digital handheld recorder.

KEY DATA

REAL/FULL NAME Lois Joanne Lane

FIRST APPEARANCE *Action Comics* #1 (June 1938)

OCCUPATION Journalist and media executive

AFFILIATIONS *Daily Planet*, Galaxy Communications

POWERS/WEAPONS Great tenacity and courage, a deductive mind, and a passion for the truth. Lois is also a trained martial artist.

LANA LANG

Clark Kent's teenage love, Lana Lang learned Clark's greatest secret when he shared the existence of his superpowers with her and took her on a flight above the fields of Kansas. Lana encouraged Clark to leave his hometown and seek out the broader horizons of Metropolis. She has remained a good friend ever since.

LYLA LERROL

Lyla Lerrol was a media star on Krypton just prior to its destruction. An alien empath used this information to copy her appearance and attempt to start a relationship with Superman. The alien hoped that she could steal Superman's powers and become a goddess on Earth.

LUMA LYNAI

In a former timeline, Luma Lynai was a celebrated super heroine on her homeworld of Staryl. She attracted the notice of Supergirl who, attempting to match-make, arranged for her to go on a date with Superman. The romance ended in tragedy when Superman discovered that Luma couldn't survive under the rays of Earth's yellow sun.

LOIS LANE

Clark Kent's colleague at the *Daily Planet* has long been the object of his affections. At first their relationship remained strictly professional, though Lois made no secret of her interest in Superman. They grew closer as time went by, and in one version of the timeline, Clark revealed his secret identity and married Lois. Years of wedded bliss followed, until the Flashpoint crisis erased all their romantic history, as well as Lois' knowledge of Clark's double life. Lois is still one of Clark's closest friends, even if they often clash over the ethics of journalism.

LORI LEMARIS

A mermaid from Atlantis, Lori Lemaris met Clark Kent in college, where she hid her mermaid's tail beneath a blanket on her wheelchair. Their romance didn't last long, but Lori remained in Clark's life and gained the magical ability to assume the form of a human being while on land.

SUPERMAN IN LOVE

Superman's crime-fighting crusade can be a lonely one. Over the years he has sought and found love in the arms of women from all sorts of backgrounds—human, alien, even Atlantean! Curiously, many of Superman's loves have shared the same initials: "L. L."

NEAR MISSES...

OBSESSION

Dana Dearden gained magic powers from the Greek Gods, and became infatuated with Superman. She initially called herself Superwoman, but soon switched to a more appropriate name: Obsession. With super-speed, super-strength, and flight, she could keep up with Superman.

MAXIMA

An alien princess from the planet Almerac, Maxima came to Earth looking for a mate worthy of her status. Superman refused her, but her rage was tempered by the hero's role in saving her planet from Brainiac. She later helped Superman in the fight against Imperiex.

ENCANTADORA

She has tried many times to start a romance with the Man of Steel, but her greed means she can rarely be trusted. Encantadora has vast magical abilities and hires out her services out as a superpowered mercenary and treasure seeker, sometimes getting just close enough to Superman to stab him in the back. Encantadora has repeatedly failed to deliver on her promises to reform.

> "People like us are really alone, aren't we?"
>
> Wonder Woman

A NEW LOVE...

In The New 52, Superman and Lois Lane have never been a couple. Instead, the Man of Steel has found romance with his Justice League teammate Wonder Woman, who understands the isolation that is the fate of the super hero.

SUPERBOY

"I'M GOING TO ASK YOU TO TURN YOURSELF IN TO THE AUTHORITIES. BECAUSE I'M SUPERBOY. THAT'S MORE THAN REASON ENOUGH."

Superboy was a clone grown from Kryptonian and human DNA. His hybrid origins meant that he didn't share all of Superman's powers, nor did he have any family connections to Krypton. Superboy sought to live up to the heroic expectations of those who wear Superman's symbol.

After the Young Justice team disbanded, Superboy became a founding member of a new Teen Titans grouping. The members included Bart Allen (Kid Flash) and Cassie Sandsmark (Wonder Girl).

ORIGINS

The scientists of Project Cadmus grew Experiment 13 from Superman's genetic code crossed with DNA from a human donor, later revealed to be Lex Luthor. Their experiment, nicknamed Superboy, escaped and performed media-friendly stunts in Metropolis. Because the true Superman had died fighting Doomsday, Superboy (along with Steel, the Eradicator, and the Cyborg Superman) became one of the Man of Steel's possible successors during the "Reign of the Supermen." Once the resurrected Superman reclaimed his role, Superboy relocated to Hawaii and eventually moved to Smallville, Kansas. Living with Jonathan and Martha Kent, he posed as Clark Kent's cousin, Conner Kent, and attended Smallville High School. Conner made Superman proud by becoming a leader of the Teen Titans, and he received the name "Kon-El" to mark his symbolic adoption into Krypton's House of El. Superboy died during the Infinite Crisis but wasn't down for long, returning to lead the fight during the Blackest Night and the war against General Zod's New Krypton soldiers.

Superboy appeared in the weeks after Doomsday killed Superman.

Superboy shared Lex Luthor's DNA and Luthor had implanted a method of forcing Superboy to attack his teammates.

They started out as teammates, but Conner Kent and Cassie Sandsmark shared a special connection. Their romance appeared to end when Conner died during Infinite Crisis.

Under the guidance of Red Tornado, the teenage heroes of Young Justice formed a youthful counterpart to the JLA.

During the battle against Krypton and Darkseid...

Through the S symbol N.O.W.H.E.R.E. hoped to gain acceptance for its project. It also reminded Superboy of his Kryptonian clone heritage.

Superboy's consciousness extends throughout his entire cellular structure, giving him enhanced awareness of threats.

THE NEW 52: SUPERBOY

The covert agency N.O.W.H.E.R.E. cloned Superboy from Kryptonian and human DNA and then raised him within a virtual reality simulation under the orders of the mysterious Lord Harvest. Sent to capture Wonder Girl for N.O.W.H.E.R.E., Superboy met the Teen Titans and made his first friends. Lord Harvest's programming threatened to force Superboy into reenacting the clone uprising that once shook Krypton.

On ancient Krypton, a clone rebel named Kon led his fellow worker drones in a violent uprising against the ruling class. From that moment, Kryptonians viewed clones as abominations.

Superboy's tactile telekinesis allows him to fly, accelerate to incredible speeds, and levitate heavy weights.

KEY DATA

REAL/FULL NAME None (has been called Kon-El)

FIRST APPEARANCE *Adventures of Superman* #500 (June 1993)

OCCUPATION Super hero, covert operative

AFFILIATIONS N.O.W.H.E.R.E., Teen Titans, Superman family

POWERS/WEAPONS Tactile telekinesis allows flight, enhanced strength, super-speed acceleration, projection of force blasts, and the levitation and disassembly of objects.

Tactile telekinesis gives Superboy resistance to injury, though he needs to maintain control for this to work.

SUPERGIRL

"MY OLD LIFE IS OVER. MY HOME IS GONE. AND I HAVE ONLY ONE PLACE LEFT TO GO."

When Superman's cousin Kara Zor-El came to Earth, she shared Superman's Kryptonian powers but lacked his familiarity with Earth's customs. Throughout her various incarnations, Supergirl has proven herself a worthy bearer of the familiar S-shield.

The first Supergirl perished battling the Anti-Monitor during the Crisis event.

ORIGINS

Superman wasn't the only survivor of Krypton's destruction. Zor-El, brother of Superman's father Jor-El, managed to save Argo City by enclosing it in a force field dome. In an echo of Superman's own journey, his daughter Kara then left Argo City inside a rocket. On her arrival on Earth, she gained amazing powers. Wearing a costume similar to Superman's, she took the name Supergirl and became one of the planet's greatest heroes. The Crisis on Infinite Earths saw her sacrifice her life to stop a great evil, and in the post-Crisis timeline her role was filled by a protoplasmic creation called Matrix from a Pocket Universe. Matrix had the ability to shapeshift and become invisible and adopted an appearance similar to that of the original Supergirl. After demonstrating her bravery during the Panic in the Sky event, the Matrix Supergirl gave way to a new Supergirl embodied by Linda Danvers. She was in turn supplanted by the post-Crisis version of Kara Zor-El. The Flashpoint event cleared the decks of all previous histories, and established a new status quo for Supergirl.

Lex Luthor briefly posed as his own son, and exploited the deception to start a romantic relationship with the Matrix Supergirl.

The Matrix Supergirl from the pocket universe sacrificed her life when she merged with Linda Danvers. A new Supergirl was created with the powers of an Earth-born angel. As Linda Danvers came to grips with her role, she exhibited the ability to teleport and to manifest wings of flame.

After Linda Danvers left the scene, a space capsule from Krypton crashed in Gotham Harbor carrying the true Kara Zor-El. Batman, who discovered this Supergirl, remained suspicious of her motives. But Superman helped Kara acclimate to life on Earth.

To help Supergirl control her powers, Superman enrolled her in Amazon combat training on Themyscira, under the guidance of Wonder Woman and Artemis.

Lex Luthor received a gift of Black Kryptonite from Darkseid and unintentionallly used it to split Supergirl into good and evil versions. Wonder Woman used her Golden Lasso of Truth to restore Supergirl's warring halves by forcing her to remember all the people who loved her.

Supergirl received mental conditioning as part of her training for the Kryptonian Finals Trials. She was unprepared for the unfamiliar culture of Earth.

The indestructible uniform displays the crest of the House of El. Supergirl received it from her father as a gift just before her homeworld exploded.

On Krypton, Supergirl was given training in martial arts from a robot combat master. Her father told her to get back on her feet after every knockdown.

THE NEW 52: SUPERGIRL

The timeline reset after the Flashpoint incident. After years orbiting Earth's yellow sun, the new Supergirl landed in the wastes of Siberia. Superman, whom she'd last seen as a baby, saved her from soldiers sent to capture her. Kara overcame his suspicions and settled into her new home. Industrialist Simon Tycho and the Worldkillers of Krypton provided opposition, but Kara found an unlikely friend in Siobhan Smythe, the Silver Banshee.

Supergirl's father Zor-El placed the unconscious Kara into an escape ship. "Krypton will die," he said. "My daughter will not."

KEY DATA

REAL/FULL NAME Kara Zor-El

FIRST APPEARANCE *Action Comics* #252 (May 1959)

OCCUPATION Super hero

AFFILIATIONS Superman family

POWERS/WEAPONS Flight, super strength, super speed, invulnerability, heat vision, X-ray vision, enhanced senses. Has the ability to superheat her entire body and release the energy in a solar blast.

WORLD'S FINEST

...AND THE TRINITY

The duo of Superman and Batman are known as the World's Finest. They were among the first costumed adventurers, and although their powers, their costumes, and their personalities couldn't be more dissimilar, they realized that they could accomplish far more as colleagues than as competitors. Superman and Batman helped found the Justice League, working out their differences while facing a worldwide invasion from Darkseid and his Parademon legions assembled on Apokolips. Wonder Woman joined them; ever since the Amazon warrior has become the third component of the team, which is sometimes called the Trinity. Recently, Wonder Woman has been romantically involved with the Man of Steel.

Throughout the Silver Age, Superman frequently dropped in on the Dynamic Duo of Batman and Robin the Boy Wonder.

Wonder Woman helped Superman to battle monsters summoned by diabolical sorceress Morgaine Le Fay.

Under the principles of the Trinity, Superman represented the pinnacle of heroism, Batman stood as the ultimate achievement of human development, and Wonder Woman personified the spirit of inspiration. The three heroes were the cornerstones of Earth's defense, but that same strength meant that the world would become an easy target if their bond should falter. During the Infinite Crisis, tensions among the members of the Trinity weakened their bond and left Earth vulnerable to the reality-erasing assault of Alexander Luthor and the Superman of Earth-Two. The three heroes renewed their friendship during the aftermath; however, their commitment to each other was then tested by the sorceress Morgaine Le Fay.

The villain Hush forced Batman to run a gauntlet of his worst enemies. Hush sprang his biggest surprise by arranging for Poison Ivy to brainwash Superman with her mind-altering pheromones. Batman needed all his wits to free his friend from Poison Ivy's malign influence.

> "IF CLARK WANTED TO HE COULD USE HIS SUPER-SPEED AND SQUISH ME INTO THE CEMENT. BUT I KNOW HOW HE THINKS. EVEN MORE THAN THE KRYPTONITE, HE'S GOT ONE BIG WEAKNESS. DEEP DOWN CLARK'S ESSENTIALLY A GOOD PERSON... AND DEEP DOWN I'M NOT." **Batman**

> "You said it yourself once, Kal. We are warriors." **Wonder Woman**

AGAINST ALL ODDS

Superman and Batman have complementary fighting styles. Batman has a knack for exploiting weak points and is armed with a technological gadget for every occasion. Superman has an array of powers and can attack at super-speed. By working together, the two heroes are able to combat powerhouse enemies such as Solomon Grundy and Doomsday, or the mind games of mad geniuses like Lex Luthor and the Joker.

**Batman: "We'll never change."
Superman: "I wouldn't want it
any other way."**

"Divided we may fall...
but united, we can stand.
Now and forever...
as the JUSTICE LEAGUE!"
Superman

Before The New 52 origin, the Justice League was formed in response to an extraterrestrial threat. The League's membership has varied over the years, but is built around the core roster of Batman, Superman, Wonder Woman, Aquaman, Green Lantern, and The Flash.

The earliest incarnation of the League operated from a cave near Happy Harbor, Rhode Island, with the non-powered Snapper Carr serving as the team's tech specialist. The League later moved to a headquarters aboard an orbital satellite and welcomed new blood in Zatanna, Red Tornado, and the Elongated Man.

After Aquaman's short-lived Detroit-based lineup, the team found new fame under financier Maxwell Lord as Justice League International. With Superman absent, heroes like Fire, Ice, Guy Gardner, Blue Beetle, and Booster Gold became the new faces of the organization.

Recognizing their influential status among Earth's super heroes, Superman, Batman and Wonder Woman resumed active status in a Justice League lineup that eventually included stretchy prankster Plastic Man and the second-generation versions of Green Lantern and the Flash. Later incarnations of the League saw other younger heroes join the team.

The ripples of the Flashpoint crisis erased previous events from the timeline and allowed the Justice League of America to form anew. Once again guided by Superman's example, this Justice League banded together to face the world-ending threat of Darkseid's legions.

THE JUSTICE LEAGUE

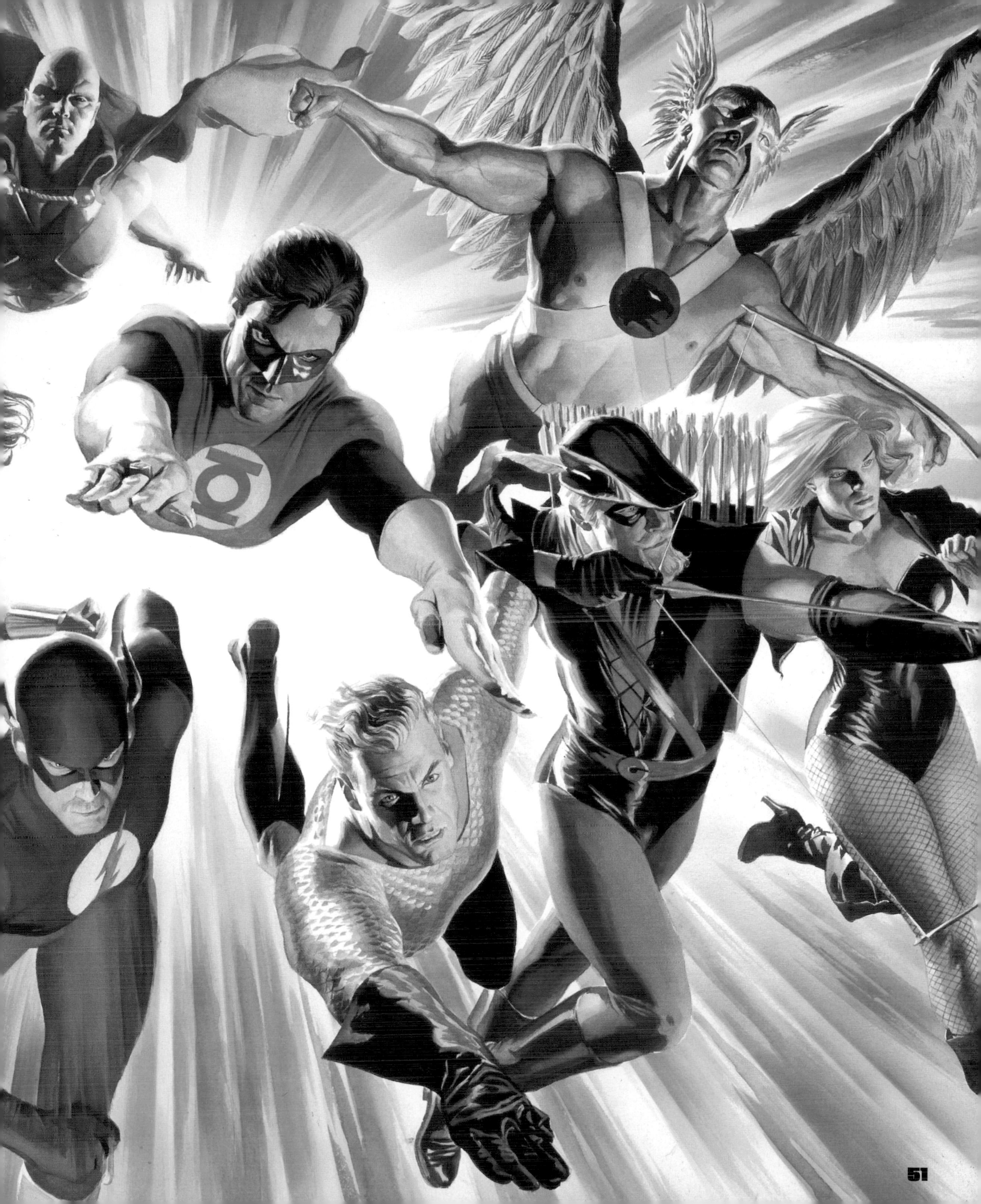

The Second World War saw America's greatest heroes unite under the banner of the Justice Society of America to fight enemy spies and saboteurs. Superman served on the team, but his contributions—as well as those of Batman and Wonder Woman—were erased by the new timeline established after the Crisis on Infinite Earths. The Justice Society remained in continuity, however, its core members including Doctor Mid-Nite (whose inverted vision allowed him to see in total darkness) and the Golden Age versions of Green Lantern, Hawkman, and The Flash.

THE JUSTICE SOCIETY OF AMERICA

As Superman's chronological adventures took him farther and farther away from the World War II era, his wartime service was categorized as having occurred on the alternate world of Earth-Two. There, the Earth-Two Superman aged gracefully with his fellow Justice Society veterans, some of whom parented the heroes of the next generation. Earth-Two's Superman married his world's Lois Lane.

During the Lightning Saga, Superman and his fellow Justice League members teamed up with the Justice Society to shut down a threat from the future. At the abandoned swamp headquarters of the Secret Society of Super-Villains, the twin teams defeated the artificial intelligence Computo.

The Legion of Super-Heroes first appeared when teens from the future Cosmic Boy, Lightning Lad, and Saturn Girl traveled back 1,000 years to offer membership in their super hero club to Superboy. On the Earth of the future, the Legion worked alongside the Science Police to keep peace throughout the United Planets. Few Legionnaires were Earth natives; the team's rules stated that all members needed to possess natural superpowers (not technological substitutes). Their ranks included Chameleon Boy, Triplicate Girl, Shrinking Violet, Phantom Girl, Bouncing Boy, Ultra Boy, and Braniac 5, all of them sporting special flight rings.

THE LEGION OF SUPER-HEROES

Cosmic Boy, Lightning Lad, and Saturn Girl traveled to a point in time before Clark Kent had become Superman. Their meeting inspired the hero who had inspired the Legion.

THE LEGION IN FLUX

The Legion of Super-Heroes has experienced dramatic changes following universe-altering events. After the Crisis on Infinite Earths erased Superman's history as Superboy, the Legion traced its origins to a "pocket universe" that soon disappeared. The Zero Hour event gave the Legion an overhaul, with many members bearing new costumes and code names. A third version saw the Legion become outlaw teenagers who represented symbols of rebellion in a repressive society. After the Flashpoint event, the Legion of Super-Heroes started anew.

When Superman followed the Legion into the 31st century, he became powerless under the red sun that now shone on Earth. Using a Legion flight ring, Superman helped the Legionnaires overthrow the regime of Earth-Man, a reject from the Legion who had whipped the public into an anti-alien frenzy.

OUT OF THIS WORLD

Some of Superman's closest friends come from distant galaxies and far-off timelines, while others have fantastic powers and gadgets. All of them are happy to help whenever the Man of Steel requires an extraordinary assist.

BATMAN
The Dark Knight is one of Superman's closest friends. With an arsenal of high-tech toys, including the Batmobile and Batplane, he guards Gotham City.

WONDER WOMAN
Diana of Themyscira is an Amazon warrior. Armed with bullet-deflecting bracelets and the Lasso of Truth, she has been romantically linked to Superman.

SUPERBOY
A clone created with both Kryptonian and human DNA, Superboy has outgrown his laboratory origins to become a hero and a core member of the Teen Titans.

SUPERGIRL
Superman's cousin Kara Zor-El departed Krypton as a teenager and traveled to Earth. She still carries memories of her lost homeworld.

THE FLASH
Barry Allen is the Fastest Man Alive. A forensic scientist in Central City, he gained his powers from the combination of a lightning strike and a chemical spill.

GREEN LANTERN
Hal Jordan is a test pilot selected by the Guardians of the Universe to be the Green Lantern of Earth. His power ring creates objects from solid light.

POWER GIRL
Power Girl Karen Starr is a Kryptonian from Earth-Two. She is the friend of Helena Wayne, the Huntress and the pair are super hero crime-fighting partners.

MON-EL
A Daxamite member of The Legion of Super-Heroes with the same powers as Superman. He survived lead poisoning by exiling himself to the Phantom Zone.

CYBORG
Man/machine hybrid Vic Stone is able to hack into any computer network. He can also fire blasts of white noise from his arm cannon.

AQUAMAN
The king of undersea Atlantis, Arthur Curry can communicate telepathically with aquatic life and survive the pressures of the ocean depths.

KRYPTO
To escape the destruction of his home planet, Krypto the Super-Dog of the House of El hid in the Phantom Zone. Krypto is loyal to his master, Superman.

STEEL
Inspired by Superman's example, John Henry Irons built a suit of power armor and fought crime as Steel. He operates the Steelworks complex in Metropolis.

MARTIAN MANHUNTER
One of Earth's most respected heroes, J'onn J'onzz is the last survivor of Mars. Martian Manhunter can read minds, shapeshift, and become invisible.

GANGBUSTER
Ex-boxer Jose Delgado became Gangbuster to keep order in Metropolis' Suicide Slum. Gangbuster fights using batons and nunchaku.

SPECTRE

God's Spirit of Vengeance, the Spectre is a near-omnipotent being usually bonded to a mortal. His current host is former police officer Jim Corrigan.

SUPERMEN OF AMERICA

After Doomsday's attack, a group of superpowered teens led by Outburst formed the Supermen of America to protect Metropolis.

STARMAN

Many heroes have been called Starman, including Will Payton, who gained superpowers after being struck by a beam from outer space.

BOOSTER GOLD

A time-traveler from the 25th century, Booster Gold hopes his super hero career will bring him fame and fortune. He has a robot sidekick named Skeets.

CAPTAIN ATOM

Nathaniel Adam of the US Air Force volunteered for an experiment that transformed him into Captain Atom. He can now manipulate nuclear energy.

MR. MAJESTIC

Kheran warlord Mr. Majestic has the powers of flight, super-strength, and invulnerability. Superman believes his law enforcement methods are too strict.

ICON

An alien who arrived on Earth in the 1800s, Icon is an extremely powerful hero who prefers to keep a low profile. His sidekick is named Rocket.

METRON

One of the New Gods, Metron is a seeker of knowledge who travels through time and space in his Mobius Chair. He prefers not to take sides.

ALPHA CENTURION

Abducted from Ancient Rome by aliens, Marcus Aelius returned to Earth as the Alpha Centurion. He wears futuristic armor and carries an energy sword.

BIG BARDA

Born on Apokolips, Big Barda was one of Darkseid's Female Furies until she met future husband Scott Free, Mr. Miracle. Big Barda's weapon is the Mega-Rod.

ORION

Born to Darkseid but raised among the heroes of New Genesis, Orion is a brooding warrior with a short temper. He flies an Astro-Harness into battle.

MR. MIRACLE

Darkseid's adopted son Scott Free abandoned Apokolips to become famous escape artist Mr. Miracle. He is married to Big Barda, who is also a New God.

STARGIRL AND S.T.R.I.P.E.

As Stargirl, Courtney Whitmore entered into a super hero partnership with her stepfather Pat Dugan, who wore a suit of armor as the rocket-powered S.T.R.I.P.E.

GIRL 13

Daughter of supernatural skeptic Doctor Thirteen, Traci Thirteen is one of the world's most powerful magic users. She loves the "urban magic" of Metropolis.

STRANGE VISITOR

Clark's old friend Sharon Vance merged with the spirit of Kismet, becoming Strange Visitor. She sacrificed herself during the battle against Imperiex.

CIR-EL

She believed she was Clark Kent and Lois Lane's daughter from an alternate future and adventured as Supergirl. However Brainiac 13 had created her.

LOIS LANE

Lois Lane has always played a pivotal role in the life of both Clark Kent and Superman. As Clark's fellow reporter at the *Daily Planet*, she developed a professional rivalry with him that was charged with romantic attraction. In *Superman*, Lois saw the biggest news story of the decade—her exclusive interviews with the Man of Steel appeared on the *Daily Planet*'s front page and won her a string of journalistic accolades. In the timeline erased by the Flashpoint event, Lois and Clark were married, but in current continuity the two have never had a serious relationship. After Morgan Edge purchased the *Daily Planet,* he promoted Lois to Executive Vice President, a role which Clark believed to represent a betrayal of her journalistic principles.

LANA LANG

Lana Lang had a teenage romance with Clark Kent in Smallville. In a previous timeline, Lana married Clark's friend Pete Ross and became CEO of LexCorp.

RON TROUPE

One of the *Daily Planet*'s top journalists, Ron Troupe won the respect of editor Perry White for his hard-hitting investigative pieces. Ron has a careful, meticulous approach—a nice contrast to the more impulsive Lois Lane's methods. In a previous timeline, Ron married Lois' sister Lucy Lane and the couple raised a son together.

PETE ROSS

One of Clark's best friends from their childhood in Smallville. In a former timeline, Pete married Lana Lang and became a US senator, with his political career culminating in the Vice Presidency under Lex Luthor.

CAT GRANT

Flirtatious Catherine Grant worked for the *Daily Planet* as an entertainment reporter and gossip columnist. She and Clark Kent recently left the *Daily Planet* to start an independent news-gathering organization.

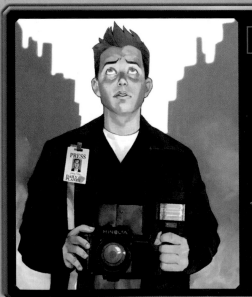

JIMMY OLSEN

A young, enthusiastic photographer for the *Daily Planet*, Jimmy Olsen became Clark Kent's first friend in Metropolis after Clark moved there from Smallville. Initially, Clark worked for the rival *Daily Star* newspaper, but Jimmy introduced him to Lois Lane and cleared the way for Clark's employment at the *Daily Planet*. Jimmy even moved in with Clark when bedbugs forced him to temporarily abandon his apartment. In his time at the *Daily Planet*, Jimmy has risen from the ranks of freelancers to become a camera operator covering live remote television broadcasts. He has earned even more status under his new boss, Morgan Edge of Galaxy Communications.

PERRY WHITE

The *Daily Planet*'s editor in chief, White hired both Lois Lane and Clark Kent as reporters. Though the *Daily Planet* has since been sold to Morgan Edge of Galaxy Communications, Perry has remained at his post.

MAGGIE SAWYER

Maggie Sawyer once headed up the Metropolis Police Department's Special Crimes Unit, responsible for dealing with super-villain and extraterrestrial threats. She and Superman have a relationship of mutual respect.

DAN TURPIN

An officer with the Metropolis police department and one-time second-in-command of the city's Special Crimes Unit, Dan "Terrible" Turpin is a tough, resourceful fighter with a reputation for brutal honesty.

DAVID CORPORON

The new commissioner of the Metropolis Police Department, Corporon works closely with the mayor to contain superpowered threats. His job requires him to work closely with Superman, whom he views with suspicion.

BIBBO

Bibbo Bibbowski is a big-hearted, no-nonsense former boxer who owns the Ace O'Clubs bar in Metropolis' Suicide Slum. He respects Superman, his "fav'rit" super hero, for his ability to take a punch.

PROF. EMIL HAMILTON

Professor Hamilton worked for S.T.A.R. Labs until he opened his own workshop in Metropolis.

CHLOE SULLIVAN

A friend of Clark Kent's from Smallville, journalist Chloe Sullivan is Lois Lane's cousin. She works for the website *Metropolitan* and dated Jimmy Olsen, once teaming up with him to investigate an alien menace.

NEWSBOY LEGION

Originally a gang of orphans who sold papers in Metropolis' Suicide Slum, the second Newsboy Legion are clones created by Project Cadmus. Led by Tommy Tompkins, the team includes Gabby, Scrapper, and Big Words.

LUCY LANE

Lois Lane's younger sister, Lucy has dated Clark Kent. In a previous timeline, she married Ron Troupe.

CLAIRE FOSTER

Claire Foster is a Metropolis psychiatrist who specializes in treating super heroes, including Superman. She understands the pressures and responsibilities of the job, and treats her patients with empathy and humor.

NATASHA IRONS

The niece of John Henry Irons, the super hero Steel, Natasha Irons shares her uncle's gift for engineering and worked as his assistant in his Steelworks complex. When an injury temporarily sidelined her uncle, Natasha forged her own suit of armor and took to the streets as the new Steel. She later volunteered to become a test subject for Lex Luthor's "Everyman Project" which aimed to give ordinary citizens superpowers. Before Luthor took her powers away, Natasha was the super hero Starlight. A lingering result of Luthor's experiment gave Natasha the ability to transform into an intangible mist and she briefly adopted the identity of Vaporlock.

BARBARA GORDON

Better known as Batgirl, Barbara Gordon is the daughter of Gotham police commissioner Jim Gordon and an information expert. She formerly aided the super hero community as the computer hacker Oracle.

LEX LUTHOR

"Superman isn't here to save us, Lois Lane. Fortunately, I am."

Lex Luthor is a scientific genius and the billionaire head of LexCorp. Until Superman arrived, he was the most important person in Metropolis, but his hatred of the Man of Steel is more than simple jealousy. Luthor believes he is humanity's defender against Kryptonians and other alien threats.

An obsession with beating Superman caused President Luthor to inject himself with the superhuman Venom serum and construct a jet-propelled armored battle suit. Luthor was soon run out of office following a string of scandals that tarnished his reputation.

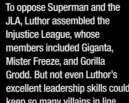

While in Smallville, Luthor discovered the secrets of Green Kryptonite.

In the version of the timeline established after the Infinite Crisis, Lex Luthor spent his childhood years in Smallville as Clark Kent's schoolmate—Luthor was bullied by the other students for his strange genius. Luthor arranged the death of his abusive father, Lionel, and used the insurance money to found the multinational corporation LexCorp. Luthor resented Superman stealing the spotlight from his own grand works for Metropolis, and plotted to eliminate the Man of Steel by funding his own corps of superpowered agents. He wore a Kryptonite ring that kept Superman from getting too close, but the green radiation claimed his hand before taking his life. Luthor, however, had staged his death so that he could secretly transfer his brain into a healthy, cloned body. For a time, he claimed to be his own son, but the demon Neron enabled him to return to his original appearance. Luthor scored his greatest victory over Superman by becoming US President, but suffered blows to his fortune and reputation after he left office. Just prior to the timeline-rewriting Flashpoint incident, Luthor undertook a quest to seize the energy used by the Black Lantern Corps, a search that brought him into the realms of the gods.

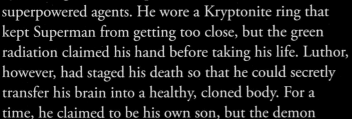

Radiation from Luthor's Kryptonite ring left him with an artificial hand.

After the Infinite Crisis, Luthor sponsored the Everyman Project, which promised to bestow superpowers on ordinary humans. His best-performing subjects became members of a new Infinity, Inc. team. He pulled the plug on the others, causing hundreds to plunge from the sky to their deaths.

To oppose Superman and the JLA, Luthor assembled the Injustice League, whose members included Giganta, Mister Freeze, and Gorilla Grodd. But not even Luthor's excellent leadership skills could keep so many villains in line.

Luthor hoped to win the public's love as President of the United States.

Luthor's intellect is unmatched on Earth. He can also be charming and is an excellent liar—human qualities that give him an edge against alien geniuses such as Brainiac.

THE NEW 52: LEX LUTHOR

When the mysterious hero Superman burst onto the Metropolis scene, General Sam Lane hired Lex Luthor to help the government trap and study the new arrival. Luthor put his genius and his fortune behind uncovering Superman's secrets, convinced that the alien was an advance scout in what would soon become a full-scale Kryptonian invasion. He allied himself with Brainiac to gain even greater power.

Luthor had Superman brought to a secret government lab for experimentation.

Luthor is so wealthy that he can buy anything he wants. He keeps his look classy yet understated, preferring to let his actions do the talking.

KEY DATA

REAL/FULL NAME Alexander "Lex" Luthor

FIRST APPEARANCE *Action Comics* #23 (April 1940)

OCCUPATION Corporate executive, government researcher, criminal mastermind

AFFILIATIONS LexCorp

POWERS/WEAPONS Lex Luthor's genius-level intellect has made him a master of multiple fields, including mathematics, physics, economics, linguistics, sociology, and engineering. Through the financial resources of LexCorp, he can obtain anything that money can buy.

MAIN ENEMIES

Superman's most dangerous foes possess an array of incredible mental and physical skills. If the Man of Steel did not stand in their way, any one of them could conquer the world.

LEX LUTHOR

He has invented hundreds of revolutionary technologies and amassed a multibillion dollar fortune. Soon after Superman arrived in Metropolis, General Sam Lane hired Lex Luthor to capture the vigilante. Luthor is convinced that Superman is an alien threat to Earth who will undermine the position of humans as the planet's dominant species.

BRAINIAC

An artificial intelligence also known as the Collector of Worlds. Prior to Krypton's destruction, Brainiac miniaturized the city of Kandor. In league with Lex Luthor, he later miniaturized Metropolis, until Superman stopped his plans. Brainiac can exist as pure information and is able to control electronics from a distance or transfer his consciousness into a mechanical host.

DARKSEID

Ruler of the fiery planet Apokolips, Darkseid is a New God who possesses the infinite power of the Omega Force. He has often clashed with Superman as he pursues the Anti-Life Equation, believing it will give him mental control of all lifeforms. Darkseid's rule over Apokolips has endured for centuries. The Omega Beams he fires from his eyes can disintegrate any form of matter.

GENERAL ZOD

Prior to Krypton's destruction, Zod led a failed revolution against the Kryptonian Council. As punishment, he and his collaborators were sent to the Phantom Zone; they thus escaped their planet's fate. Zod and his Kryptonian henchmen emerged to wreak havoc on Earth. Superman's father, Jor-El, sent Zod into the Phantom Zone, and Zod has vowed revenge on Jor-El's son.

DOOMSDAY

Created thousands of years ago on Krypton to be the ultimate killing machine, Doomsday actually killed Superman. After Superman's return from the dead, Doomsday re-emerged to launch several berserker rampages. Despite seemingly terminal injuries, Doomsday's regenerative powers enable him to come back stronger than ever. The spikes on his body can pierce Kryptonian skin.

BIZARRO

Created as an imperfect duplicate of Superman, Bizarro is a backwards-speaking, slow-witted creature who causes more harm from carelessness than cruelty. Many of his powers are the opposite of Superman's, including fire breath and freeze vision. Bizarro created Bizarro World and populated it with Bizarro versions of key people from Superman's life in Metropolis.

MONGUL

The brutal, merciless ruler of Warworld, Mongul is a supremely powerful alien conqueror who believes in the principle of "rule by the strong." Aboard Warworld's intergalactic megalopolis, Mongul held regular gladiatorial contests in which his strongest slaves fought to the death. When Superman joined the games, he fought his way through Warworld's warriors without taking a single life. Mongul had no choice but to face the Man of Steel one on one and suffered a humiliating defeat. Now consumed with thoughts of revenge, Mongul allied with the villainous Cyborg Superman and annihilated Coast City on his enemy's home planet of Earth. Superman defeated Mongul's attempt to turn Earth into another Warworld. Mongul was later killed during a furious confrontation with the demon Neron.

During later conflicts between Mongul and the Man of Steel, the role of super-villain fell to Mongul's son, who shared the same name and appearance as his father.

METALLO

US soldier John Corben once had a relationship with Lois Lane. When she broke it off, he became obsessed with rekindling their romance. He volunteered for the Steel Soldier project run by Lois' father, General Sam Lane, hoping to gain closer ties to the Lane family. When Superman escaped from government custody, Corben agreed to bond with the experimental "Metal 0" armor. In his new cybernetic state, he tried to recapture Superman, but the alien intelligence Brainiac took control of Metallo's systems and made him do his will. After this ordeal, the military repaired Metallo's injuries by replacing his heart with a reactor powered by Green Kryptonite.

PARASITE

Parasite has the ability to absorb the superpowers of other beings, sometimes gaining access to their memories and intelligence. Before his transformation he was Rudy Jones, a janitor at the *Daily Planet* who jumped at the chance to receive a new life in Lex Luthor's laboratories. An accident at LexCorp mutated him into the Parasite; side-effects of his new state included purple skin and a circular mouth lined with teeth. When Parasite absorbs a super hero's powers, he temporarily becomes a formidable opponent. Superman's Kryptonian powers offer a never-ending food source, so he is Parasite's ultimate target.

CYBORG SUPERMAN

A close encounter with a solar flare mutated astronaut Hank Henshaw's cells and sent his body into a rapid spiral of deterioration. Reduced to a skeleton, Henshaw discovered that he could transfer his consciousness into machinery. The shock of seeing her husband in the form of a skeletal robot led his wife to commit suicide. Paranoid and delusional, Henshaw decided that Superman was to blame for his fate. When the Man of Steel died stopping Doomsday's rampage in Metropolis, Henshaw decided to destroy Superman's heroic reputation. As the Cyborg Superman, he forced Mongul into an alliance and orchestrated the destruction of Coast City, until the true  Superman returned and put an end to his schemes. The Cyborg Superman later joined the ranks of the Sinestro Corps, and was also targeted by the Doomslayer as part of a plan to clone Doomsday and lay waste to the Earth.

OTHER ENEMIES

Superman's foes vary from small-time to universe-shaking, but each has a special talent that cannot be underestimated. Superman takes them all seriously, whether there are a billion lives at stake or just one.

ATOMIC SKULL

A metahuman mutation turned the Atomic Skull's flesh invisible, making him look like a living skeleton and giving him the ability to fire radiation blasts. He has become dangerously mentally unstable.

BRUNO MANNHEIM

Nicknamed "Ugly," Bruno Mannheim is a major figure among Metropolis' organized crime families and the leader of Intergang. He sometimes strikes deals with Darkseid and is a follower of the twisted cult the Religion of Crime.

BLACK ADAM

Ancient Egyptian pharoah's son Teth-Adam received magical powers from the wizard Shazam. Corrupted by his gifts, Teth-Adam lay in a sarcophagus for millennia until his resurrection in modern times. Now called Black Adam, he is nearly as strong as Superman. His magic-based powers allow him to bypass Superman's Kryptonian defenses.

TOYMAN

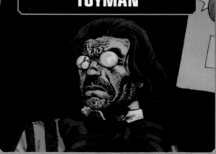

Winslow Schott is a brilliant inventor who specializes in children's toys. He learned to use his talents in the service of crime, constructing intricate, miniature models of jack-in-the-boxes or toy soldiers that frequently featured nasty surprises, such as high explosives or live ammunition. The Toyman tries to avoid injuring people, but he pulls out all the stops when he faces Superman.

PRANKSTER

Former TV host Oswald Loomis is a connoisseur of practical jokes, employing a customized arsenal for his Prankster crimes. He sometimes sells his services to other super-villains, who pay him to distract Superman with his pranks while they carry out their crimes.

ERADICATOR

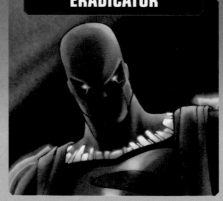

A Kryptonian artifact created more than 200,000 years ago, the Eradicator became self-aware after Superman brought it back to Earth. When Superman died in battle with Doomsday, the Eradicator inhabited a duplicate of Kal-El's body, leading some people to believe that Superman had returned from the dead. The Eradicator later joined the Outsiders. When the Doomslayer tried to destroy the Earth, the Eradicator sacrificed itself to cast the enemy into a bottomless singularity.

DOMINUS

The alien priest Tuoni hoped to possess the omnipotent Kismet force, but saw it granted to his lover instead. Exiled to the Phantom Zone, he gained the power to warp reality and returned as Dominus, using Superman in his revenge scheme.

JAX-UR

Jax-Ur was a brilliant Kryptonian scientist, sentenced to exile in the Phantom Zone after he accidentally destroyed Krypton's moon. Jax-Ur then fell under the influence of General Zod.

MR. MXYZPTLK

Imp from the fifth dimension Mr. Mxyzptlk has control over our three-dimensional reality. His wife posed as Clark Kent's landlady Mrs. Nyxly during Clark's early years in Metropolis, following Mr. Mxyzptlk's defeat by the fifth-dimensional sorcerer Lord Vyndktyx.

LIVEWIRE

Metropolis radio host Leslie Willis began a life of crime as Livewire, using her ability to turn into living electricity and fire lightning bolts. Livewire has teamed up with Superman, notably during his coast-to-coast walk across the US.

CONDUIT

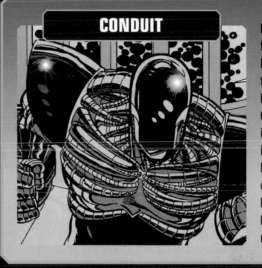

Kenny Braverman, Clark Kent's classmate from Smallville, received a dose of Kryptonite radiation from the same rocket that first brought Kryptonian infant Kal-El to Earth. After Kenny became the villain Conduit, he discovered Clark's secret identity, and tormented Jonathan and Martha Kent and Lois Lane in an effort to break Superman's spirit. Conduit wears a cyborg suit with gauntlets that fire blasts of Kryptonite energy and rockets that allow him to fly. He also has an army of mercenaries on his payroll.

SILVER BANSHEE

Siobhan Smythe is the most recent member of the Smythe family to fall victim to an ancient Celtic curse, the same curse that turned her father into the sinister Black Banshee. To flee her past, Siobhan left Dublin and moved to Metropolis. Thanks to her ability to comprehend alien languages, she befriended Supergirl shortly after the Kryptonian arrived on Earth. Siobhan became the Silver Banshee to fight her father and reclaim the soul of her brother Tom. She has the magical ability to emit ear-shattering sonic screeches.

IMPERIEX

The cosmic entity Imperiex appears in the form of a gigantic armored being, containing a near-limitless reservoir of energy. When Imperiex attacked the Earth, Superman united with Lex Luthor and Darkseid to defeat this powerful being and its legion of drones.

MORE ENEMIES

Weird mutations and alien invaders are nothing new for the Man of Steel, who always stays on full alert to defend the people of Metropolis.

SUPERBOY-PRIME

Prior to the Crisis on Infinite Earths, the Clark Kent of the alternate world of Earth-Prime was his planet's only super hero. He survived the multiverse's collapse and, seething with resentment, emerged during the Infinite Crisis to wreak havoc. His abilities are more powerful than Superman's.

ULTRA-HUMANITE

The first Ultra-Humanite's real name is unknown. The second, real name Gerard Shugel, is also a scientific genius. Stricken with a degenerative disease, he transplanted his brain into a new body. He has extended his life by taking over the bodies of innocent victims, but his most common form is that of a mutated albino gorilla.

TITANO THE SUPER-APE

Titano was once a normal chimpanzee, but a mad scientist used him as a test subject for experimental DNA mutations during Superman's earliest years in Metropolis. Grown to gigantic proportions, Titano caused trouble until the Man of Steel confined him to a secure facility. Alien nanites impersonating Superman, seemingly executed Titano believing he might pose a threat in the future.

NEUTRON

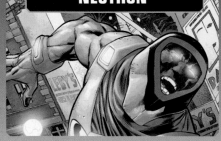

An accident at a nuclear power plant reduced security guard Nathaniel Tryon to a cloud of nuclear energy. Holding his shape in a containment suit, he became the super-villain Neutron. He can fly, is immune to most forms of damage, and can fire bolts of energy from his hands.

INSECT QUEEN

Ruler of alien insectoids the All-Hive, she travels the galaxy looking for planets to colonize. She can fly, secrete a narcotic substance, metamorphose, and exert telepathic control. She has used her powers to take over Lana Lang's body.

KALIBAK

One of the New Gods of Apokolips, the first-born son of Darkseid is desperate for his father's approval and jealous of his half-brother Orion. Kalibak is invulnerable to most forms of attack, his Beta-Club fires energy blasts, and he has access to Fourth World boom tube technology.

SATANUS

The demonic Lord Satanus is a high-ranking figure in the infernal underworld. He has often targeted Superman, hoping to ensnare his soul. Satanus has posed as Colin Thornton, the Metropolis-based publisher of *Newstime* magazine.

KRYPTONITE MAN

Scientist K. Russell Abernathy hoped to use Kryptonite as an alternative energy source, but an explosion infused his body with radiation. As the green-skinned Kryptonite Man, he can counter the natural superpowers of Kryptonians.

RIOT

Attempting to live up to his family's monster-making legacy, Frederick von Frankenstein used an experimental phase shifter to split himself into multiple copies. As the villain Riot, he joined the Superman Revenge Squad.

THE FEMALE FURIES

The elite strike force of Apokolips is commanded by Granny Goodness. Its changing roster includes cruel Mad Harriet, earthquake-generating Stompa, whip-wielding Lashina, and Bernadeth, whose fahren-knife burns victims from the inside out.

MORGAN EDGE

The billionaire CEO of Galaxy Communications is one of Metropolis' most powerful figures. His holdings include television station WGBS and the *Daily Planet*. He is rumored to have connections with organized crime and alien warlords.

AMBUSH BUG

This oddball character wears a protective suit and can teleport. At first he annoyed the Man of Steel, but he has since tried to become Superman's friend. He carries a doll named Cheeks, the Toy Wonder, which he claims is his sidekick.

RAMPAGE

A lab explosion temporarily turned meek scientist Kitty Faulkner into Rampage, a towering, violent, orange-skinned creature. Dr. Faulkner holds a high-ranking post at S.T.A.R. Labs, but has reverted to Rampage from time to time.

BLOODSPORT

Robert DuBois suffered a breakdown when his brother was severely injured serving in the US Army. DuBois believed he should have taken his brother's place and succumbed to Lex Luthor's suggestion that Superman was to blame. Bloodsport's automatic weapons fire Kryptonite bullets; a teleporter enables him to escape with ease.

ADVERSARY

Young Cary Richards made a deal with Lord Satanus to fix his paralyzed legs and become like the super heroes he saw on television. As the Adversary, Richards sports a black costume with metal spikes and chews on a cigar, all part of a child's idea of a super-villain.

THE NEW 52
TIMELINE

WHAT IS "CONTINUITY"?

The DC Universe is an interconnected setting that changes over time. But sometimes previous histories have been overwritten by new ones, usually explained as the fallout from epic "Crisis" events. All of Superman's adventures since 1938 occurred within their respective timelines, but The New 52 continuity is the only one fans need to follow to understand the Man of Steel.

• During the height of Kryptonian civilization, a violent uprising led by a clone named Kon brings death to thousands.

• Jor-El, a leading scientist on Krypton, discovers the Phantom Zone. The criminal Xa-Du is the first Kryptonian to be sentenced to exile within its endless void.

• Despite the warnings of Jor-El, the planet Krypton is destroyed in a catastrophic explosion. Jor-El and his wife Lara send their son Kal-El to Earth in a tiny spacecraft. Jor-El's brother Zor-El launches his teenage daughter Kara Zor-El in a separate craft. Kal-El's rocket crashes in a field near Smallville, Kansas, where it is found by Jonathan and Martha Kent. They raise the alien baby as Clark Kent.

• Jonathan and Martha Kent pass away. After burying his parents, Clark Kent departs Smallville to attend college.

• Clark Kent moves to Metropolis and takes a job as a reporter for the *Daily Star*. He begins secretly adventuring as a hero, though his superpowers are still developing.

• Wearing his early uniform of t-shirt, jeans, and cape, Superman scares corrupt Metropolis businessman Glen Glenmorgan into confessing his illegal business practices. General Sam Lane and Lex Luthor devise a trap to capture the vigilante.

• Clark saves a boy from a train collision. Lois Lane and Jimmy Olsen publicize the rescue in the pages of the *Daily Planet*, introducing the world to Superman.

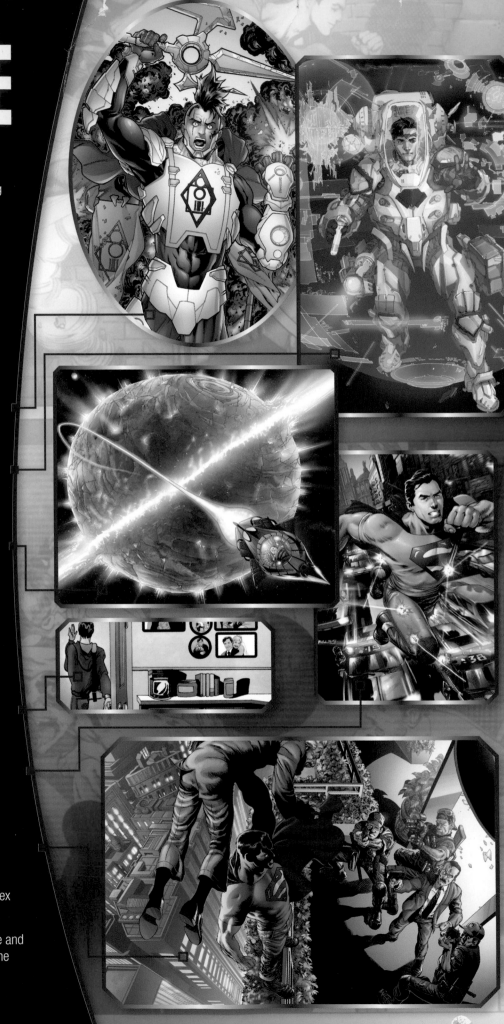

- As part of the efforts to stop Superman, John Corben is turned into the cyborg Metallo. John Henry Irons dons a suit of powered armor and fights Metallo as a new hero, Steel.

- Brainiac shrinks Metropolis, bottles it, and stores it in his spaceship. Superman defeats him and obtains a new costume of Kryptonian design.

- After Metropolis is restored to full size, the mayor gives Superman the key to the city, publicly praising him as a hero.

- Superman meets Batman, Green Lantern, The Flash, Aquaman, Wonder Woman, and Cyborg when they unite to stop Darkseid's invasion of Earth. They stay together as the Justice League.

- After constructing the Fortress of Solitude in the Arctic, Superman fights the Phantom Zone criminal Xa-Du and rescues his family's dog, Krypto.

- The fifth-dimensional being Lord Vyndktvx recruits villains into the Anti-Superman Army, and attacks a Mars colony to force Superman to fight his agents, the Multitude.

- Superman defeats a number of threats to Metropolis including Titano, the Sky Raiders, and the giant robots of Professor Fleischer.

- Superboy is created in the laboratories of N.O.W.H.E.R.E., implanted with the memories of the Kryptonian clone Kon by the sinister Lord Harvest.

- The *Daily Planet* is sold to Morgan Edge of Galaxy Communications. Its iconic building is demolished to make room for a new one.

- After years spent orbiting the sun, Kara Zor-El's rocket finally lands on Earth. She emerges from Stasis, still as a teenager, and is met by her cousin Kal-El, now a grown man. Kara eventually takes up the identity of Supergirl.

- In the Himalayas, Superman meets Helspont of the Daemonites, who fails in his attempt to lure Superman to his side.

- The Justice League defeats the villain Graves. In the aftermath, Superman and Wonder Woman share their first kiss.

- A being called H'el intrudes on the lives of Superman, Supergirl, and Superboy, claiming to have a connection to Krypton.

THE GOLDEN AGE

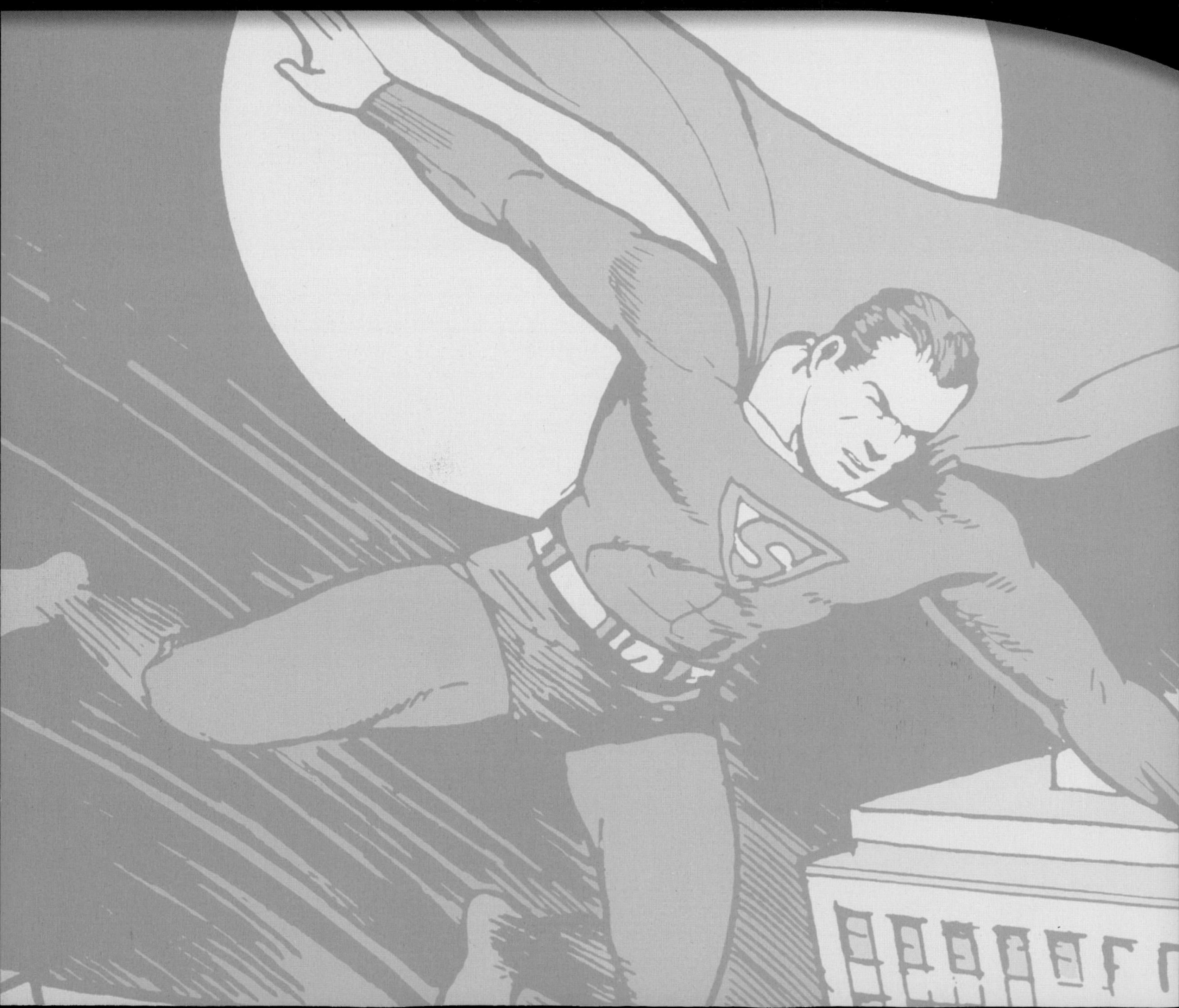

Without Superman, there never would have been a Golden Age. The term describes the explosion in American super hero comics that began in 1938 and echoed through the following decade. The spark that lit the fuse was DC Comics' Superman.

Other companies followed Superman's lead after his star turn in *Action Comics* #1. Soon, newsstands across the country were advertising the comic book adventures of their own heroes, from Captain Marvel to Captain America. But DC wasn't about to surrender its head start. Superman became the head of an army of DC Golden Age heroes that included Wonder Woman, Hawkman, Green Lantern, Aquaman, the Flash, and Batman. Notably, DC chose to place all its super heroes into a shared fictional continuity, which became known as the DC universe. The Justice Society of America was the first multi-hero team in comics, and Superman made its roster as an honorary member.

As newspaper headlines chronicled World War II in Europe and in the Pacific, readers on the home front took comfort from their super heroes. In due course, wartime paper shortages forced DC to reduce publication frequency of some of its titles and drop pages froml others. Superman, however, remained a bright spot.

The character's runaway success in *Action Comics* inspired a separate, self-titled *Superman* series. The Man of Steel also appeared in *World's Finest Comics*, starting in 1941. Superman's younger self, Superboy, had been appearing in *Action Comics* since 1945. In 1949, Superboy received his own series, commencing with *Superboy* #1 (March-April), which chronicled Superman's childhood adventures in Smallville.

By the close of the 1940s, sales of super hero comics were flagging, indicating that the genre's boom years were ending. Neither Superman nor Superboy titles were in danger of cancellation, but the disappearance of several other super hero series signaled the end of comics' Golden Age.

OVERLEAF *Action Comics* #131 (April 1949): Luthor, Superman's nemesis, seems to have the Man of Steel at his mercy with a ray that can make him vanish into the fourth dimension. No wonder Lois Lane looks concerned. Cover art: Al Plastino

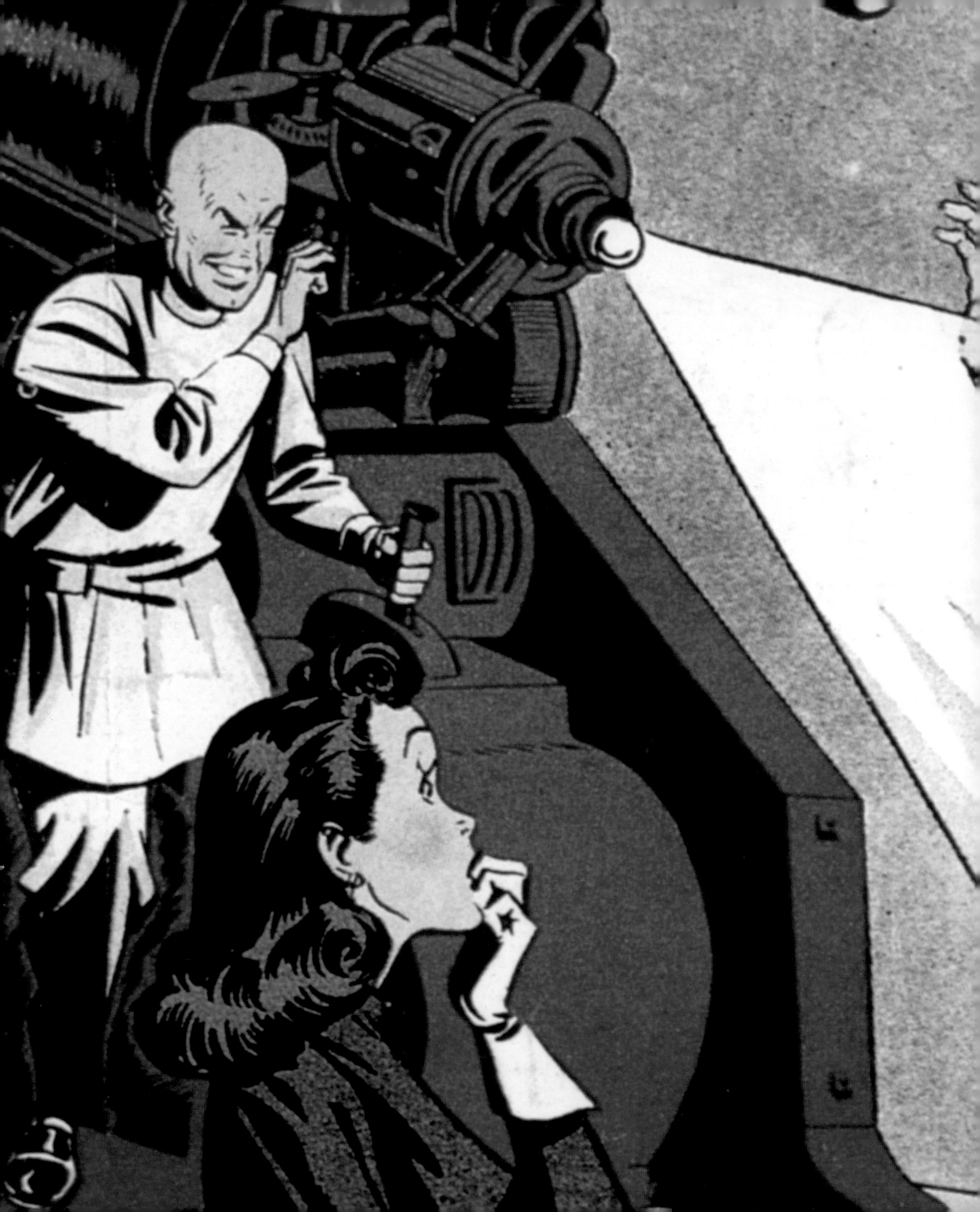

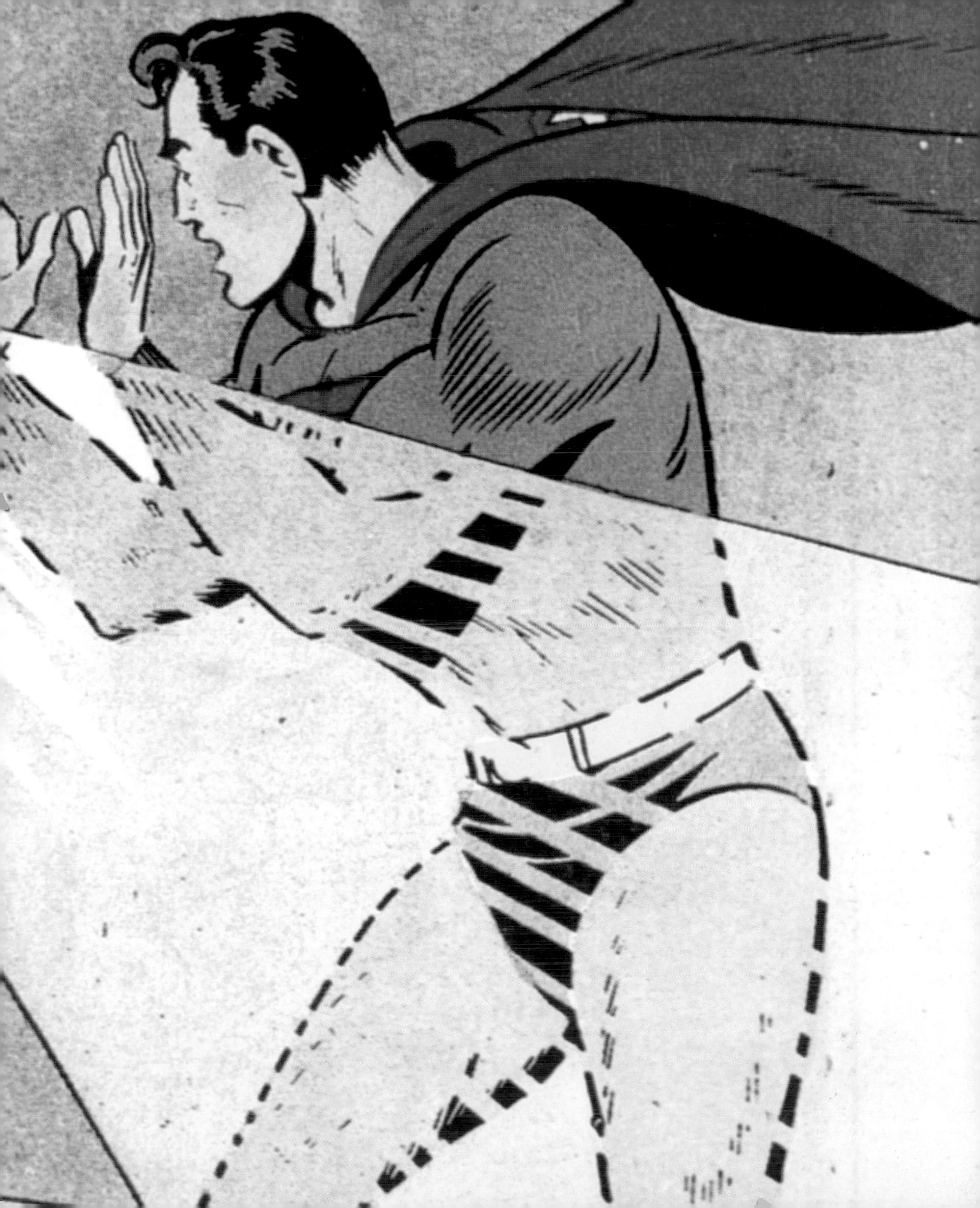

GOLDEN AGE ADVENTURES

ACTION ALLIES

Superman was the star of *Action Comics* from its first issue, but the comic's anthology format allowed other heroes to shine: Tex Thomson, Mr. America, carried a whip and later changed his name to the Americommando; the Vigilante wore Old West trappings like a kerchief and six-shooter; Zatara, sporting a top hat, performed feats of magic by speaking his spells backward; Congo Bill adventured in the African jungle. Although Superman didn't co-star in their tales, all the characters co-existed in the same shared universe.

KRYPTON NO MORE

The destruction of Krypton and the sacrifice of Superman's parents was part of the legend from the start, though the story gained more details throughout the Golden Age. In some versions, all Kryptonians had superpowers on their own planet; later, Superman's abilities were attributed to Earth's lower gravity. At first, Superman had no inkling of his extraterrestrial origins, but an investigation of a mysterious green rock that weakened him led the Man of Steel to trave back in time to Krypton to witness the world of his birth.

ROLE MODEL
Thanks to his popularity with young readers, Superman served as a role model for kids in need. DC also started an official Superman fan club during in 1939 called the Supermen of America, which called on each member to "do everything possible to increase his or her strength and courage and to aid in the cause of justice."

HAVING SOME FUN

As Superman's powers became clearly defined, writers found new ways to challenge the hero. Imaginative storylines, which would become even more outlandish during the Silver Age, included Superman and Lois Lane discovering a tribe of cavemen who used dinosaurs as pack animals. Superman also stopped giant robots on more than one occasion, and gained intriguing new powers, such as super-hypnotism. In one tale, a greedy promoter tried to get the Man of Steel to endorse a series of questionable products, including "Superman gasoline for super-power."

THE ATOMIC AGE

As the US entered the post-war era, Superman could be seen in a new light as a symbol of limitless power. In a story published after the US had begun atomic bomb testing at Bikini Atoll in the Pacific, the force of an atomic blast cures Superman of the effects of a drug that drives its victims insane. Restored to his normal self, Superman remains in the area to film a second test, hoping the footage will serve as "a warning to men who talk against peace."

A GALLERY OF ROGUES

Superman started out fighting corrupt politicians, but gradually acquired his own rogues gallery of bizarre villains. Mad scientist the Ultra-Humanite was the first; the far more cunning Luthor (he only became Lex Luthor in 1960) soon followed; Mr. Mxyzplk [sic], an imp from the Fifth Dimension, pestered Superman with his magical abilities; and the Prankster and the Toyman created dangerous playthings to surprise the Man of Steel.

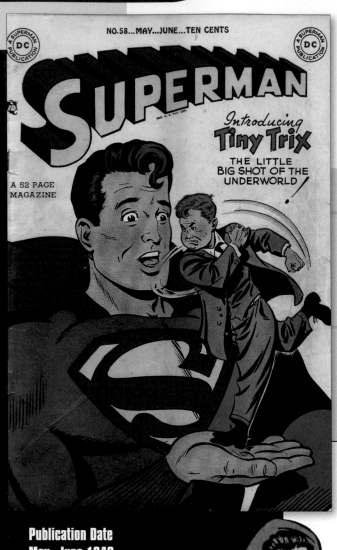

NO. 58...MAY...JUNE...TEN CENTS

SUPERMAN

Introducing **Tiny Trix**

THE LITTLE BIG SHOT OF THE UNDERWORLD!

A 52 PAGE MAGAZINE

Publication Date
May–June 1949

Editor
Whitney Ellsworth

Cover Artist
Al Plastino

Writer
William Woolfolk

Penciller
Wayne Boring

Inker
Stan Kaye

SUPERMAN

Vol. 1   #58

"Lois Lane Loves Clark Kent!"

> "Newspaper reporting is my first love, Superman was my second. But you're only third!"
>
> **Lois Lane to Clark Kent**

Main Characters: **Superman, Lois Lane**
Main Supporting Characters: **Perry White**
Main Locations: **Metropolis, psychiatrist's office, *Daily Planet* Building**

BACKGROUND

Unlike most super heroes of the era, Superman had a consistent love interest. What's more, Superman had a love triangle!

The relationship between Lois Lane, Superman, and Clark Kent provided the foundation for countless stories. Lily-livered Clark failed to win Lois' affections while she mooned over square-jawed Superman. But, since the "men" in her life were keeping a vital secret, Lois had the deck stacked against her from the start. Clark, armed with superpowers and an inside track on his ever-curious co-worker's habits, always remained one step ahead of Lois' attempts to better understand the Man of Steel.

This plotline would be given an additional twist in later stories when writers introduced Lana Lang, Superman's former flame from Smallville, as Lois' romantic rival. Between Lois' attempts to trick Superman into proposing marriage and her efforts to stop Lana from doing the same, it's a wonder that Lois had any time left over to file her stories for the *Daily Planet*.

But "Lois Lane Loves Clark Kent!" from *Superman* #58, doesn't forget that readers first met Lois inside a newsroom. When Lois begins a romantic pursuit of Clark on a psychiatrist's questionable advice, she discovers her *true* love—journalism.

THE STORY

Lois Lane loves Superman, but is her hopeless, unreciprocated devotion damaging her mental health? One therapist believes so and advises Lois to transfer her affections onto someone a little closer to home. Clark Kent becomes the object of Lois' undivided attention, until he thinks of a way to demonstrate where Lois' loyalties truly lie.

Lois Lane is so preoccupied with thoughts of Superman that she wanders into traffic on a busy Metropolis street. Just in time, Clark Kent changes into his Superman costume and saves her **[1]**. Concerned for her well-being, Superman recommends that Lois visit a psychiatrist in order to clear her head.

The doctor plays a simple word-association game with Lois, and every topic he suggests gets the answer: "Superman." He decides that Lois has been pining over an unattainable goal, and is suffering from heartbreak. If she transfers her feelings onto someone who might actually reciprocate, he suggests, she might find happiness. Someone like her co-worker, Clark Kent **[2]**.

Lois isn't happy about asking Clark out on a date, but she resolves to act as if she loves Clark, in the hope that genuine emotions will follow. Their candlelit dinner goes well **[3]**, but Clark—who can't break character under such close scrutiny—resorts to trickery to stop a purse-snatcher from making off with Lois' valuables. A similar scene plays out at the movies, where Clark uses his super-speed to slip away and collar a gang of thieves raiding the box office, without Lois noticing his absence **[4]**.

Lois discovers that her efforts are paying off. She feels closer to Clark every day. When she starts giving him love notes and expensive presents, Clark starts to worry. A glance at Lois' scrapbook reveals the reason for her sudden behavior change **[5]**. He decides to stop things before they get out of hand.

An opportunity arises when a derailed train releases a cargo of cattle in downtown Metropolis. Superman stops the stampede by ripping up the tracks of a decommissioned cable car network, laying down the steel beams around the herd and erecting a makeshift corral **[6]**.

Lois witnesses the whole thing, and realizes that the Man of Steel's latest stunt is a guaranteed front-page feature. She races back to the *Daily Planet* and types up her story as quickly as she can, unaware that Clark is doing the very same thing **[7]**.

Perry White rejects her story, explaining that he has already accepted Clark's version. Lois confronts her co-worker, who innocently explains that he had watched Superman's cattle roundup by pointing a telescope through his office window **[8]**.

Furious at getting scooped, Lois realizes that she doesn't love Clark. And furthermore, that there isn't anything she loves more than her career—not even Superman. With an icy glare she tells Clark that their romance is over **[9]**.

But being a reporter doesn't mean that she has to give up on Superman entirely. Back in her apartment, Lois stares longingly at her framed Superman photo and dreams of the day when the Man of Steel will sweep her off her feet **[10]**.

BOOSTING MORALE

DC faced a dilemma when it came to Superman's monthly adventures. After all, if someone with the abilities of the Man of Steel were actually unleashed against the Axis powers, World War II would be over in days. To maintain the suspension of disbelief, DC explained that Clark Kent had failed his draft board examination due to a poor score in his eye test. Clark remained in Metropolis to chronicle the war for the *Daily Planet*, while Superman fought spies and saboteurs at home. Meanwhile, the covers of *Superman* and *World's Finest Comics* promoted war bonds and victory gardens, and 1944's *Superman* #29 cover depicted Lois Lane with a trio of admirers she dubbed "my supermen"—a soldier, a sailor, and a US Marine.

Superman became a potent symbol of wartime patriotism.

With his X-ray vision, Clark accidentally read the eye chart in an adjoining room, causing him to flunk his draft physical.

At the height of the Superman boom, the world faced the specter of global war. Thanks to his optimistic embodiment of American resolve, Superman helped to keep spirits high.

THE WAR YEARS

Hitching a ride in the back of a jeep, Superman shared stories with American GIs during their stateside training.

THE TRUE HEROES

Superman's behind-the-scenes role allowed DC to focus on the US armed forces. In 1943's *Superman #23*, the Man of Steel assisted in a training exercise. Superman aided the red team by using his X-ray vision to report on the blue team's positions, and he tunneled through a mountain to allow the red team to get the drop on its opponent. But what really impressed Superman was what he called "America's secret weapon"—the courage of the nation's soldiers.

> "HOORAY FOR THE AMERICAN FIGHTING MAN—THE REAL CHAMPION ON LAND, ON THE SEA, AND IN THE AIR!"

With Hitler in one hand and Stalin in the other, Superman streaked toward an appointment with the League of Nations.

WINNING THE WAR

"How Superman Would End the War" appeared as a special feature in *Look* magazine. In this imaginary tale, Superman smashed the German defenses along the Siegfried Line, punched a Luftwaffe fighter right out of the sky, and plucked Adolf Hitler from his fortified bunker. Telling the Führer, "I'd like to land a strictly non-Aryan sock on your jaw," he hauled his prisoner to Moscow where he also collared Joseph Stalin (at the time of the story's publication in 1940 the US hadn't even entered the war, let alone forged an alliance with Stalin's Russia). Superman deposited both dictators before a League of Nations tribunal in Geneva, Switzerland.

THE SILVER AGE

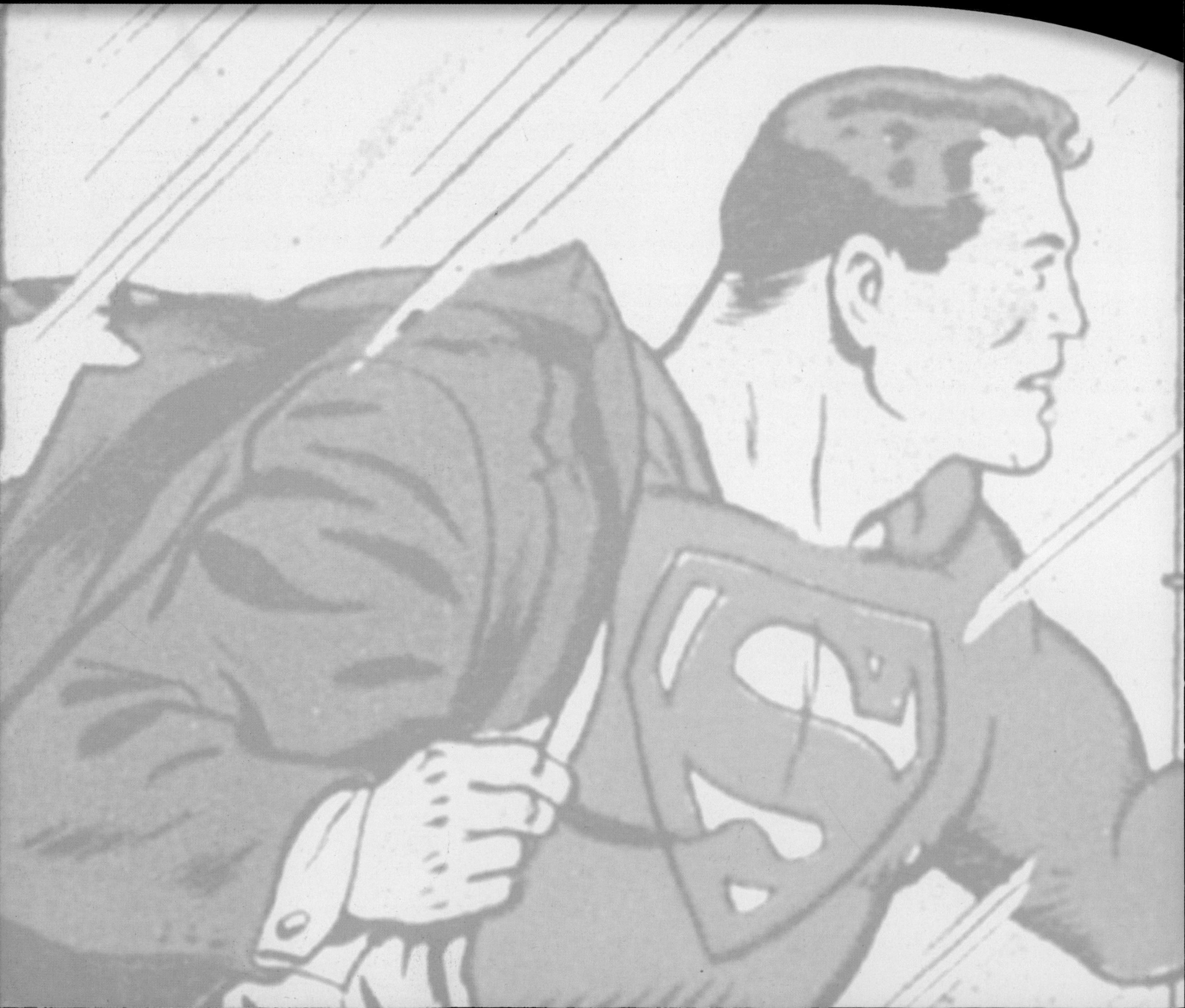

Were super heroes just a fad? That's what many publishers started to think when low-selling super hero comics disappeared from newsstands at the end of the 1940s. Romance stories, funny animal antics, and other genre experiments took their shelf space. However after a few barren years in the early 1950s DC brought super heroes back in a big way and ignited a whole new era of spectacular creativity.

The first appearance of Barry Allen as the Flash in 1956's *Showcase* #4 is widely considered the landmark event of the Silver Age of comics (1956–c.1970), ushering in new interpretations of classic characters such as Green Lantern, Hawkman, and the Atom. Superman's popularity had kept him in continuous publication, but cultural changes would soon give even the steadfast Man of Steel an eye-opening makeover.

The publishing industry's adoption of the Comics Code Authority, intended to shield children from excessive violence and sexual themes, had the byproduct of creating a sanitized super hero universe. Meanwhile, the growing public fascination with atomic power and its potentially terrifying or bizarre side-effects, flying saucers and "little green men" from outer space, and a prevailing 1950s craze for sci-fi movies full of outlandish monsters of every kind, helped shape DC's Silver Age output and give it a distinctly science-fictional flavor.

Unlike some heroes, sci-fi suited Superman just fine. He was already a strange visitor from another planet, so battling space invaders and mutant apes hardly seemed outside his jurisdiction. The Man of Steel soon gained some extraterrestrial friends: his cousin Supergirl, his dog Krypto, his space monkey Beppo, and the time-traveling teenagers of the Legion of Super-Heroes. The radiation of Kryptonite could potentially give Superman the head of an ant or the power to breathe fire; happily he could recover from his often bizarre adventures in his arctic Fortress of Solitude.

Superman's Pal, Jimmy Olsen cast the *Daily Planet*'s cub reporter as an everyman character caught up in the Man of Steel's adventure-filled world. Another new title, *Superman's Girl Friend, Lois Lane* spotlighted the strength of Superman's supporting cast and focused on Lois' frequent romantic entanglements.

OVERLEAF *Action Comics* #226 (March 1957): During the 1950s, Superman's enemies increasingly came from the realms of science fiction. The "petrified spaceman" came from an ice world and had been immobilized by Earth's warmth—until Luthor brought him to life. Cover art: Wayne Boring, Stan Kaye

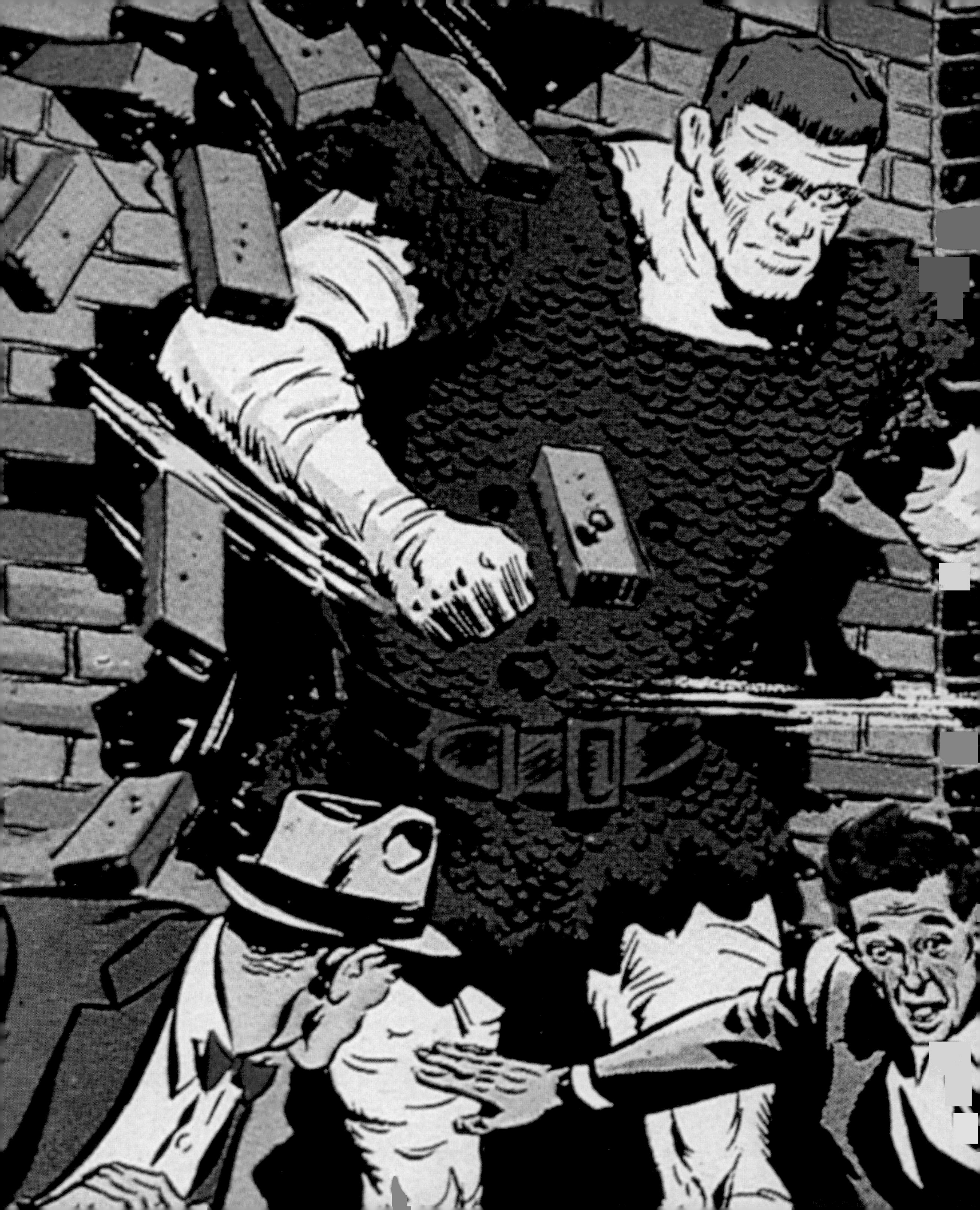

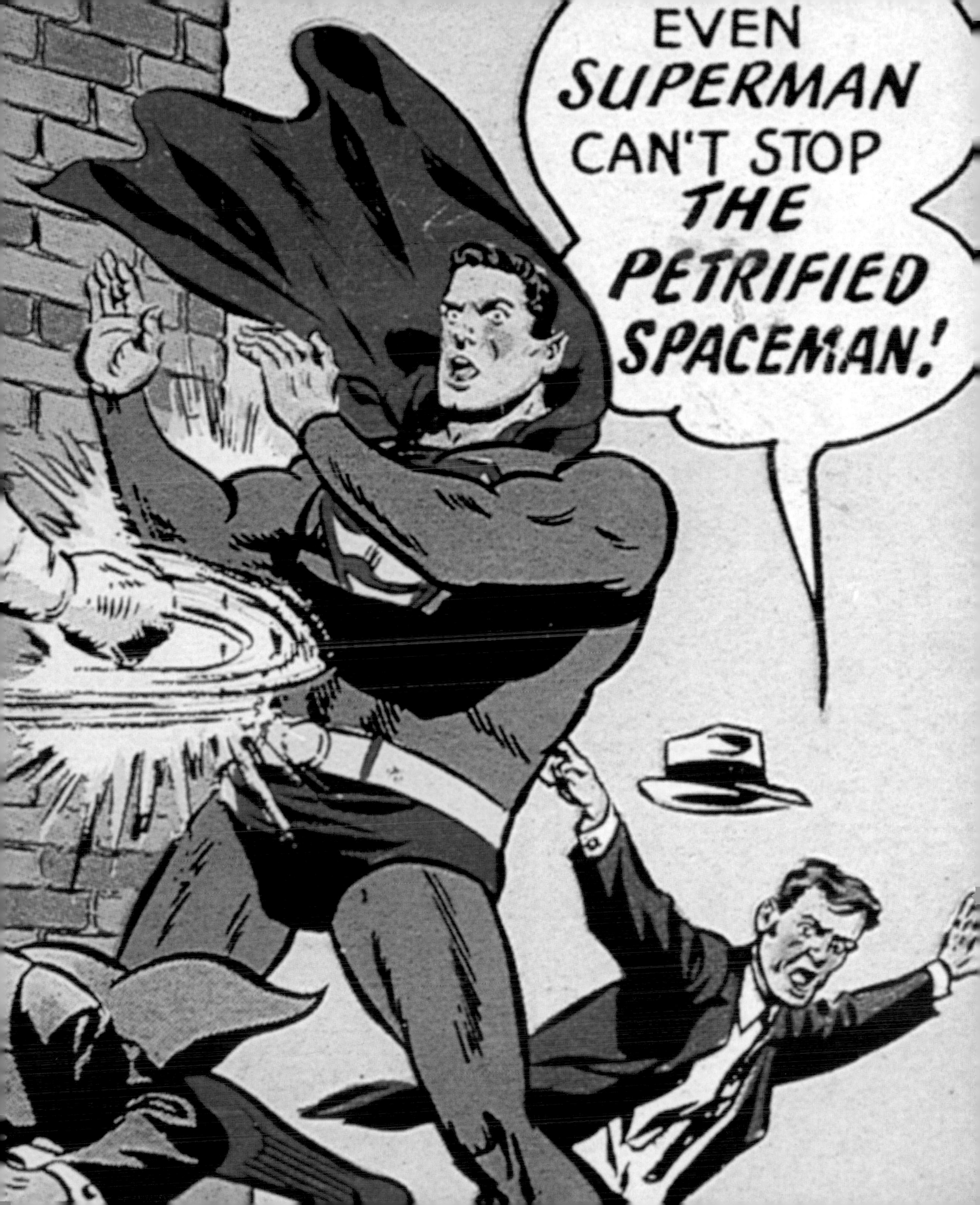
EVEN SUPERMAN CAN'T STOP THE PETRIFIED SPACEMAN!

SILVER AGE ADVENTURES

THE FORTRESS OF SOLITUDE

Superman's arctic hideaway, a repository for trophies, Kryptonian technology, and crime-fighting souvenirs, became part of his legend during the Silver Age. In time, the Fortress housed an intergalactic zoo and a squad of Superman robots. It also held the Kryptonian bottle city of Kandor, preserved prior to the planet's destruction. The tiny inhabitants of Kandor sometimes assisted their host by assembling as the Superman Emergency Squad. A spectacular science-fiction headquarters, the Fortress of Solitude emphasized Superman's alien nature.

SUPERGIRL

When Supergirl joined the fun as Superman's cousin Kara Zor-El, the Man of Steel had the makings of an extended Kryptonian family. Other additions to his supporting cast during the Silver Age included Krypto the Super-Dog and Beppo the Super-Monkey.

BRAINIAC AND MORE

Superman's enemies had a distinctly local feel at the start of the Golden Age; however, as the Silver Age embraced the Space Age, his rogues gallery became increasingly exotic. Brainiac was an alien collector with a passion for bottling cities, while Titano, a gigantic, mutated chimp, towered over Metropolis. Other dangers included Metallo, a human in a robot body, and the backwards-talking but well-meaning Bizarro. Superman often teamed up with Batman during this era, pulling the Caped Crusader out of his dark comfort zone and into sunnier, more fanciful environments.

SUPERMAN AND LOIS

During the Silver Age, Lois Lane's focus on getting a marriage proposal from Superman bordered on obsession. Her fervent desire to become "Mrs. Superman" was fertile soil for comedy, particularly when Superman's former flame, Lana Lang, started appearing in the comics as a rival for the Man of Steel's romantic affections. Lois received her own comic with the 1958 publication of *Superman's Girl Friend, Lois Lane.*

SPACE INVADERS

Superman found himself starring in increasingly bizarre adventures, reflecting the tone of the times and the popularity of B-movie sci-fi thrillers. Writers found that different colors of Kryptonite made convenient plot-drivers for strange events. For example, in *Action Comics* #296, Red Kryptonite endowed Superman with an ant's head so he could communicate with giant ants. Other outlandish scenarios played for laughs included Superman's transformation into a lion and his regression into a baby.

SAVING THE PLANET

Superman continued his double life as *Daily Planet* reporter Clark Kent, but he made an extra effort to assist his co-workers in times of need. He also helped the *Planet* indirectly, because his heroics resulted in scoops that boosted sales of the paper.

SUPERMAN
Vol. 1   #164

> "For the first time, there's not one person rooting for me in a fight! On this world, I'm a villain and Luthor is a hero!"
>
> **Superman**

Main Characters: Superman, Lex Luthor
Main Supporting Characters: Lois Lane, Jimmy Olsen
Main Locations: Metropolis, unnamed battle planet

Publication Date
October 1963

Editor
Mort Weisinger

Cover Artist
Curt Swan

Writer
Edmond Hamilton

Penciller
Curt Swan

Inker
George Klein

BACKGROUND

One of the core reasons that Lex Luthor uses to justify his hatred of Superman is the belief that his alien nemesis is somehow cheating—that his incredible powers are unearned, and that they steal the spotlight from Luthor's unmatched brilliance. Surprisingly, this tale concluded that Luthor's rationale might not be entirely misguided.

Luthor cunningly appeals to Superman's innate sportsmanship by challenging him to a fair fight. A planet orbiting a red sun—which robs the Man of Steel of his superpowers—proves to be the ideal site for bringing a Kryptonian into Luthor's weight class.

Even with his handicap, Superman scores a knockout in the first round. However Luthor's battle with Superman soon becomes a test of character rather than strength. On the planet, Superman cannot use his powers to save the planet's population from a drought; but Luthor's genius can revive irrigation and help save lives. For once, Luthor uses his gifts for the greater good with no expectation of a reward.

By the end of the tale, the Man of Steel deposits Luthor back in his jail cell. Yet something has changed between them. The grudging appreciation they show for each other's talents looks almost like…respect.

THE STORY

In a fair fight, who would win: Lex Luthor or Superman? That's the question that Luthor poses to the public, and an honor-bound Superman is forced to arrange a championship bout. Luthor can throw a punch, but the day will be won by ingenuity and compassion.

Stewing in his jail cell, Lex Luthor rages against being locked behind bars, sure that his intellect could accomplish so much. He persuades the warden to give him access to the prison's malfunctioning stamping machine **[1]**, transforms it into a tank **[2]**, and smashes through the prison wall.

Luthor's next move is to hijack the nation's airwaves and challenge Superman to a one-on-one bout with no superpowers allowed, to determine once and for all who is the better man **[3]**. Superman accepts Luthor's terms **[4]**. Only the rays of a red star can drain Superman's powers. Luthor and Superman board a spacecraft and set off toward a suitable planet for the main event **[5]**.

On the planet's surface, Luthor blacks Superman's eye and staggers him with body blows **[6]**. Superman eventually realizes that he can hit back with power and knocks Luthor out cold.

Luthor recovers, and continues the fight across the strange landscape of this alien world. He dislodges a rolling boulder to try to flatten his enemy, but Superman—unable to pulverize the rock with his fists—calculates some quick geometry and deflects the danger **[7]**. Superman becomes lost in a sandstorm **[8]** and suffers from dehydration and exhaustion. In his delirium, he hallucinates the ghosts of long-dead Kryptonians **[9]**.

Luthor, meanwhile, has discovered that the planet's people have fallen victim to a drought. He reactivates an ancient pump to chase a flock of birds away from the withered crops **[10]**. The people hail Luthor as a hero, and capture his enemy, Superman.

Luthor renews his challenge to fight Superman in the arena. But while the Man of Steel familiarizes himself with the gadgets stored in the arena's arsenal **[11]**, Luthor powers up the natives' digging machines, hoping to locate fresh sources of water **[12]**. He fails.

The day of the re-match arrives. Luthor and Superman duel with exotic weapons, including an anti-gravity tornado and a wall of darkness. Luthor tops them all by unleashing an automaton bloodhound on his foe **[13]**. The weakened Superman is at his enemy's mercy **[14]**, but on the brink of victory Luthor remembers the natives' plight and, surprisingly, surrenders.

Superman and Luthor depart **[15]**. But instead of heading for home, Luthor diverts their spaceship to a nearby planetoid and asks Superman, his superpowers now restored, to hurl vast chunks of ice toward the world they have just left **[16]**. Luthor knows that the ice will melt and spread water across the planet through the network of canals excavated by his digging machines.

Superman realizes that Luthor deliberately conceded their fight so that he could save the people's lives. Once Luthor is back in prison, Superman brings him a snapshot taken by a powerful telescope in the Fortress of Solitude. A giant statue now stands on the planet where Lex Luthor has become a legendary hero **[17]**.

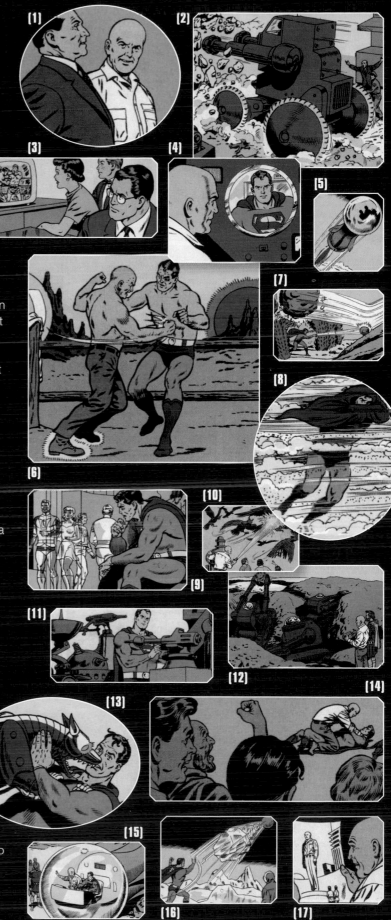

THE BRONZE AGE

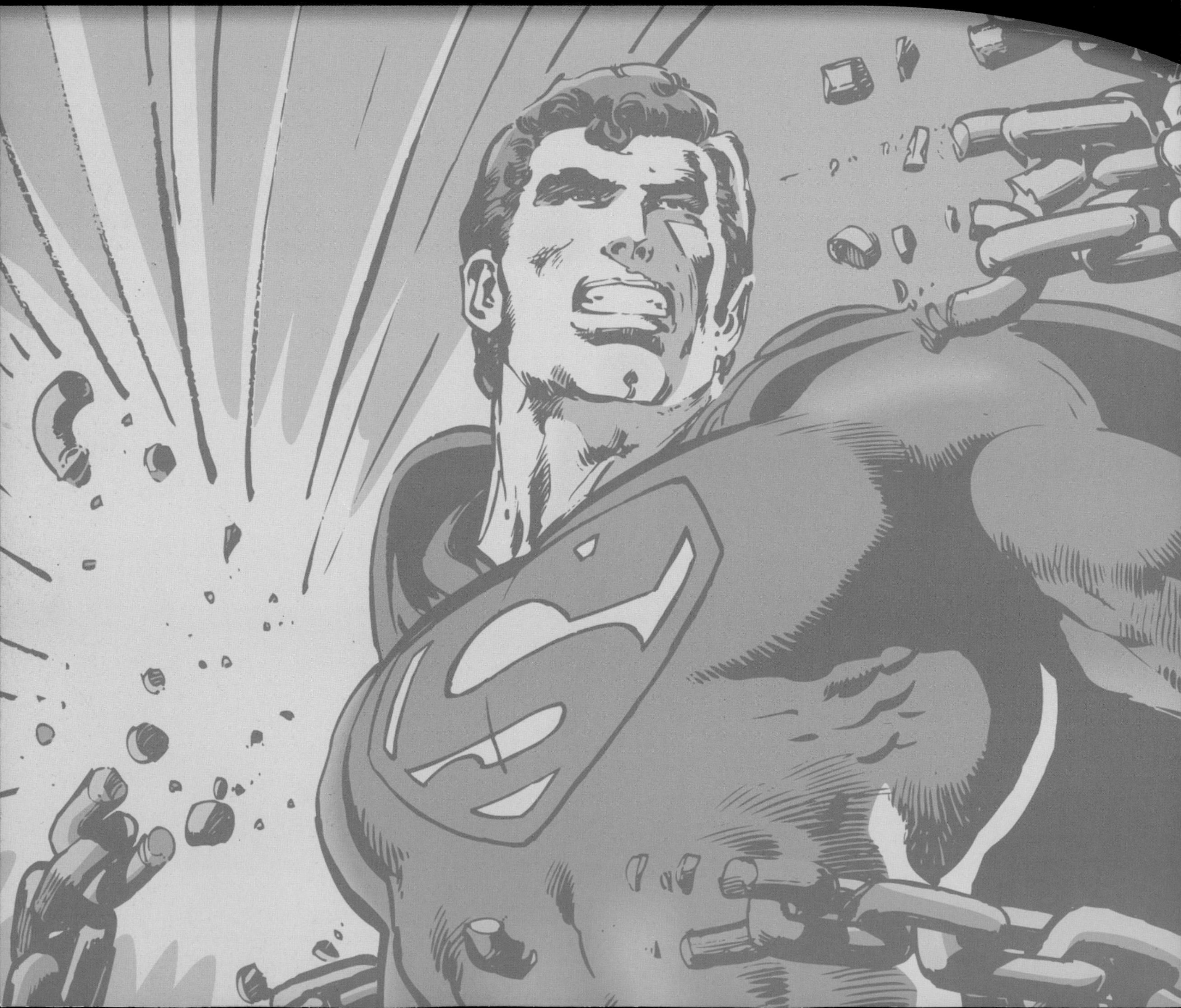

The 1960s ended in an explosion of psychedelia and social and political unrest and upheaval fuelled by the deeply controversial war in Vietnam. American mores and popular culture were undergoing a series of seismic shifts, and the traditional heroes of comic books suddenly looked hopelessly square. Action would be needed if super heroes were to remain relevant in this new, uncertain, turbulent world.

As the standard bearer for DC's super heroes, Superman was not immune to the widespread reinvention affecting other comic book heroes. While DC pursued societal relevance in titles like *Green Lantern*, its writers and artists made a series of tweaks to the Superman franchise to better align the Man of Steel with the new sensibilities of the so-called Bronze Age of comic books (generally judged to run from 1970 to 1985).

With a 1971 cover declaring "Kryptonite Nevermore!," Superman saw the removal of his traditional weakness, but his power was temporarily downgraded in the process. The Superman universe also saw an invigorating injection of new concepts, in particular the introduction of Darkseid and the mythology of the Fourth World.

In the early 1970s, Superman's alter-ego Clark Kent left the *Daily Planet* to become a television anchorman at news station WGBS, and traded in his blue suit for a contemporary wardrobe. Meanwhile, Lois Lane joined the women's liberation movement and stopped pining for Superman's hand in marriage. Over in *Superman's Pal, Jimmy Olsen*, the junior reporter became a stand-in for the youth movement and teamed up with freaks and outcasts like the Hairies—hippies who had evolved beyond modern-day human beings.

By 1985, DC had decided to clear the decks of nearly a half-century of shared continuity and start over again from scratch. Shortly after *Crisis on Infinite Earths* reconfigured the DC universe and ushered in a new age of comics, DC bid farewell to the hero who had started it all with the classic crossover tale in *Superman* #423 and *Action Comics* #583, "Whatever Happened to the Man of Tomorrow?"

OVERLEAF *Superman vs. Muhammad Ali* (1978): From the 1960s onward, real-life celebrities were regularly featured in comic books. This oversize, one-shot comic book matched the Man of Steel with the heavyweight champion of the world. After knocking out Superman, Ali teams up with the Man of Steel to save the world from aliens. Cover art: Neal Adams, Dick Giordano

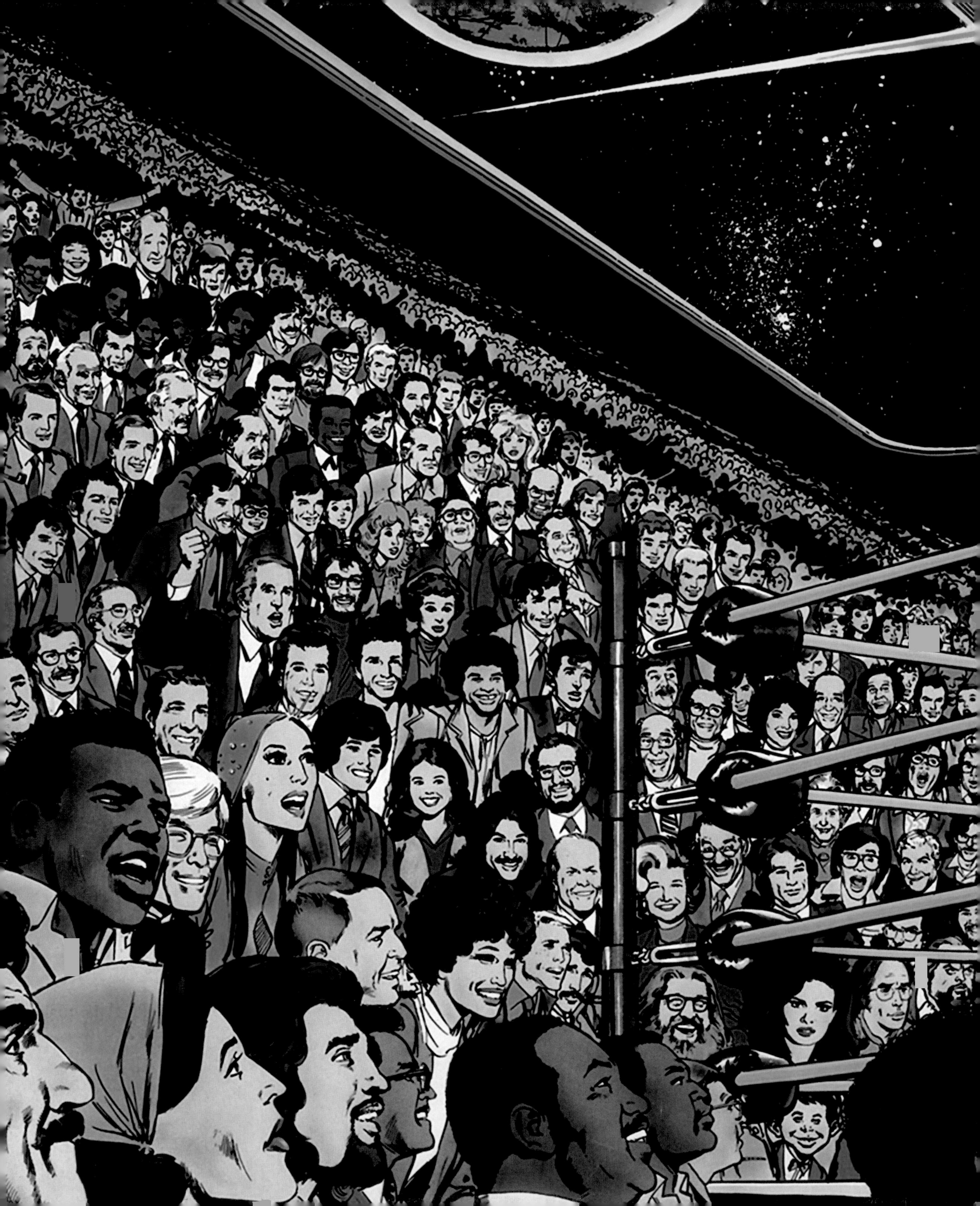

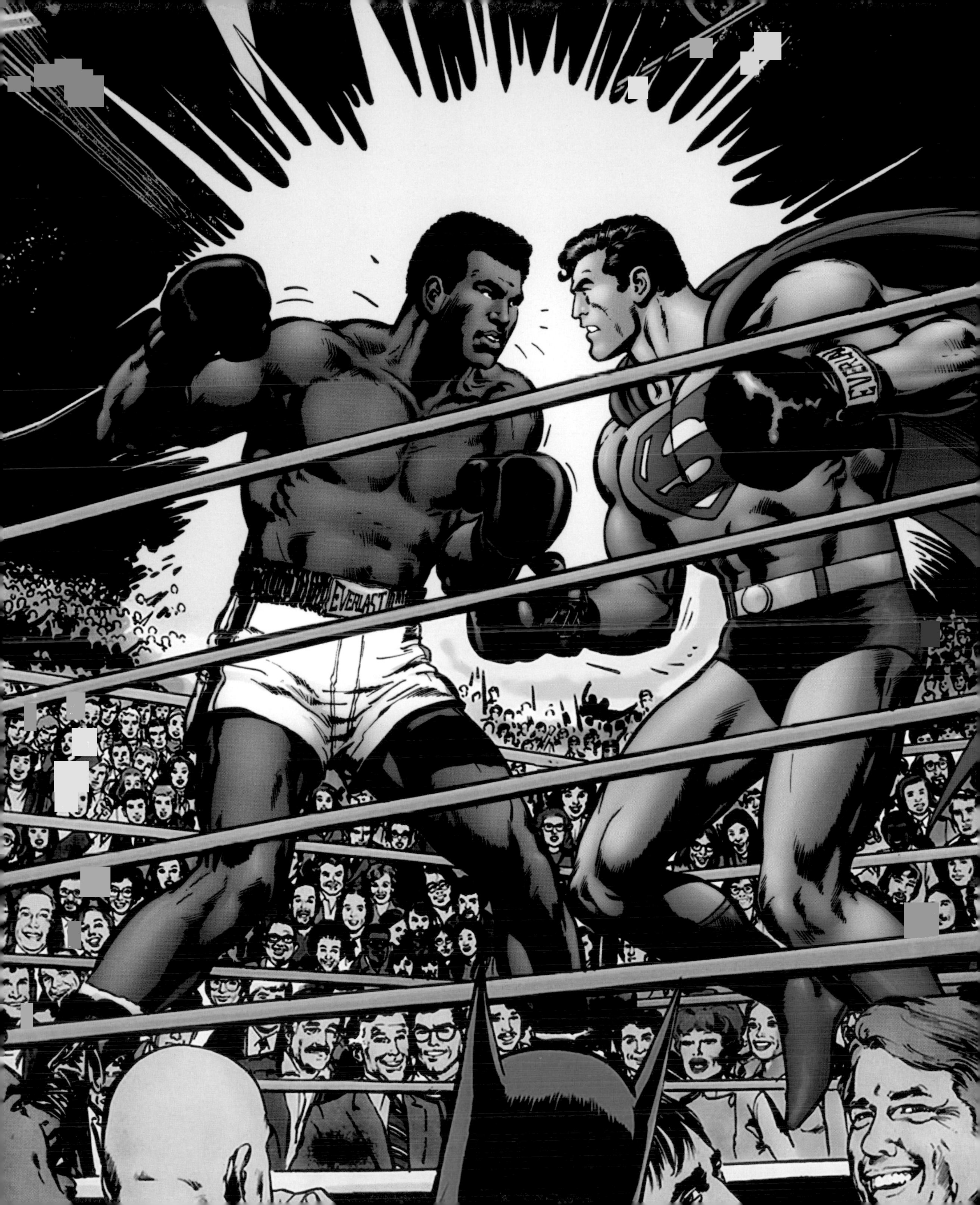
EVERLAST

BRONZE AGE ADVENTURES

KRYPTONITE NEVERMORE

A new era of Superman stories opened with a change to the status quo. When a scientist tried to use Kryptonite as an alternative energy source, an explosion triggered a chain reaction that turned all Kryptonite into harmless iron. Superman humiliated a would-be assassin by grabbing a chunk of this harmless "Kryptonite" and taking a bite out of it. Although genuine Kryptonite and its side effects would return to the comics in time, its temporary removal indicated that Superman's writers were looking for new, more inventive ways to challenge the Man of Steel.

THE FOURTH WORLD

A major addition to Superman's mythology came with the creation of the Fourth World, a pantheon of bizarre New Gods who hailed from the twin planets of New Genesis and Apokolips. These immensely powerful beings became an outlet for imaginative storytelling and futuristic design. The cruel Darkseid dominated the people of Apokolips and quickly emerged as one of Superman's greatest foes, while Clark Kent found time to rub elbows with New Gods like Lightray in the pages of *Superman's Pal Jimmy Olsen*.

CLARK KENT REPORTING

In a sign of the times, Clark Kent left the *Daily Planet* to work at local television station WGBS. His first assignment saw him covering the live launch of a space rocket. In time he took over as anchorman for the WGBS' nightly news broadcast. Fortunately, Clark's TV visibility didn't compromise his secret identity as the Man of Steel.

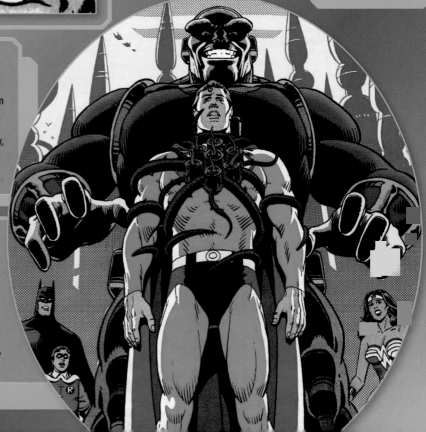

THE BEST OF HEROES

Superman's relationships with his fellow heroes were true friendships, and sometimes writers focused on this aspect. In the short story "For the Man Who Has Everything," Batman, Robin, and Wonder Woman arrived at the Fortress of Solitude to celebrate Superman's birthday, only to discover that the intergalactic conqueror Mongul had beaten them there. In the end, Robin saved Superman from a mind-altering illusion.

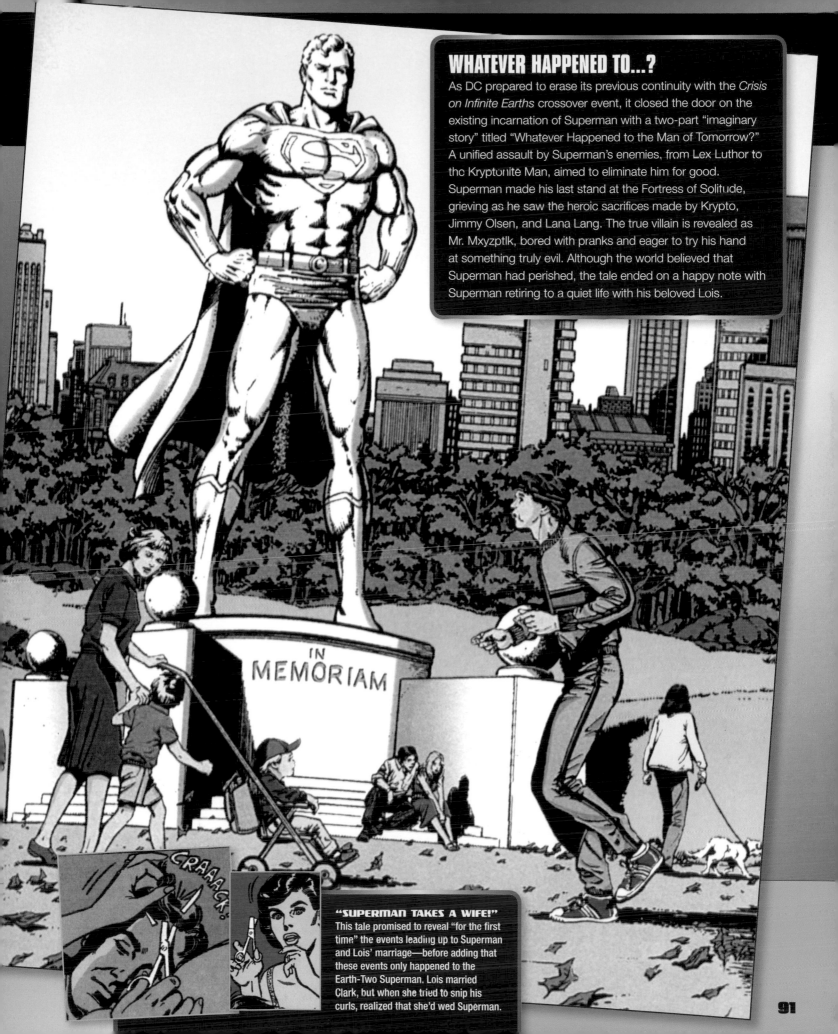

WHATEVER HAPPENED TO...?

As DC prepared to erase its previous continuity with the *Crisis on Infinite Earths* crossover event, it closed the door on the existing incarnation of Superman with a two-part "imaginary story" titled "Whatever Happened to the Man of Tomorrow?" A unified assault by Superman's enemies, from Lex Luthor to the Kryptonite Man, aimed to eliminate him for good. Superman made his last stand at the Fortress of Solitude, grieving as he saw the heroic sacrifices made by Krypto, Jimmy Olsen, and Lana Lang. The true villain is revealed as Mr. Mxyzptlk, bored with pranks and eager to try his hand at something truly evil. Although the world believed that Superman had perished, the tale ended on a happy note with Superman retiring to a quiet life with his beloved Lois.

"SUPERMAN TAKES A WIFE!"

This tale promised to reveal "for the first time" the events leading up to Superman and Lois' marriage—before adding that these events only happened to the Earth-Two Superman. Lois married Clark, but when she tried to snip his curls, realized that she'd wed Superman.

THE AMAZING ADVENTURES of SUPERMAN

48 pages ONLY 25¢

DC SUPERMAN

NO. 247 JAN. 30675

APPROVED BY THE COMICS CODE AUTHORITY

WE...THE GUARDIANS OF THE UNIVERSE...FIND SUPERMAN OF EARTH GUILTY...

...GUILTY OF CRIMES AGAINST HUMANITY!

EXTRA! INTRODUCING A NEW SERIES... "The PRIVATE LIFE of CLARK KENT"

SPECIAL! A "SUPERMAN OF TOMORROW" CLASSIC!

Publication Date
January 1972

Editor
Julius Schwartz

Cover Artists
Curt Swan &
Murphy
Anderson

Writer
Elliot S. Maggin

Penciller
Curt Swan

Inker
Murphy Anderson

SUPERMAN
Vol.1 #247

"You don't need a Superman! What you really need is a super-will to be guardians of your own destiny!"

Superman to striking workers

Main Characters: Superman, Guardians of the Universe
Main Supporting Characters: Katma Tui, Mr. Harley, Manuel
Main Locations: Interstellar space, Oa, California

BACKGROUND

The Guardians of the Universe, fixtures in the *Green Lantern* comics, popped up on Superman's turf in this issue. Their roles as cosmic judges give their words extra authority when they pose a question about the Man of Steel's very existence: "Must There Be a Superman?" They seed doubts in Superman's mind about the rightness of his mission and whether his never-ending battle against injustice might be deterring the people of Earth from personal improvement and self-reliance.

The moment he returns to Earth, Superman takes a new approach, refusing to take sides in a labor dispute. However, he does step in to stop an earthquake and fix some of the damage it has caused. Superman concludes that he's best suited for intervening in natural disasters, but smaller-scale problems should be entrusted to those directly involved.

Superman didn't always stick to this plan in subsequent stories, but "Must There Be a Superman?" remains a thought-provoking exploration of a character in the process of becoming an everyday hero instead of an invincible god.

THE STORY

An injured Superman is discovered by a representative of the Green Lantern Corps, who brings him to the Guardians of the Universe on Oa. Superman's actions as Earth's greatest hero are questioned, forcing him to wrestle with the idea that his deeds might be holding back humanity's progress.

Superman's deep-space scans of extraterrestrial threats have turned up a colony of alien spores bound for Earth **[1]**. Realizing that the spores might upset Earth's ecology, Superman resolves to construct an isolated ecosystem for them. The red rays of a nearby star sap his strength, but he fuses asteroids into a planetoid and scoops up a gaseous soup to form an atmosphere **[2]**. Exhausted, Superman falls unconscious as the spores settle around their now home **[3]**.

Katma Tui, one of the interstellar peacekeepers of the Green Lantern Corps, finds Superman and brings him to the headquarters of the Corps on planet Oa. There, the Guardians of the Universe **[4]** reveal that they had intended Superman to tackle the spores, because Green Lantern rings are ineffective on anything colored yellow.

After healing Superman's injuries **[5]**, the Guardians discuss whether the Man of Steel should be allowed to operate freely in the affairs of Earth **[6]**. They speak to him about unintended consequences and the possibility of cultural stagnation, driving their message home by showing him a recording of the JLA's recent mission to the planet Kalyarna **[7]**. In that scenario, Superman had angrily rejected the Kalyarnans for expecting him to save them from an ecological catastrophe. He had used his powers to clean their polluted seas **[8]**, but had also warned them that taking care of their planet in the future was solely their responsibility. Superman takes his leave of the Guardians and departs Oa with a lot on his mind.

Upon arriving in California, Superman witnesses a standoff between striking fruit-pickers and their boss, Mr. Harley. When Harley slaps a boy, called Manuel, who dares to stand up to him **[9]**, Superman intervenes **[10]**. But he is quick to accuse the other men of not doing their part and showing the same backbone as Manuel.

Superman brings the boy home, amazing his mother **[11]**. Soon the residents of the housing development surround Superman, demanding favors and miracles. Suddenly, disaster strikes as an earthquake rattles the hillsides. Superman, recognizing that this is a true test of his talents, burrows beneath the Earth's crust to excavate around the fault line **[12]**. This relieves the subterranean pressure and quiets the tremors.

Many workers have lost their homes during the quake. Superman replaces them in the blink of an eye with some high-speed carpentry **[13]**. He then explains that not every problem calls for a heroic intervention. "You must not count on a Superman to patch up your lives every time you have a crisis or disaster," he says **[14]**, and leaves the workers to sort out the labor dispute.

Many light-years away, the Guardians of the Universe celebrate the Man of Steel's actions, sure that a hands-off hero will be better for everyone. Superman flies off to rescue a pleasure craft from a waterspout **[15]** and the Guardians smile, realizing that this is truly a job for Superman.

THE DARK AGE

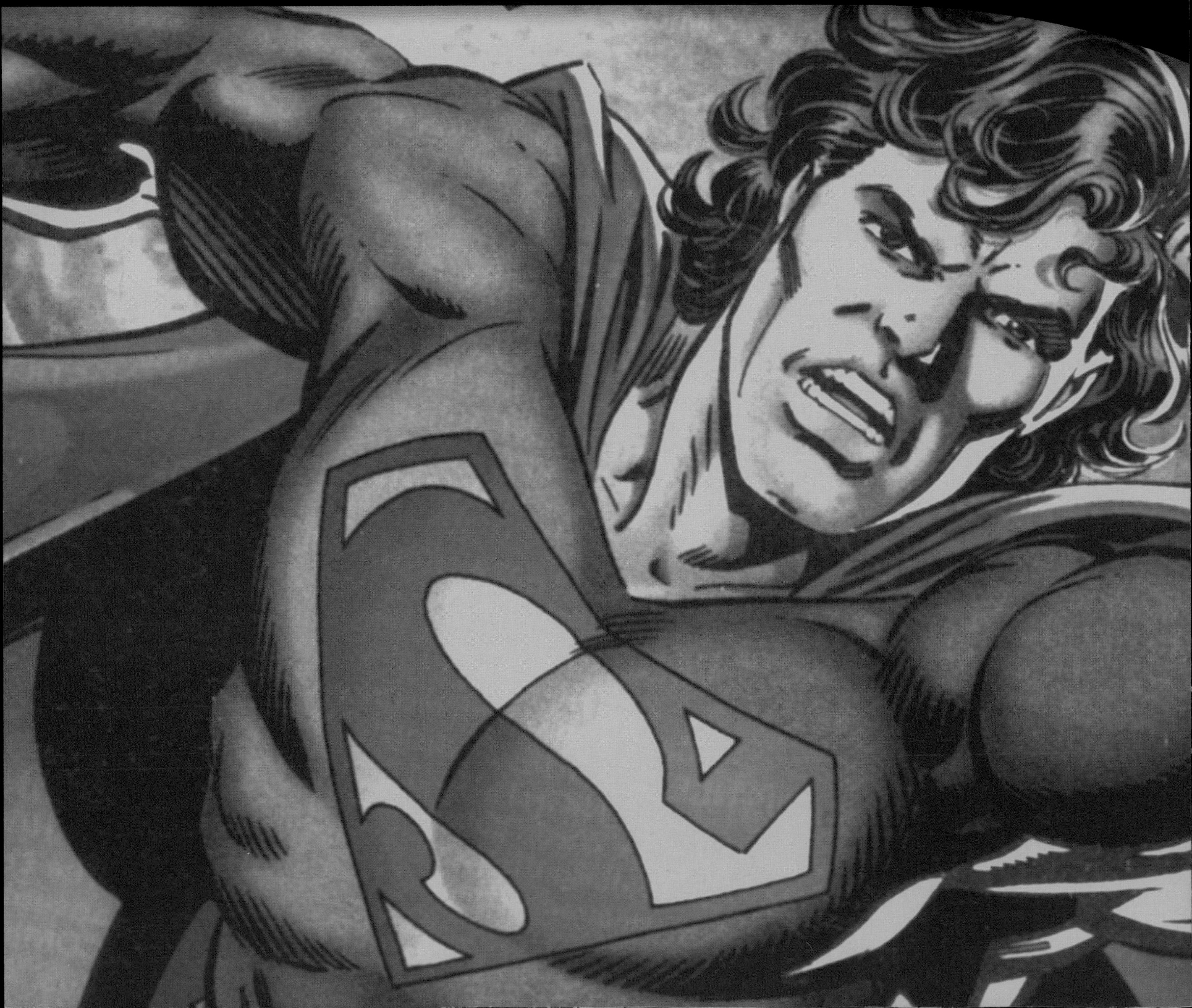

The crossover series *Crisis on Infinite Earths* established a new status quo within the DC Universe. No longer obligated to uphold old storylines, DC had a blank canvas upon which to create fresh mythologies. Helped along by visionary writers and artists, the stories of this new era emphasized realism, maturity, and sometimes a touch of darkness. It was Superman, of course, who led the way.

The world's first super hero now had a much simpler backstory, one that jettisoned his childhood career as Superboy and left him with a more realistic (but still super) range of abilities. His archenemy Lex Luthor now wielded a subtler sort of influence as Metropolis' wealthiest businessman, though his ruthless ambition hadn't diminished one whit.

Superman now had three ongoing titles—*Action Comics*, *Superman*, and *Adventures of Superman*. The business of selling comics had moved into specialty comics shops, which attracted an older clientele with a willingness to sample darker, grimmer stories that cast familiar heroes in new, unexpected roles.

By the early 1990s, Superman had got his hands dirty. He contravened his personal moral code of not killing enemies by executing a trio of genocidal Kryptonian war criminals. Superman himself became the target of an execution—one planned by his editors. The bestselling "Death of Superman" saga introduced the unstoppable villain Doomsday, and provided the opportunity for DC to bring back Superboy, this time as a teenaged clone created from Superman's own DNA. Death for comic book heroes is nearly always a temporary condition and, true to form, Superman didn't stay dead for long.

After more than 50 years of off-on romance, Superman finally revealed his secret identity to Lois and popped the question. The big event happened in 1996's *Superman: The Wedding Album*, setting the stage for Lois and Clark to explore the unfamiliar territory of married life.

OVERLEAF *Superman: The Man of Steel* #20 (February 1993): The death of Superman was one of the most dramatic events of the aptly named Dark Age of comics. A procession of super hero mourners followed Superman's coffin. Jimmy Olsen comforted Lois Lane amid the griefstricken crowd.
Art: Jon Bogdanove, Dennis Janke, Glenn Whitmore

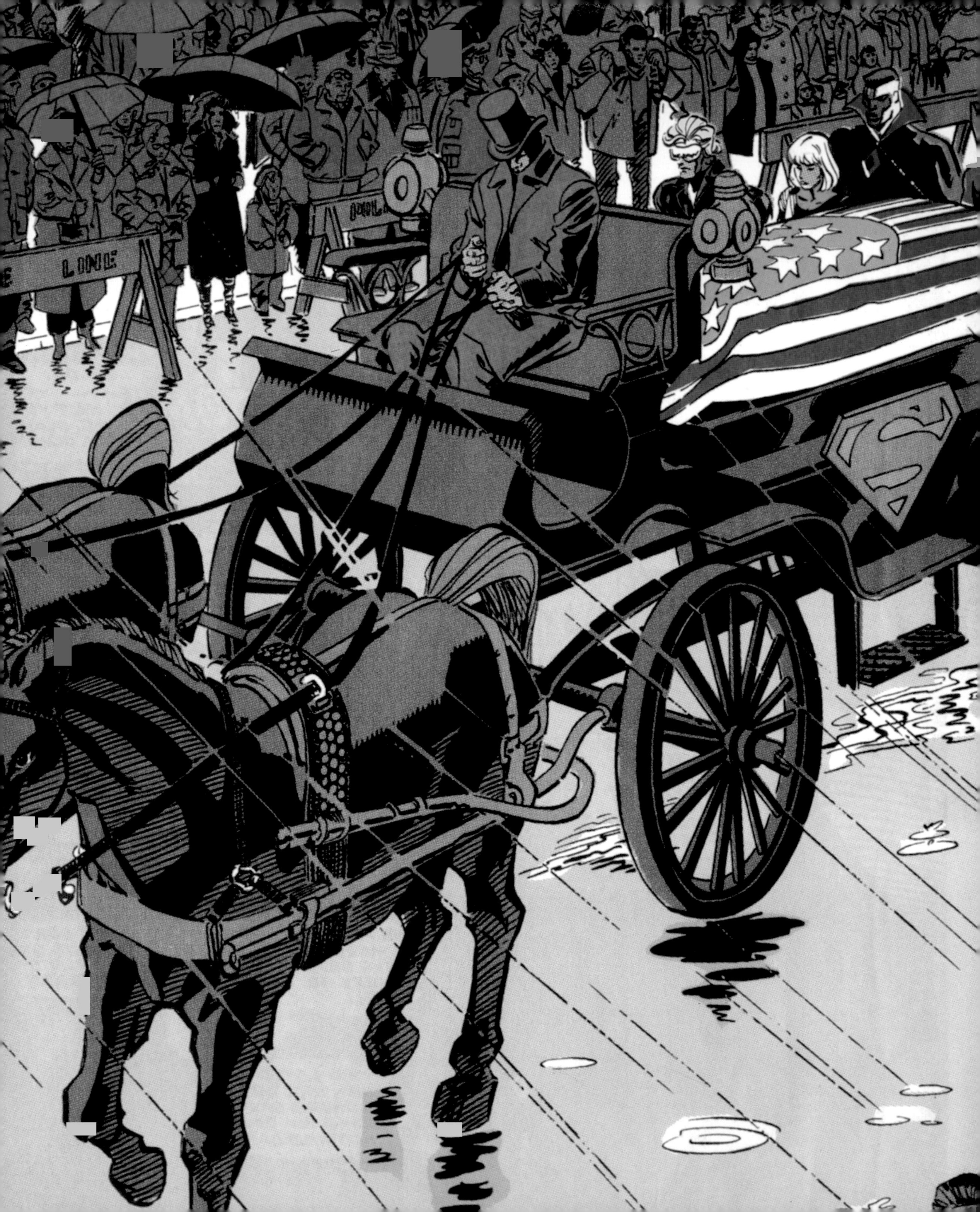
LINE

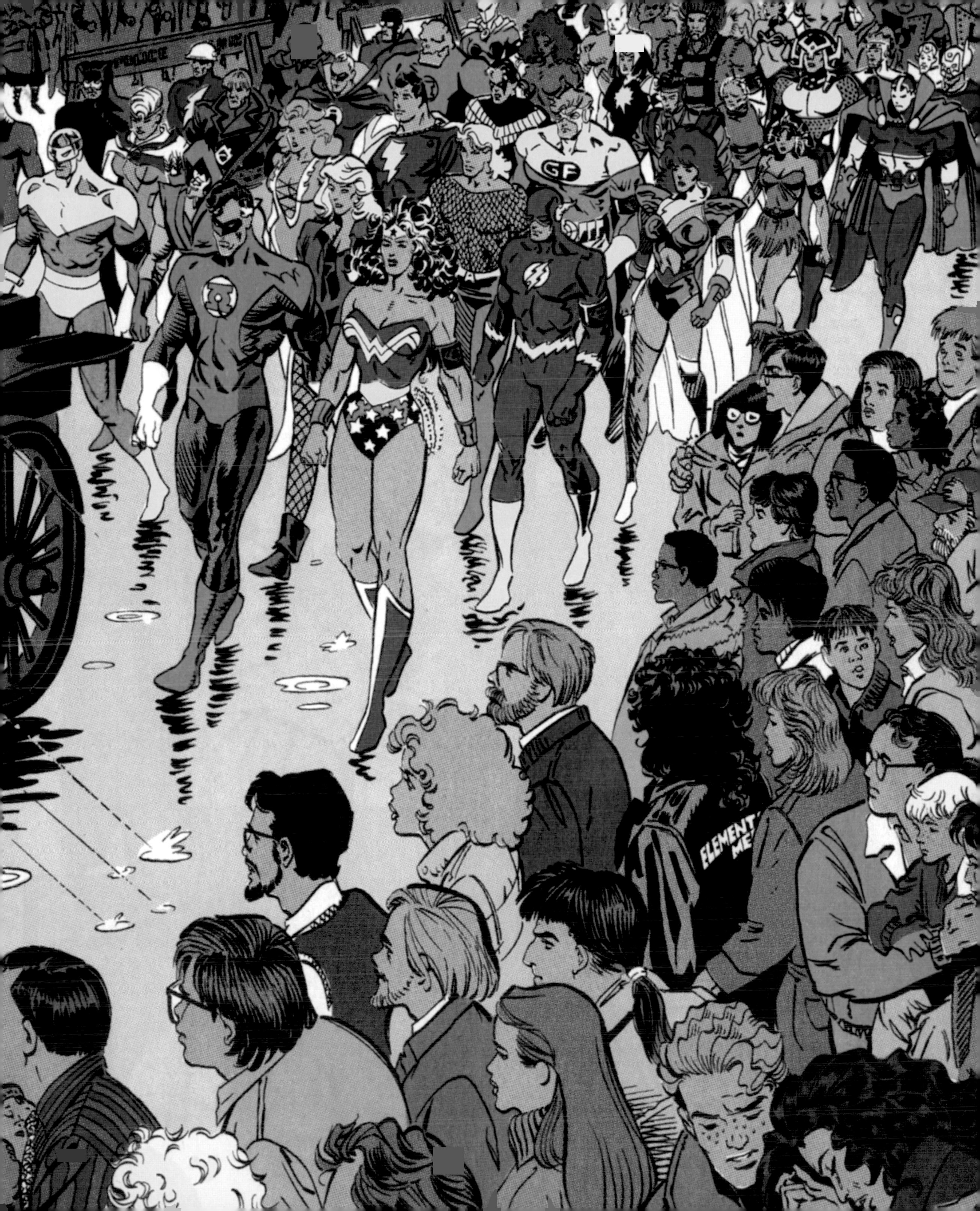
POLICE

To prevent the destruction of all reality, the Monitor plucked heroes from different periods of history. He briefed them for battle aboard his orbital HQ.

Within the multiverse, an endless number of universes existed side by side. The Anti-Monitor's threat to erase them all was a crisis too grave for one Superman to handle.

CRISIS
ON INFINITE EARTHS

UNIVERSES COLLAPSING

Superman had long been aware of the existence of parallel Earths. Another Superman, active during World War II, lived on Earth-Two, while heroes such as Captain Marvel and the Blue Beetle inhabited their own worlds. When the near-omnipotent Anti-Monitor blanked entire universes out of existence with waves of anti-matter, his counterpart, the Monitor, was forced to gather together history's greatest heroes to make a stand. Superman and his Earth-Two equivalent fought alongside champions from the Old West and the 30th century. The war claimed the lives of Supergirl and the Flash but, by the midpoint of the Crisis, five universes had been saved from obliteration. Then, as the barriers separating dimensions and time periods started to erode, Lex Luthor saw an opportunity to seize power by uniting super-villains from across all five Earths. Superman struggled to stay focused as the fate of everything hung in the balance.

The Anti-Monitor enlisted the Weaponers of Qward, who ruled the antimatter universe and provided the energy source for the Anti-Monitor's reality-extinguishing attacks.

The Monitor chose the woman called Harbinger to help him in his crusade, but she killed him while under the Anti-Monitor's influence. The Monitor had prepared for this event, however, and Harbinger's action saved the five remaining universes from extinction.

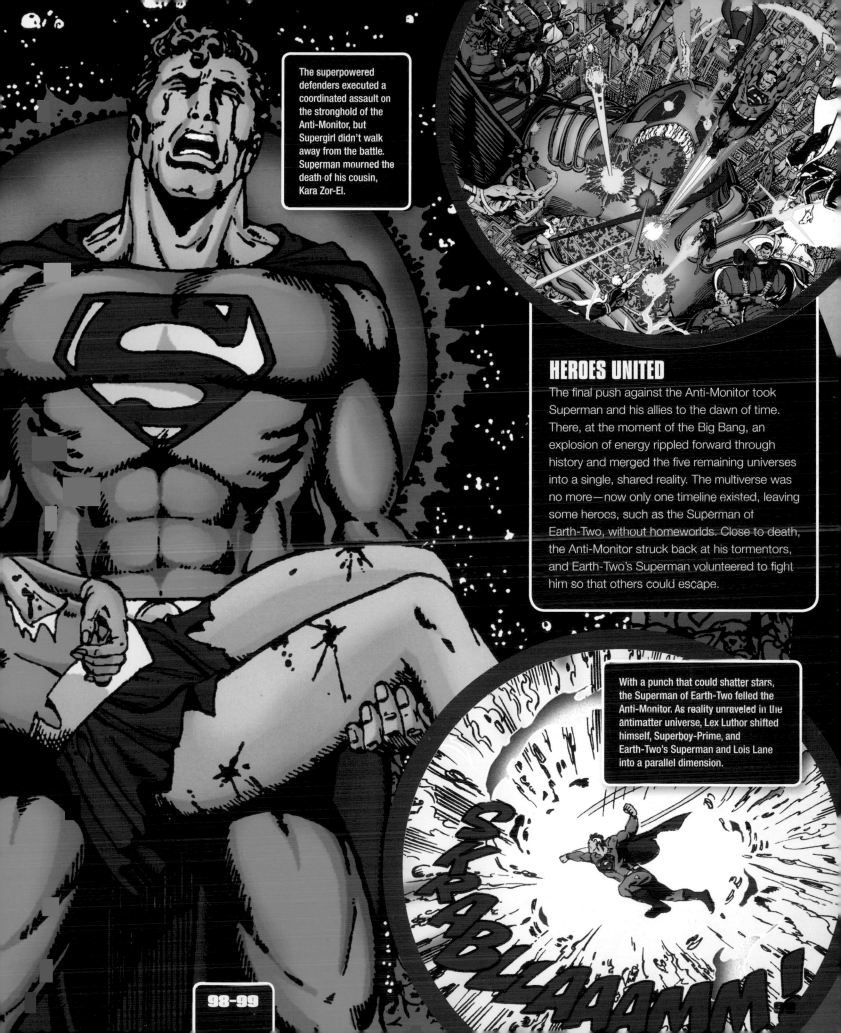

The superpowered defenders executed a coordinated assault on the stronghold of the Anti-Monitor, but Supergirl didn't walk away from the battle. Superman mourned the death of his cousin, Kara Zor-El.

HEROES UNITED

The final push against the Anti-Monitor took Superman and his allies to the dawn of time. There, at the moment of the Big Bang, an explosion of energy rippled forward through history and merged the five remaining universes into a single, shared reality. The multiverse was no more—now only one timeline existed, leaving some heroes, such as the Superman of Earth-Two, without homeworlds. Close to death, the Anti-Monitor struck back at his tormentors, and Earth-Two's Superman volunteered to fight him so that others could escape.

With a punch that could shatter stars, the Superman of Earth-Two felled the Anti-Monitor. As reality unraveled in the antimatter universe, Lex Luthor shifted himself, Superboy-Prime, and Earth-Two's Superman and Lois Lane into a parallel dimension.

ROCKETED FROM KRYPTON

Only Superman's father, Jor-El, realized that cold, sterile Krypton had entered its final days. He placed genetic material from himself and his wife Lara into a birthing matrix and fired the vessel in the direction of Earth.

MAN OF STEEL

The post-Crisis on Infinite Earths retelling of Superman's origins emphasized his Kansas upbringing instead of his Kryptonian roots. Ma and Pa Kent remained a vital presence, and Lex Luthor became more dangerous than ever.

FOUND BY THE KENTS

Jonathan and Martha Kent of Smallville, Kansas discovered the crashed alien craft, which released its newborn passenger into their arms. They took the infant home, and a long blizzard provided the necessary cover for Martha to claim the baby as a natural birth. They named him Clark and, as he grew, the Kents helped their son deal with the gradual emergence of his superpowers.

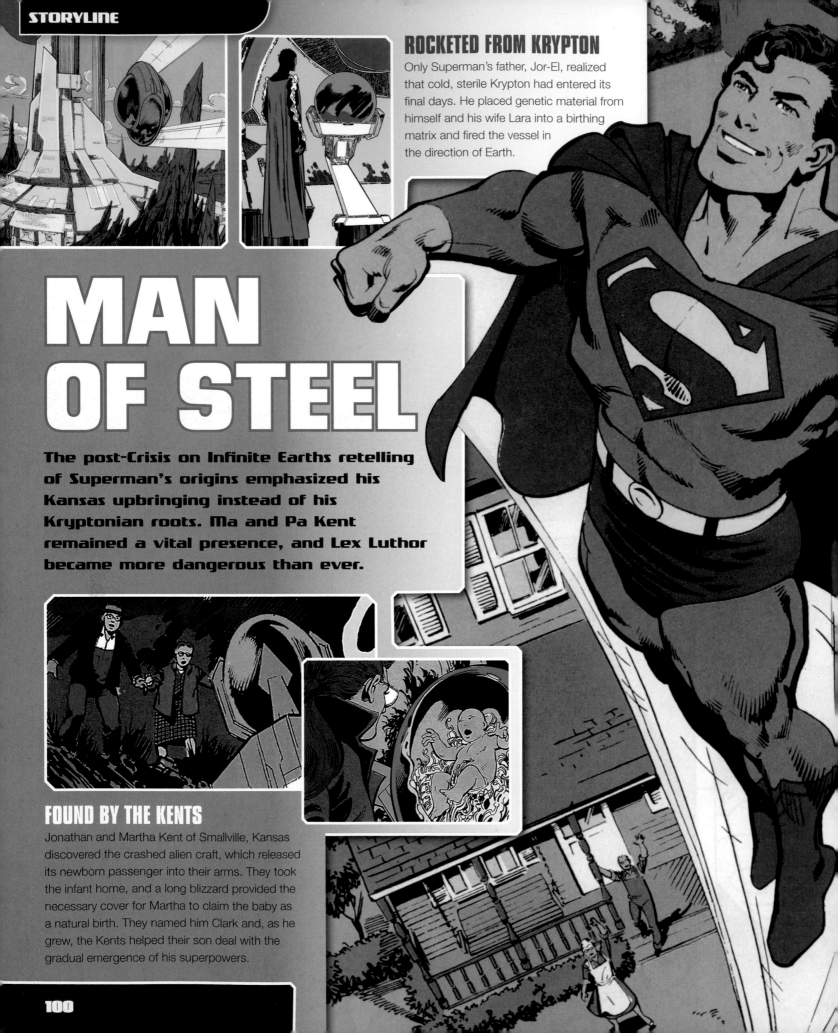

The power of flight didn't appear until Clark had nearly reached adulthood. He discovered it entirely by accident.

In his first public appearance, Clark saved a prototype space plane and met *Daily Planet* reporter Lois Lane, who named him "Superman." Martha Kent sewed the world's newest hero an eye-catching uniform. The aura that gave Clark his invulnerability protected the suit from damage.

> "It was Krypton that made me Superman, but it is the Earth that makes me human!" Superman

As the most powerful figure in Metropolis, Lex Luthor deeply resented this new rival to his power. If he couldn't bribe or blackmail Superman, he would eliminate him.

A Bizarre Duplicate

In a private laboratory, Lex Luthor's scientists used a tissue sample from Superman to grow a full-sized clone. But the skin of Luthor's pet Superman crystalized on contact with the air, turning him into a monster. The clone shared enough of Superman's memories to try out its own "Clark Kent" disguise. Although Superman didn't mean to destroy the strange being, a super-speed collision shattered it into powder.

Superman confronted Bizarro, disguised as Clark Kent, in the Daily Planet Building—and took a surprise hit.

THE DARK KNIGHT RETURNS

> "They'll kill us if they can, Bruce. We must not remind them that giants walk the Earth." Superman

THE FINAL SHOWDOWN

In an alternate future, super heroes had been driven into hiding by a public that had come to fear them. Superman, now an authorized agent of the United States government, was the only hero still in business. When Batman decided to put his costume back on after a ten-year retirement, his heroics soon started to capture the attention of the news media. The US president ordered Superman to bring Gotham City's notorious vigilante under control.

Their confrontation took place in Crime Alley, the same Gotham street where young Bruce Wayne had witnessed the murders of his parents. Superman coped with the middle-aged Batman's various high-tech gadgets and endured the pain of the Dark Knight's sonic screamers, but then Batman played his trump card—he exposed Superman to synthetic Kryptonite, and delivered a knockout blow to his weakened opponent.

The strain of the battle told on Batman, who seemingly suffered a fatal heart attack at his moment of victory. Superman detected a faint heartbeat and decided to let his old friend live in peace.

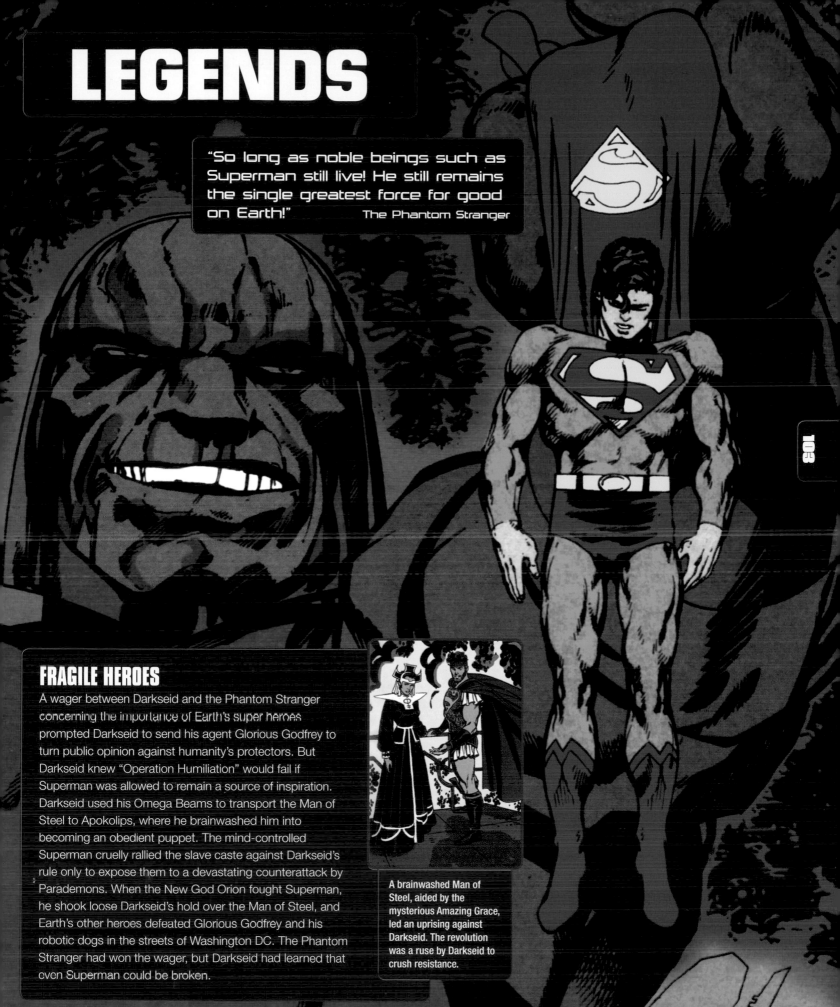

LEGENDS

"So long as noble beings such as Superman still live! He still remains the single greatest force for good on Earth!"
The Phantom Stranger

FRAGILE HEROES

A wager between Darkseid and the Phantom Stranger concerning the importance of Earth's super heroes prompted Darkseid to send his agent Glorious Godfrey to turn public opinion against humanity's protectors. But Darkseid knew "Operation Humiliation" would fail if Superman was allowed to remain a source of inspiration. Darkseid used his Omega Beams to transport the Man of Steel to Apokolips, where he brainwashed him into becoming an obedient puppet. The mind-controlled Superman cruelly rallied the slave caste against Darkseid's rule only to expose them to a devastating counterattack by Parademons. When the New God Orion fought Superman, he shook loose Darkseid's hold over the Man of Steel, and Earth's other heroes defeated Glorious Godfrey and his robotic dogs in the streets of Washington DC. The Phantom Stranger had won the wager, but Darkseid had learned that even Superman could be broken.

A brainwashed Man of Steel, aided by the mysterious Amazing Grace, led an uprising against Darkseid. The revolution was a ruse by Darkseid to crush resistance.

SUPERMAN
Vol.2 #22

> "As the last representative of law and justice on this world, it falls to me to act as judge, jury... and executioner."
>
> **Superman**

Main Characters: Superman, Supergirl (Matrix), Zod, Quex-Ul, Zaora

Main Supporting Characters: Lex Luthor (Pocket Universe), Jonathan Kent, Martha Kent, Lana Lang

Main Locations: Pocket Universe Earth, Smallville

Publication Date
October 1988

Editor
Mike Carlin

Cover Artist
John Byrne

Writer
John Byrne

Penciller
John Byrne

Inker
John Byrne

Colorist
Petra Scotese

BACKGROUND

Crisis on Infinite Earths streamlined Superman's continuity by erasing his adventures as Superboy. Rewriting history in this way resulted in some storytelling loose ends. Because the members of the Legion of Super-Heroes were said to have gained their inspiration from Superboy's example, post-Crisis continuity introduced a "Pocket Universe" copy of Superboy.

Leaving this Pocket Universe intact would have undermined the whole point of the Crisis, so writer/artist John Byrne wiped it out and also presented Superman with a crucial moral decision. In issue #22 of the relaunched *Superman* title, the idyllic Pocket Earth had been rendered a lifeless moonscape by the Kryptonian criminals Zaora, Quex-Ul, and General Zod. Superman was the only surviving being with the will and moral authority to pass judgment on the murderers of more than five billion people.

Superman's decision to invoke the death penalty broke his longstanding code against killing. Byrne made sure this act had grim repercussions in future stories.

THE STORY

A single Kryptonian is immeasurably powerful, but the Pocket Universe Earth suffered under an assault from *three* of them. General Zod, Zaora, and Quex-Ul gloated after they had killed billions. Superman determined that, in this instance, the punishment should fit the crime.

The Pocket Universe Earth was now a lifeless scar after the genocidal rampage of Quex-Ul, Zaora, and General Zod **[1]**. The three Kryptonian super-villains found their only remaining opposition from Superman and the planet's versions of Supergirl **[2]**, plus human heroes Lex Luthor, Bruce Wayne, Oliver Queen, and Pete Ross. Above the wasteland that used to be Smallville, the survivors rallied for their last stand.

The attack fighters are swatted out of the sky, killing their human pilots. General Zod and Zaora give Supergirl a double blast of heat vision that leaves her near death **[3]**.

The brutal Quex-Ul attacks Superman **[4]** in the ruins of a laboratory that had once belonged to the Pocket Universe's Superboy. There, Superman finds the one item capable of turning the tide in his favor: a lead-lined canister containing a chunk of gold Kryptonite. By focusing its radiation on Quex-Ul, Superman permanently drains him of his powers, rendering him no more dangerous than a human being **[5]**.

After doing the same to General Zod and Zaora, Superman builds a cubical, metallic prison to keep the trio out of trouble while he checks on his allies **[6]**.

Lex Luthor is still breathing. He apologizes to Superman for thinking he could stop the Kryptonians on his own. Before he dies, Luthor urges Superman to make sure a crime on this scale can never happen again **[7]**.

Superman returns to his makeshift prison to pass judgment on Zod, Quex-Ul, and Zaora for the murders of five billion innocents **[8]**. They laugh in his face **[9]**, believing Superman won't kill them and vow to escape and commit the same atrocities upon the Earth that Superman calls home.

Superman, however, has arrived at his verdict, and he announces that the sentence is death. Opening a canister of Green Kryptonite, he aims its lethal rays at his victims **[10]**. In their last moments the three criminals beg for their lives, but Superman carries his duty through to the end **[11]**.

Superman buries the bodies of Zod, Quex-Ul, and Zaora, then discovers that a single life still remains within the wasteland of the Pocket Universe. Supergirl who, in this world, had been grown out of artificial protomatter, hadn't died but had instead reverted into an inert state so she could regenerate.

Superman carries this "Matrix Supergirl," back to his own universe. Realizing that she would need time to heal, he left her in Smallville in the care of Lana Lang **[12]** and Jonathan and Martha Kent. He had faith that his parents would provide a loving home for Matrix and teach her the ways of her new Earth, but Superman couldn't shake his guilt over deliberately taking the lives of others. He flew off in search of spiritual peace **[13]**.

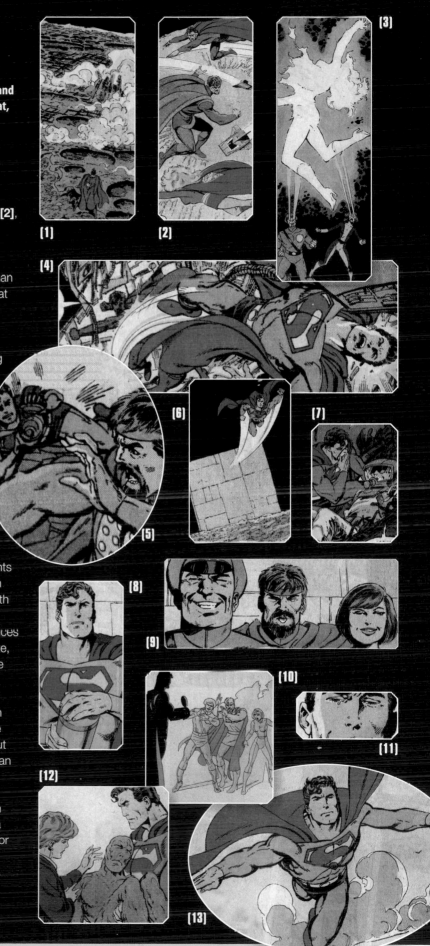

[1] [2] [3] [4] [5] [6] [7] [8] [9] [10] [11] [12] [13]

Superman feared he would do more harm than good if he remained on Earth. He set off into space in search of a place where he could never again injure another living being.

Collector of Brains

Superman found himself on the spacecraft belonging to Hfuhruhurr the Word Bringer. It contained thousands of living brains—Hfuhruhurr wished to bring everyone's brain into timeless telepathic union. Superman fought him over the right to individual self-determination.

Flooded Out

One planet shared the same rolling plains and fertile soil as Kansas. Superman spent weeks tilling the land and growing his own crops—until a terrible storm washed his hopes away. He continued his lonely journey, wondering if he would ever again find peace.

EXILE

BANISHED BY CHOICE

Fearing he could no longer control his actions, Superman resolved to leave Earth before he hurt someone. Professor Emil Hamilton gave him a breathing mask and an oxygen belt to provide air for a lengthy space voyage. Superman set out in search of a world where he could live out his life as a hermit.

Tormented by Guilt

Months before, in an alternate reality, Superman had executed the Kryptonian criminals Zod, Quex-Ul, and Zaora for genocide. The trio had murdered five billion people and threatened to destroy Earth. Superman knew he had done the right thing, but his conscience gave him no rest, leading him to lose control during a fight with Brainiac. Superman later discovered that his subconscious mind had made him moonlight as a new, violent Gangbuster.

Haunted by Visions

On a nightmarish world teeming with phantoms, Superman faced his greatest challenge. The ghosts of Zod, Quex-Ul, and Zaora rose from the dust to accuse their executioner. The exhausted Superman passed out and was found by a scout ship from Warworld.

Thrown into Warworld's gladiator pits, Superman beat opponents but refused to kill them. One vanquished champion, Draaga, vowed to win back his honor at a later date. Mongul, tyrannical leader of Warworld, then faced the newcomer, but suffered shameful defeat.

The Cleric of Krypton

An alien cleric had long ago come to Krypton to speak out against the practice of creating clones for use as spare parts for Kryptonians. His followers clashed with the traditionalists of the High Council, prompting the cleric and his converts to leave Krypton aboard a giant space ark. But the Kryptonians aboard his vessel were genetically locked to their birth world and they perished when they left planetary orbit. The grieving cleric lived for thousands of years in penitent solitude, until a gladiator on Warworld turned out to be the Last Son of Krypton.

The Eradicator, a technological relic from Krypton's lost age, had been in the cleric's possession for millennia. With it, the cleric opened a telepathic link with Superman, and restored the Man of Steel's familiar costume. A psychic vision caused Superman to relive his guilt over the execution and the negative feelings that had led to his exile. He emerged spiritually cleansed, ready to return to Earth.

His mission finally complete after 200,000 years, the Cleric passed away peacefully. Superman laid his body to rest on a barren planetoid, and marked the gravesite to show his gratitude.

PARTNERSHIP

Luthor was in no mood to play around with Red Kryptonite. He was apprehensive of overly lowering exposure of Gold Kryptonite radiation, but once Mr. Mxyzptlk proved that Red Kryptonite would not transform a normal human being, Luthor agreed to cooperate but there remains the greater threat.

The Krimson
Kryptonite Crisis

RED KRYPTONITE

The Red Kryptonite created by Mr. Mxyzptlk could drain Superman's powers similar to the effect of normally occurring Gold Kryptonite. With Red K, Luthor could knock Superman down a peg, clearing them of the each other in proper results.

Professor Hamilton

Superman rushed to his friend Prof. Emil Hamilton, who confirmed that Superman's Kryptonian cells had become 100 per cent human. As a temporary fix, Hamilton lent Superman a force-field belt. However, it only had a 20-minute activation limit.

A Super Beat-Down

Luthor activated the chunk of Red K after Superman had taken flight, and his mystified foe plunged into the icy waters of Metropolis harbor. Mxyzptlk's powers teleported the half-drowned Superman into Luthor's LexCorp penthouse suite, allowing Luthor to pummel his exhausted enemy and leave him bruised and bleeding.

STARMAN

The rookie hero Starman arrived as soon as he got Superman's call. In Professor Hamilton's Metropolis lab, Starman tried to transfer his solar-based abilities into Superman by using an experimental reflector field. When that failed, Starman changed his face to become an exact duplicate of the true Man of Steel.

Posing as Superman, Starman retrieved the Red K from Luthor's office. But Superman's powers remained dormant.

MXYZPTLK'S MONSTER

When Lex Luthor angered Mxyzptlk, the fifth-dimensional imp called off their partnership. Just like that, Superman was back up to full power. As a parting shot, Mxyzptlk grew a flake of Luthor's skin to gargantuan proportions. When Superman fought back—in essence, punching out Lex Luthor—a satisfied Mxyzptlk blinked back to his home dimension.

Superman's Power Suit

Luckily, Professor Hamilton had built an armored power suit, based on blueprints from LexCorp. The suit's servomotors simulated super-strength, and provided bulletproof shielding. When the maximum-security Stryker's Island prison erupted in a hostage crisis—and Starman fell victim to a trap and required rescuing—Superman put the suit into action. Killgrave, the mastermind behind the prison takeover, hoped that the fact that Superman was wearing armor meant that the Man of Steel might be vulnerable. He was soon to be disappointed.

The criminal kingpin Killgrave threw everything he had at his armored enemy, but Superman kept on coming.

With the Red K chunk serving as its brain, the skin creature menaced downtown Metropolis.

THE END OF LUTHOR?

Defeated once again, Lex Luthor decided to make history in a different way in the time he had remaining. He took the controls of an experimental aircraft to complete a pole-to-pole flight around the world. Luthor's plane went down over the Andes. All Superman found was his artificial hand.

THE DEATH OF CLARK KENT

"All these years I thought I was getting beat by Clark Kent! But I was getting beat by Superman!"

CONDUIT

Conduit taunted Clark by letting him know that his dual identity had been compromised.

The super-villain Conduit had grown up in Smallville and knew Superman's greatest secret. Clark Kent's days were numbered!

CHILDHOOD VENDETTA

Kenny Braverman and Clark Kent grew up in Smallville, with both of them hiding the fact that they had started to develop incredible powers. Braverman, who could emit Kryptonite energy, had been irradiated by the same rocket that brought Superman to Earth. All his life, Braverman had resented Clark. Braverman even believed that his father would have preferred Clark as his son. Once Braverman learned Clark's secret, he set out to ruin his rival. He began by hanging a Superman effigy on Clark's apartment door and targeting Clark's friends and loved ones.

Superman hauled Perry White's booby-trapped roadster away from rush-hour traffic and tossed it off a bridge. Moments later, it exploded.

CONDUIT'S TRAP

Now the mechanically-augmented villain Conduit, Braverman kidnapped Jimmy Olsen to force Superman into a confrontation. Superman got the upper hand, but Conduit distracted him by threatening Clark's loved ones. Conduit's mercenaries destroyed the Kents' farmhouse and targeted Lois. Meanwhile, Conduit's hired goons, including Neutron and Metallo, caused more chaos.

REVENGE SERVED COLD

Conduit waited for an opening before hitting the emotionally-drained Man of Steel with a sneak attack. He hadn't stopped pursuing his other victims either. Lois Lane seemingly died beneath the rubble of a collapsing building, while the Kents vanished after the destruction of their cabin safehouse.

Kenny had always come in second. He blamed this on Clark's hidden superpowers.

A FIGHT TO THE FINISH

Tormented by his failure to protect his loved ones, Superman vowed to abandon his heroic role. When he later learned that the Kents and Lois had survived, he tried to keep them safe by maintaining a low profile in the Pacific Northwest. However, Conduit refused to leave Superman in peace. He engineered a bizarre showdown inside a replica of the Smallville High School football stadium, with a crowd of humanoid robots programmed to cheer "Kenny" to victory.

KRRRZZHZZT!

Superman ripped up live power cables and gave Conduit a direct jolt. His cybernetic parts overloaded and his organic body fried.

"YOU'RE AN OPINIONATED, STUBBORN WOMAN LOIS LANE... WILL YOU MARRY ME?"
Clark Kent

THE WEDDING

Fresh from her investigation into an international drug-smuggling ring, Lois Lane returned to Metropolis with a new appreciation for the unshakeable love that she and Clark Kent shared. Lois accepted Clark's proposal a second time and the couple set to work planning a whirlwind ceremony.

Lois endured dress fittings and bridal showers, while Clark tried to keep Jonathan Kent and Lois' father, General Sam Lane, from butting heads. Clark had temporarily lost his powers, so small complications turned into big headaches, including a bachelor-party brawl at the Ace O'Clubs bar and a surprise visit from Mr. Mxyzptlk. Nevertheless, the big day went without a hitch. Jimmy Olsen and Lucy Lane served as best man and maid of honor, with Lana Lang, Pete Ross, and Lori Lemaris also among the wedding party. Perry and Alice White's adopted son Keith served as ring bearer. The happy couple started their honeymoon vacation knowing that Batman and a squad of super hero volunteers would ensure Metropolis was in safe hands.

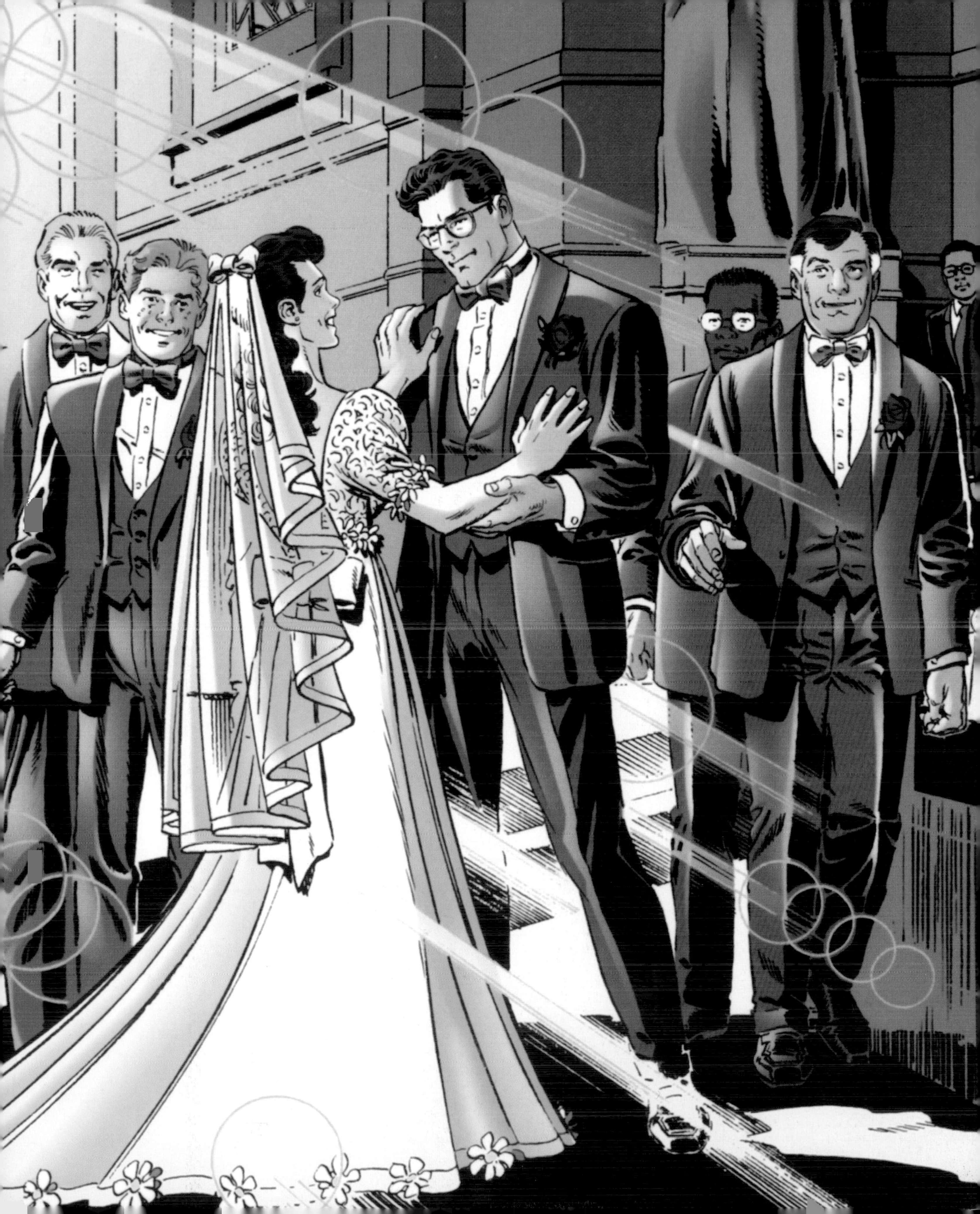

During Superman's exile in space, he had made some powerful enemies. Now his foes sought revenge, and planet Earth would be their field of battle.

PANIC IN THE SKY

ENEMY ALLIANCE

Draaga had lost to Superman in the Warworld gladiatorial games (see pp.106–7). He hoped to defeat Superman in a rematch and restore his honor. Maxima of Almerac had come to Earth in search of a worthy mate, only to be rejected by Superman. She sought revenge on the man who had dared to spurn her affections.

Supergirl hypnotised

This Supergirl was an artificial life form known as Matrix. She could duplicate most of Superman's powers and shapeshift; she had even been masquerading as Superman. A punch from Draaga reverted her to her Supergirl form, and her mind proved vulnerable to Brainiac's manipulations. A spellbound victim, she joined the enemy team.

First Strike

Brainiac had taken control of Warworld, and he steered it toward Earth to launch a full-scale invasion. But first he softened up his target, activating one of his skull ships and destroying downtown Metropolis. Brainiac then used his telepathic powers to reach out to Superman's mind, threatening that he would destroy everyone Superman cared for and warning: "Warworld is coming."

Brainiac used persuasion and brainwashing to recruit three colossally-powerful beings—Maxima, Draaga, and Supergirl—as his chief lieutenants.

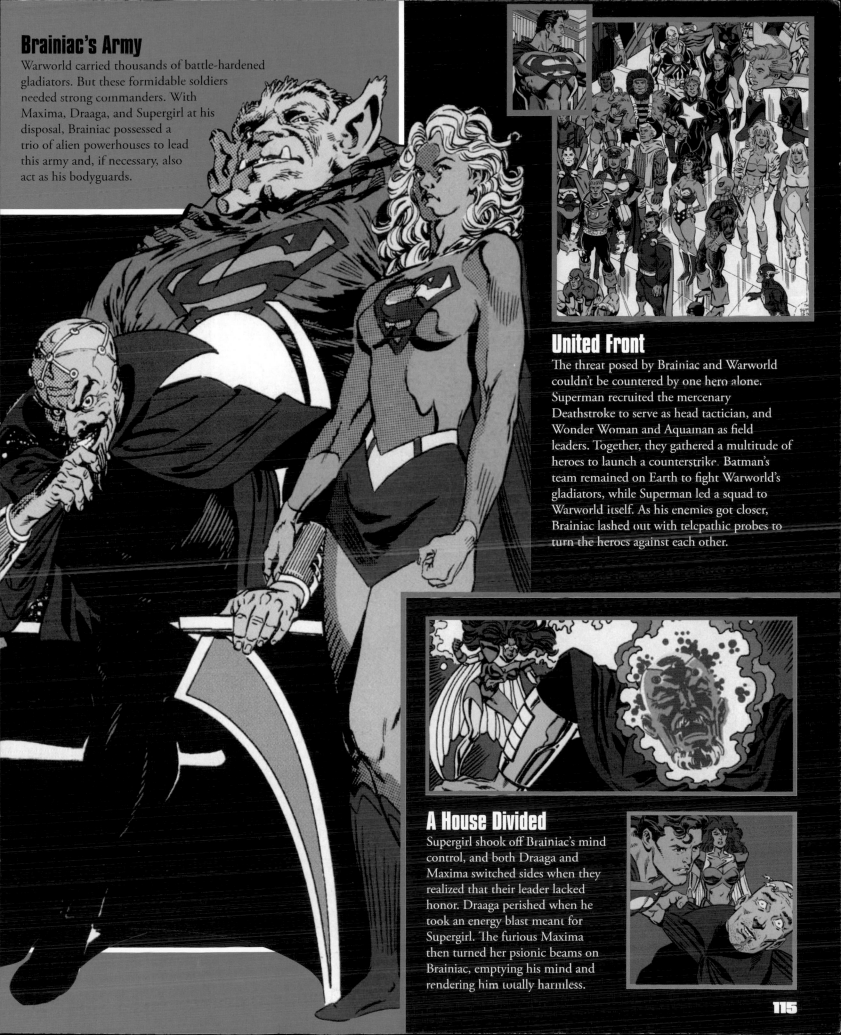

Brainiac's Army

Warworld carried thousands of battle-hardened gladiators. But these formidable soldiers needed strong commanders. With Maxima, Draaga, and Supergirl at his disposal, Brainiac possessed a trio of alien powerhouses to lead this army and, if necessary, also act as his bodyguards.

United Front

The threat posed by Brainiac and Warworld couldn't be countered by one hero alone. Superman recruited the mercenary Deathstroke to serve as head tactician, and Wonder Woman and Aquaman as field leaders. Together, they gathered a multitude of heroes to launch a counterstrike. Batman's team remained on Earth to fight Warworld's gladiators, while Superman led a squad to Warworld itself. As his enemies got closer, Brainiac lashed out with telepathic probes to turn the heroes against each other.

A House Divided

Supergirl shook off Brainiac's mind control, and both Draaga and Maxima switched sides when they realized that their leader lacked honor. Draaga perished when he took an energy blast meant for Supergirl. The furious Maxima then turned her psionic beams on Brainiac, emptying his mind and rendering him totally harmless.

DOOMSDAY

"Hrrarrrgh!"

Doomsday achieved the impossible when he killed Superman. Since then, the unstoppable monster has emerged multiple times to finish what he started and permanently silence the Man of Steel. Because Doomsday can regenerate despite catastrophic injuries, it seems that his rampages will never end.

President Lex Luthor mobilized Doomsday to fight the cosmic menace of Imperiex. A blast of energy reduced Doomsday to a charred skeleton, but even this wasn't enough to stop the creature's regeneration.

Doomsday's intellect has varied over the years, but generally he cannot speak other than grunting a few mimicked words. He can be out-thought, but not out-fought.

ORIGINS

Thousands of years ago, Kryptonian scientist Bertron undertook a twisted experiment in "forced evolution." Bertron subjected an infant to a series of increasingly violent deaths. With each resurrection, the subject gained resistance to whatever had killed it.

By putting a baby through an endless cycle of death and rebirth, Bertron hoped to create an invincible killer. He didn't concern himself with the child's emotional well-being.

In time, Bertron created a hulking, mindless monster with incalculable strength and an invulnerable hide covered with bony spikes. This creature, Doomsday, murdered Bertron, escaped Krypton, and spread destruction across the stars.

An alien champion called the Radiant seemingly killed Doomsday. The spacegoing barge carrying Doomsday's body crashed on Earth. After centuries of dormancy, Doomsday reawakened and began a campaign of destruction that ended in Metropolis. There, Superman stopped Doomsday, but lost his life.

Superman came back, but so did Doomsday, more cunning and dangerous than ever. Eventually Doomsday was cloned into multiple bodies possessing different powers.

After Doomsday's defeat at the hands of the Radiant, aliens wrapped him in funerary clothes and launched him into deep space.

The invulnerable Doomsday is immune to projectiles and energy blasts, and is even more damage-resistant than Superman. During their battle to the death, only full-force punches from Superman could have any effect on Doomsday.

One of Doomsday's clones fought the Cyborg Superman, gaining the ability to generate machinery from its own flesh. This Doomsday and its fellow clones nearly destroyed the Earth under the direction of the Doomslayer.

Doomsday seems to possess a sixth sense that helps him seek out living Kryptonians. He has a special hatred for their kind, possibly a carryover from his traumatic upbringing on Krypton.

KEY DATA

REAL/FULL NAME None

FIRST APPEARANCE *Superman: The Man of Steel* #18 (December, 1992)

OCCUPATION Superpowered killing machine

AFFILIATIONS Suicide Squad, Secret Society of Super-Villains

POWERS/WEAPONS Super-strength, super-speed, invulnerability, sharp bone spurs, and a hyper-accelerated healing factor. Given time, Doomsday can regenerate from near-complete annihilation.

Doomsday doesn't possess internal organs and thus doesn't have the same biological weak points as most humanoids. One version of Doomsday could emit Kryptonite radiation.

REIGN OF THE DOOMSDAYS

As if one Doomsday wasn't bad enough, a highly intelligent "ultimate Doomsday," calling itself the Doomslayer, cloned multiple copies of the monster. Each Doomsday clone replicated the powers of its victim. After defeating Superboy, Steel, the Eradicator, and the Cyborg Superman, they spread across the planet to initiate the Doomslayer's plan to exterminate all life on Earth.

While Superman and his allies fought the Doomsdays, the Eradicator inhabited the original Doomsday's body, pulling the Doomslayer into a miniature black hole from which neither could ever escape.

Razor-sharp bone protrusions can slice through Kryptonian skin. If the tips are snapped off they quickly grow back.

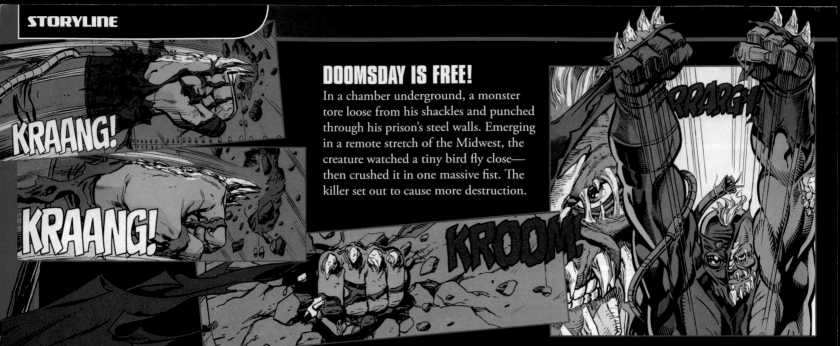

KRAANG!

KRAANG!

KROOM

RRARGH

DOOMSDAY IS FREE!

In a chamber underground, a monster tore loose from his shackles and punched through his prison's steel walls. Emerging in a remote stretch of the Midwest, the creature watched a tiny bird fly close—then crushed it in one massive fist. The killer set out to cause more destruction.

THE DEATH OF SUPERMAN

The citizens of Metropolis counted on Superman to come out on top. But the arrival of Doomsday resulted in the unthinkable—the death of the Man of Steel.

SWAKE

CRUNCH

Not even the JLA's powerful array of weaponry could slow down Doomsday's rampage.

Onward To Metropolis

The Justice League confronted the creature in Ohio, but their attacks failed. Booster Gold observed, "It's like Doomsday has arrived." Demonstrating incredible strength, Doomsday propelled himself across the US with leaps that spanned miles. Each jump took him closer to Metropolis.

METROPOLIS 50 MILES

Hearing the name "Metropolis" coming from a television set, Doomsday followed road signs toward Superman's city.

THOOM

THE FINAL BLOW

Superman and Doomsday's punches rocked Metropolis like earthquake tremors. Afraid of what would happen to the people of the city if Doomsday unleashed his full fury, Superman held nothing back in a fight that was broadcast around the world. With his last ounce of strength, Superman knocked Doomsday out cold and collapsed. As Lois rushed to his side, Superman breathed his last.

Lois Lane held Superman in her arms as the city's heroes looked on helplessly. Jimmy Olsen snapped the iconic photo that appeared on the front page of the *Daily Planet*'s memorial edition.

REIGN OF THE SUPERMEN

SUPERBOY

Project Cadmus had created a clone from a mix of Kryptonian and human DNA, but the clone escaped before it reached full maturity. Dubbed "Superboy" by the Newsboy Legion, and gifted with powers of tactile telekinesis, he soon became a famous face across Metropolis's news media.

THE ERADICATOR

Hailed as "The Last Son of Krypton," this vigilante bore a perfect physical resemblance to Superman—but his cold-blooded executions of minor criminals left no doubt that he lacked the hero's spirit. It transpired that this emotionless agent was an artificially intelligent piece of Kryptonian technology called the Eradicator, which had fashioned an organic body for itself based on Superman's template.

Superman was gone, but four challengers arose to claim his title as defender of Metropolis. The public wondered which of them—if any—might be the true Man of Steel.

STEEL

Engineering genius John Henry Irons formerly made weapons for the US military. Superman's sacrifice in stopping Doomsday inspired Irons to become an example for others. Carrying a sledgehammer and wearing a high-tech armored suit propelled by jet boots and emblazoned with the S-shield, the new Man of Steel announced his plan to carry on Superman's legacy by protecting Metropolis.

CYBORG SUPERMAN

Many believed the Cyborg Superman to be the real deal, somehow resurrected through the miracle of mechanical implants. In truth, this grim figure had been NASA astronaut Hank Henshaw, until a solar radiation accident destroyed his body and left him with the power to control machines. Blaming Superman for his condition, Henshaw set out to ruin the Man of Steel's reputation while forging a secret alliance with Mongul, the leader of Warworld.

OTHERWORLD VISIONS OF HOPE

The stress of losing Clark hit Jonathan Kent hard, bringing on a heart attack. As doctors tried to resuscitate him, Jonathan experienced visions of life after death. He found Clark and urged him to fight demons that wanted to claim his soul. Jonathan then helped Clark to enter a dark void that represented the way back to the physical world.

In the spirit realm, Jonathan Kent found himself flashing back to his time in the military when he helped rescue a downed airman.

Unable to believe that Superman was really dead, Lois demanded to see his body to put her doubts to rest. An empty coffin, however, seemed to hint at a miracle.

THE RETURN OF SUPERMAN

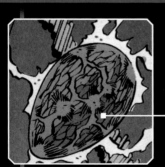

THE MATRIX

After the Eradicator brought Superman's body to the Fortress of Solitude, the Kryptonian regeneration matrix restored him to life.

Four stand-ins had emerged on the scene following the death of Metropolis's greatest hero, but the reappearance of Superman proved there was no substitute for the real Man of Steel.

Inside a suit of Kryptonian ceremonial battle armor, the weakened Superman journeyed from the Fortress across the ocean floor, emerging on the shores of Metropolis. At first, Steel mistook him for an enemy.

RECLAIMING HIS NAME

As Lois Lane, Supergirl, Steel, and Superboy watched, the massive armored suit split open to release its driver—the one, true Superman. Resurrected by Kryptonian technology, Superman had heard the news of Coast City's destruction and of his old enemy Mongul's alliance with the Cyborg Superman. His friends and allies couldn't believe he had really returned, but Superman's heroism was evident. As he had done so many times before, Superman led the charge to save the world.

The uniform might have changed, but the "S" on his chest was unmistakable. The Man of Steel was back.

CYBORG AND MONGUL

The Cyborg Superman tortured intergalactic warlord Mongul to win his obedience. From Mongul's base, Warworld, the two villains annihilated Coast City. Within the smoking crater they erected Engine City, the first beachhead for a new Warworld, that would consume Earth from pole to pole.

Hal Jordan, Earth's representative in the Green Lantern Corps, had once made Coast City his home. He had a personal reason for taking down Mongul.

Superman couldn't bring back the seven million lives lost at Coast City, but he could knock out the cyborg imposter responsible for their murders.

TOGETHER AGAIN

Superman and Lois, engaged at the time of the Doomsday tragedy, picked up right where they had left off. Superman's new, long-haired look, however, lasted only until their wedding day. Clark Kent also returned to the land of the living, explaining his disappearance by emerging from an underground shelter beneath buildings ruined during Doomsday's rampage.

Lois had watched others try to claim the mantle of Superman, but one kiss was all she needed to know that her true love had returned.

Time was unraveling. Alternate versions of heroes flickered in and out of existence. Superman was shocked to discover that the villain behind Zero Hour was former Green Lantern Hal Jordan.

ZERO HOUR

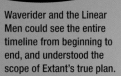

THE RISE OF EXTANT

Time-traveling heroes, including Waverider and the New Gods' Metron, urged Earth's champions to unite against the villain Extant and his vandalism of the timestream. Heroes such as Batgirl and Hawkman appeared in versions that had been erased long ago during the Crisis on Infinite Earths. Anything was possible by disassembling and reconstructing time, declared Extant. Superman and Earth's other defenders couldn't leave the power of creation in a madman's hands.

Waverider and the Linear Men could see the entire timeline from beginning to end, and understood the scope of Extant's true plan.

HEROES FALL

Wally West, the current Flash, sacrificed himself while breaching the light-speed barrier in a failed attempt to stop the time rift. The members of the Justice Society of America reacted by stepping up to fight Extant. Although they looked young, their vigor was the result of long-term exposure to chronal energy. Time suddenly caught up to the World War II veterans when Extant restarted their biological clocks. In an instant, The JSA became a team of 80-year-olds.

One Flash mourned another when Jay Garrick believed that Wally West had died.

Extant used his powers to age the Justice Society into old men, killing Hourman and the Atom in the process.

THE POWER OF PARALLAX

Extant had merely been an agent for Zero Hour's mastermind: former Green Lantern Hal Jordan. Ever since Mongul and the Cyborg Superman had wiped out everyone in Jordan's home town of Coast City, the ex-hero had been obsessed with bringing them all back. Now, infused with chronal energy, Jordan sought to remake the universe as the omnipotent Parallax. He couldn't understand why his former heroic teammates failed to share his vision.

> "You've set yourself up as a god, Hal! You've killed billions!"
> **Superman to Parallax**

FOUND GUILTY

For Parallax, erasing time to Zero Hour was a necessary step toward his ultimate goal. But Superman couldn't let Hal Jordan remake reality to his liking. The heroes made their last stand against Parallax amid a blank void empty of both time and space. Their coordinated strikes against Parallax began to take their toll, clearing the field for the team's heavy hitter—the Spectre. The embodiment of God's Vengeance passed judgement on Hal Jordan and condemned him for the death of a universe.

Waverider led the heroes' counterattack against Parallax, hoping that a united effort would break through his defenses.

After the Spectre weakened Parallax, Green Arrow fired a single arrow into the chest of his old friend Hal Jordan. Parallax died and time restarted.

SUPERMAN
RED
SUPERMAN
BLUE

Superman had turned into a being of pure energy. When an old foe tried to destroy this new Superman, he faced double trouble!

In its energy state, Superman could phase through solid matter, travel at the speed of light, emit electrical bolts, and perceive the entire electromagnetic spectrum. He could transform into Clark Kent, which had no superpowers. Superman was captured by Hank Henshaw, the Cyborg Superman. Henshaw used to harness Superman's electromagnetism form and attempted to interfere, he caused the hero's energy pattern to duplicate.

An accident had caused Superman's powers to run wild. Bullets no longer bounced off him, they passed through him instead. Dr. Emil Hamilton knew that unless he found a way to harness Superman's energy, Superman would fade away forever.

SUPERMAN RED

At the moment the split occurred, Superman had been concerned about Lois Lane's safety. Superman Red represented his emotional side—impulsive, overconfident and belligerent, while openly flirtatious with Lois.

To survive, Superman desperately needed a containment suit. The Contessa, Lex Luthor's wife, donated a bolt of LexCorp polymer fabric; Dr. Hamilton lined it with Kryptonian circuitry.

RED VERSUS BLUE

Because each of the Supermen claimed to be the original, both of them showed up for work at the *Daily Planet* and returned home to the same apartment. Their wildly different personalities led to fierce arguments over how best to keep the peace in Metropolis. Meanwhile, an ancient menace stirred deep within the Earth. The Millennium Giants rose from a thousand-year slumber in Egypt, Mexico, and England, initiating the scouring of the surface world to mark the beginning of the Cycle of Ages. Superman Red and Superman Blue teamed up to lead the counterattack against the three colossi, calling on help from Aquaman, Steel, the Justice League, the Teen Titans, and the Challengers of the Unknown. The Millennium Giants followed the mystical ley lines of the planet during their march of destruction, and the two Supermen realized that the electromagnetism within their bodies might be enough to heal the ley lines and send the guardians back into dormancy. The act, however, would require the supreme sacrifice. Superman Red and Superman Blue both agreed to lay down their lives in order to save the world.

SUPERMAN BLUE

Without the extreme emotions of his red counterpart, Superman Blue calmly solved problems through logic. Both Supermen considered themselves to be the real article and neither one wanted to merge back into a single person.

As Superman Red circled the Earth at dizzying speeds, Superman Blue burrowed to the planet's core. The release of their energies fulfilled the mission of the Millennium Giants—and also restored Superman to his original body, with all his superpowers intact.

Superman had the power to be a global dictator, but no one ever thought he would go that far. When he proclaimed his authority over all the nations of Earth, Lois Lane and Lex Luthor teamed up to find out why.

SUPERMAN KING OF THE WORLD

DOMINUS

The reality-bending villain Dominus used his powers to brainwash the Man of Steel into believing that only direct intervention would save the world from disaster. Superman ordered his robot duplicates to watch over the world's capital cities, and threw half of LexCorp Tower into space when he suspected Lex Luthor had developed synthetic Kryptonite. The Justice League and the United Nations couldn't penetrate Superman's Fortress of Solitude, but Luthor scored a victory by dropping the orbiting chunk of LexCorp Tower onto Superman's stronghold—accidentally paving the way for the next phase of Dominus' plan.

DOMINUS

After throwing Superman into the Phantom Zone, Dominus assumed Superman's appearance (right) and convinced Earth's governments to help him find the mastermind behind the recent unrest. Lois Lane and Lex Luthor suspected the truth and infiltrated Superman's glittering new command center.
In a forgotten sublevel deep underground, they found and freed the true Superman.

Changes in costume marked Superman's journeys through dream states conjured by Dominus, including one inspired by the Kingdom Come reality.

While in the Phantom Zone, Superman had met others who belonged to Dominus' alien species. From them he learned the reason behind his enemy's quest for absolute power. Dominus had tried to wrest the omnipotence of Kismet away from his former love Ahti. In the process he had suffered a terrible accident and been confined to the Phantom Zone. During his long exile, Dominus had gained reality-warping abilities. To combat Dominus, Superman mastered the ancient Kryptonian meditative technique of Torquasm Vo and engaged Dominus on a purely mental plane. Though his environment shifted and rearranged, Superman maintained his focus throughout the fight. Ultimately, his mental assault shattered Dominus' physical form and banished his intellect back into the Phantom Zone. Superman had won, but he now needed to win back the trust of the people of Earth.

The powerful being Kismet had once been the priestess Ahti. Her jealous lover Tuoni had tried to gain the power of Kismet for himself. His failure triggered his transformation into Dominus. Superman didn't expect Kismet to help him, but Dominus' obsession with his lost love was a weakness he could exploit.

"I'M KING OF THE WORLD, AND EARTH IS JUST THE BEGINNING!"

SUPERMAN FOR ALL SEASONS

Spring, summer, fall, and winter always brought fresh challenges to the Kent farm. The changing seasons also marked Clark Kent's transition to adulthood, and his new life in Metropolis.

A tornado ripped through Smallville, Kansas, tearing apart a filling station. Clark shielded the attendant as the pumps exploded.

RAISED RIGHT

Clark Kent's alien superpowers made him more powerful than any Earth army that had ever existed. But Jonathan and Martha Kent brought up their adopted son to value humility, hard work, and the satisfaction of helping his neighbors. Friendship with Pete Ross and a crush on Lana Lang initially tied Clark to Smallville, but once he realized all that he could accomplish with his incredible gifts, he knew it would be a sin if he didn't devote himself fully to making the world a better place.

Before heading to Metropolis, Clark said his goodbyes to his mother Martha on the front porch of the Kent homestead.

On a return visit to Smallville, Clark demonstrated his love for Lana Lang. She knew, however, that Clark belonged in Metropolis.

CITY CHAMPION

In Metropolis, Clark worked as a reporter for the *Daily Planet* while keeping the city safe as Superman. Lex Luthor, the city's most powerful businessman, took a dim view of his rival. He created a corps of armored agents to handle civic emergencies, and when that failed he turned an innocent woman into the costumed Toxin and doused Metropolis with a virus that rendered every citizen unconscious. After using Toxin to fix the crisis, Luthor suggested that Superman's alien biology may have been the vector for the outbreak. Doubting his mission, Superman went back to Smallville, but a catastrophic flood forced him back into action. With a new commitment to his calling, Superman returned to Metropolis.

Lex Luthor tried to win back the public's affection by creating his own LexCorp legion of superpowered employees.

Superman helped the woman called Toxin dissipate the virus that had infected Metropolis, but she died when he returned her to LexCorp.

His career at the *Daily Planet* was just beginning, but Clark Kent knew that he had a one-of-a-kind colleague in Lois Lane.

Clark took in the Kansas sunset with his father one last time before heading east. He admitted that he'd never grow tired of the view.

NEW ENEMIES

MANCHESTER BLACK

Telepath Manchester Black led the Elite, a team of metahuman crime fighters. Black's ruthless methods soon brought him into conflict with Superman, who proved the superiority of his morality, thus incurring Black's hatred. Black's mind-reading abilities enabled him to discover Superman's secret identity. Unable to undermine the hero's principles Black seemingly killed himself.

IGNITION

Ignition is a bizarre melding of man and machine. His sleek black armor offers him near-complete shielding against attack. He can fly as well as Superman, due to the twin turbines on his back. He also possesses enhanced speed and strength. Very little is known of his origins, but in one version of events, Ignition aided the false General Zod in the takeover of the nation of Pokolistan.

SCORCH

The Joker, using Mr. Mxyzptlk's power, turned Aubrey Sparks into the demoness Scorch who had the ability to teleport and control fire. Originally a villain, she reformed and even started a romantic relationship with the Martian Manhunter.

RADION

A minor, power-suited Metropolis thug, Radion received an upgrade when a dunk in a reactor mutated him into a glowing monster. Radion can emit radiation and accelerate the growth of tumors in living beings. He sometimes works with the villain Neutron, who has similar powers. Radion and Neutron once worked for Intergang to carry out a hit against Clark Kent.

EQUUS

A genetically-enhanced cyborg created by a secret government agency, Equus has artificial organs, self-healing skin, a built-in targeting and communications system, and claws that can cut through steel. Equus fought Superman in the aftermath of the Vanishing, but teleported away when the Man of Steel got the upper hand.

REPLIKON

The last of his species, Replikon mirrored the appearance of Earth's heroes when he appea. help from Green Lantern, who constructed an asteroid home where the alien and his two egg-children could live. Replikon later caused destruction throughout Metropolis to catch Superman's attention, begging the Man of Steel to help its children, who had by a super-villain to fight against their will.

KANCER

An artificial being grown from Kryptonian cancer cells, Kancer can dissolve and absorb org Because it originated from a sample of K genetic material, Kancer has the same su as all Kryptonians, including flight, super-strength, and invulnerability. Kancer served in the entourage of the false General Zod after he emerged as t er of the European nation of Pokolistan.

As the Earth faced strange new threats, heroes and villains arose from the chaos. But even those who claimed to fight for justice had mixed motivations, forcing Superman to stand up for what was right.

GOG

In an alternate future, a superpowered battle devastated Kansas and turned one of the survivors into the fanatical Gog, who blamed the Superman of his world for failing to prevent the disaster. Gog set out to kill Superman again and again at different points in the timeline. On the primary Earth, Gog battled the heroes of the Justice Society of America, but also used his vast cosmic powers to grant wishes to the needy.

SUBJEKT-17

The crash of a spacecraft in the Soviet republic of Kazakhstan revealed an alien baby, who fell into the hands of Soviet scientists and became a government experiment. Labeled Subjekt-17, the alien escaped after the collapse of the Soviet Union. Subjekt-17 has the power of telekinesis and mind-reading, as well as enhanced strength and speed.

ENCANTADORA

Lourdes Lucero channels vast magical abilities through the mystical Mists of Ibella, which she wears around her neck in a vial suspended from a chain. As Encantadora, she flirts with Superman while plotting to betray him. She once introduced a deadly nanobot into Superman's body with a passionate kiss. Over time, she has developed a genuine admiration for the Man of Steel and his unflagging heroism.

HELSPONT

Helspont, an exiled Daemonite prince, longs to return the Daemonites to their previous place as galactic conquerors. He possesses the ability to alter his appearance and has a powerful array of psionic powers, including telekinesis and mind control. At his base in the Himalayas, Helspont tried and failed to recruit Superman to his dubious cause.

REACTRON

Radioactive menace Benjamin Krull donned a containment suit as the villain Reactron. Part of Lex Luthor's plot against New Krypton, Reactron received a Gold Kryptonite upgrade and killed Supergirl's father. He later activated a bomb hidden inside his body and destroyed the planet of New Krypton.

H'EL

Arriving on Earth, H'el claimed to have piloted the Kryptonian test rocket that convinced Jor-El of the viability of space travel. H'el believed that Superman had become corrupted by Earth's decadent culture, and demonstrated powers of telekinesis and telepathy.

GENERAL SAM LANE

The father of Lois and Lucy, General Sam Lane serves on secret government committees charged with containing the threats posed by aliens and metahumans. Shortly after Superman appeared in Metropolis, General Lane hired Lex Luthor to capture the alien. When that failed, he activated the first subject in his "Steel Soldier" project—resulting in the creation of Metallo.

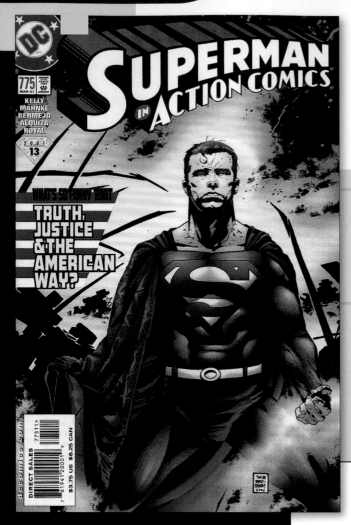

ACTION COMICS
Vol.1 #775

> "They have to know there's another way, Lois. They have to hear a voice of compassion and faith, instead of spite and anger."
>
> **Superman**

Main Characters: Superman, Manchester Black
Main Supporting Characters: Coldcast, The Hat, Menagerie, Lois Lane, Perry White, Jimmy Olsen, Jonathan Kent, Steel
Main Locations: Metropolis, Tokyo, Smallville, Jupiter's moon Io

Publication Date
March 2001

Editor
Eddie Berganza

Cover Artist
Tim Bradstreet

Writer
Joe Kelly

Pencillers
Doug Mahnke, Lee Bermejo

Inkers
Tom Nguyen, Dexter Vines, Jim Royal, Jose Marzan Jr, Wade Von Grawbadger, Wayne Faucher

Colorist
Rob Schwager

BACKGROUND

By the time super hero comics entered the new millennium they had been deconstructed, reassembled, and examined from every literary angle. Dark, gritty themes were particularly popular: DC's *Watchmen* explored the "real world" implications of heroes with godlike gifts or a hunger for vigilantism; WildStorm's *The Authority* depicted super heroes as tyrants of fictional universes. In response, Joe Kelly's "What's So Funny About Truth, Justice, and the American Way?" in *Action Comics* #775 stood out as a bold defense of Superman, the very first super hero, and the principles he stood for.

The enemies in Kelly's tale, the Elite, could have stepped out of any number of competing titles. Observers within the story praise the Elite's efficient brutality at eliminating threats to public safety. But for Superman, ends never justify means. He has to defend his methods and his philosophy, and he isn't immune to self-doubt. The Elite call him (with faint mockery) "the first, the best," but Superman proves that his brand of idealism is truly timeless.

THE STORY

The Elite are the new heroes on the scene, and they don't care much about due process or collateral damage. However, they get quick results, and the public asks why Superman doesn't use their methods. Putting his heartland morality to the test, Superman challenges the Elite to a showdown.

As Superman patrols the skies of Metropolis, his ears pick up news of a major terrorist action in Libya **[1]**. Before he can swoop into the fray, however, the incident is already over. Thousands have died in Tripoli in a fight between insurgents, Libyan troops, and a giant mutated ape **[2]**. A team of superpowered operatives calling themselves the Elite are credited with ending the crisis, but Superman thinks the death toll is unacceptable.

Polls show increasing public support for the Elite's ruthless methods, and Superman wonders if the world has moved on from the traditional values he stands for. In the Fortress of Solitude, Superman discusses these doubts with Steel **[3]**.

Another emergency arises: in Tokyo, the genetically-engineered killers of the Samurai Roshu threaten to annihilate the city **[4]**. Superman plans to take them down without anyone getting seriously hurt, but instead the Elite indiscriminately slaughter the aggressors.

The leader of the Elite, telepath Manchester Black, introduces the other members of his team: the electromagnetic-channeling Coldcast, the living bio-colony Menagerie, and the demon conjurer known as The Hat **[5]**. Black teleports Superman to the Elite's extra-dimensional headquarters, letting him know that the team's outward politeness is a courtesy extended only out of respect for his status as the world's first super hero. The future, Black proclaims, belongs to the Elite **[6]**.

In Smallville, Jonathan Kent **[7]** encourages his son to lead by example. Superman puts his methods into action against a new alien threat **[8]** by finding a solution that doesn't require killing. When the Elite point out that he's only achieved a temporary victory, Superman responds that he stops his foes as many times as it takes **[9]**.

Superman and the Elite know their philosophies can't co-exist. A showdown seems inevitable, and when Superman issues his challenge the Elite reveal their starship HQ **[10]**.

On Jupiter's moon Io, the combatants face off as the world watches on television. Coldcast gets in a cheap hit **[11]**, allowing Manchester Black to trigger a telekinetic stroke in Superman's brain.

The Man of Steel responds by ripping into Coldcast, Menagerie, and The Hat, seemingly killing them in seconds. When Black accuses him of breaking his code, Superman uses his heat vision to lobotomize the psychic nodes in Black's brain, rendering him powerless **[12]**.

Superman has won, and he then reveals that he didn't have to stoop to the Elite's level to do it. The other members aren't dead, just unconscious **[13]**, and Black's powers will return in time.

Superman says that he could be the kind of person championed by the Elite's fans, but as he puts it, "I don't like my heroes ugly and mean." As he flies away, Superman reminds Black that no matter what obstacles he faces, he'll never stop fighting **[14]**.

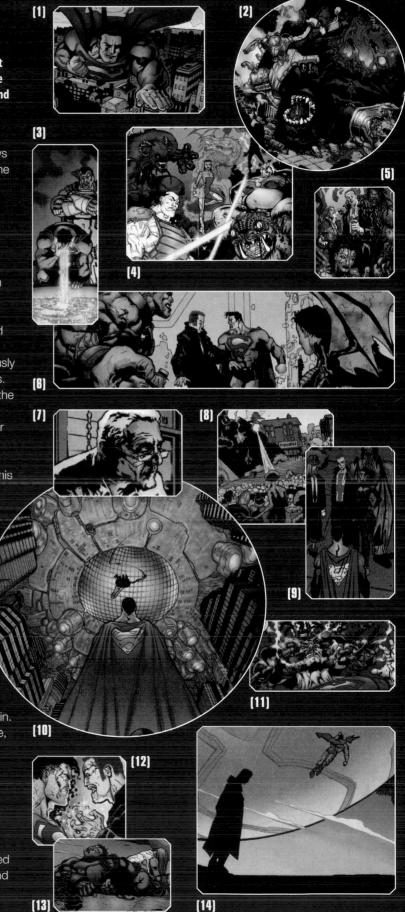

136/137

PRESIDENT LUTHOR

Superman fought for truth, justice, and the American way, but what happened when his worst enemy was elected to the most powerful office in the land? Superman had to call Lex Luthor "Mr. President."

ENVY

Lex Luthor hated Superman for hogging the attention and praise that Luthor felt were owed to him alone. The sight of a photo of the Man of Steel on the front page of the *Daily Planet* helped inspire Luthor to embark upon a new strategy for outdoing Superman: become the next President of the United States of America.

ASSASSINATION

After dealing with the threat Atlantis posed to the citizens of Metropolis, Luthor found himself looking down the barrel of a

Jenny Hubbard had hated Luthor ever since he had broken his promise to whisk her away from her dead-end job.

gun. A waitress with a grudge fired two shots. Not only did Luthor survive, he used the incident to increase his sympathy among the voting public.

Luthor bounced back from his injury and his popularity skyrocketed. Nothing, it seemed, could stand in the way of his election.

The Oval Office became President Luthor's refuge. Not even Superman dared to violate the White House.

TALIA AL GHŪL

His role as US President would take Luthor away from his duties as the head of LexCorp. But he had a successor in mind. Talia al Ghūl, daughter of the immortal Rā's al Ghūl, had been trained by the League of Assassins and inherited her father's gift for coordinating eco-terrorism cells across dozens of countries. Her relationship with Rā's al Ghūl had never been good. Luthor offered to protect Talia from her father if she took the reins of LexCorp. The lure of power proved intoxicating and Talia became the company's new CEO.

Talia remained suspicious of Luthor's motives, especially after he seemingly staged an attempt on her life to influence her decision.

With the resources of LexCorp and her father's global terrorism network, Talia held more power than ever before.

LUTHOR'S ADMINISTRATION

It was a close race, but Lex Luthor, championing technological progress, won and took office as the 43rd President of the United States. He appointed several familiar faces to his cabinet, including General Frank Rock as Chairman of the Joint Chiefs, Major Sam Lane (Lois's father) as Secretary of Defense, Jefferson Pierce as Secretary of Education, Amanda Waller as Secretary of Metahuman Affairs, and Cat Grant as White House Press Secretary. Luthor also cleaned up a loose end from his past by ordering a missile strike against his ex-wife, the Contessa Erica Alexandra Del Portenza. Superman and Batman paid visits to their new Commander-in-Chief, vowing to keep their eyes on him for the sake of the American people.

Some of Luthor's appointees—like Jefferson Pierce, the hero formerly called Black Lightning—didn't trust their boss. They watched carefully for any signs of wrongdoing.

OUR WORLDS AT WAR

FACING ANNIHILATION

Imperiex, believed to be the embodiment of entropy, had consumed entire galaxies by the time it set its sights on Earth. If Imperiex succeeded in "hollowing" the core of the planet, the reaction would trigger the collapse of the entire universe. President of the United States, Lex Luthor, saw the coming conflict as a way to guarantee his legacy as one of history's greatest leaders. He made alliances with super-villains Brainiac 13 and Darkseid, and freed potentially useful super-villains, including Manchester Black and Doomsday. Superman didn't trust these allies, but he couldn't refuse any offer of help.

"I HAVE ALL THIS POWER..."

"...AND I COULDN'T SAVE THEM"

Brainiac 13, an evolved intelligence of the original Brainiac from the 64th century, used a mind-controlled Lena Luthor to arrange a partnership with her father, President Luthor. As the war progressed, Brainiac 13 plotted his surprise betrayal.

An Imperiex probe fell from space toward the center of North America. Topeka, Kansas took most of the impact and thousands died. The damage stretched as far as Smallville; Superman believed that Jonathan and Martha Kent had also perished.

A lightning-fast flurry of punches damaged the probe that had landed in Kansas. A crack in the probe's armor released a wave of pure energy that obliterated its host.

THE HOLLOWING OF EARTH

As Imperiex took up position in Earth's orbit, it sent its hollowing probes raining down on the world below. Each probe targeted the center of a major landmass, hitting locations as far apart as Zaire, Russia, Antarctica, and even the underwater city of Atlantis.

In space, the Justice League and other heroes took the fight to the enemy, engaging Imperiex's probes in battle before they could hit the Earth. Spacegoing field hospitals called Paradocs were set up in order to treat the injured and patch their wounds. Casualties ran high. Not even the mighty Doomsday could stand up to Imperiex, who casually blasted the flesh from the bones of the monster that had once killed Superman. With his allies falling to fatigue and injury, Superman redoubled his efforts inspired by his belief that victory would honor his parents' memories.

"I'M SO LOST. PLEASE GOD... TELL ME WHAT TO DO. TELL ME HOW TO FIGHT ON..."

THE DEAD

Imperiex's probes continued their assault on Earth's resistance forces. One probe zeroed in on Washington DC, headquarters of President Luthor. General Sam Lane commanded a tank guarding the lawn of the White House. When the probe got too close he courageously detonated the reactor that powered his tank, taking out both his attacker and himself.

President Luthor offered words of comfort to Lois Lane after the death of her father, General Sam Lane. She couldn't understand why Superman hadn't arrived in time to help.

ENDGAME

After the death of Sam Lane, Superman agreed to follow President Luthor's orders if it meant the end of Imperiex. Wonder Woman nearly died fighting the probes, while her mother, Queen Hippolyta, fell in battle during the defense of Greece. Eventually, a coordinated assault opened up a seam in Imperiex's armor, rendering Imperiex helpless without a form that could house its consciousness. But in that moment of triumph, Brainiac 13 collected the stray Imperiex energy using the technology of Warworld. Only Lex Luthor's genius, Darkseid's power, Wonder Woman's spirit, and Superman's heart could turn the tide against this new foe. Superman traveled to the surface of the sun to supercharge his body's cells, gaining the strength to push Warworld through a teleport gateway back to the beginning of time. The Big Bang obliterated both Brainiac 13 and Imperiex.

His Herculean labor accomplished by eliminating Warworld, Superman returned to Kansas to mourn his parents. Jonathan and Martha Kent numbered among the missing, but they soon turned up alive.

EARLY WARNINGS

Visiting childhood friend Pete Ross at the Capitol, Clark Kent had a ringside seat for a raid by Master Jailer and the walking bomb Neutron. Was the attack linked to Pete's role as Vice President in Lex Luthor's administration? But then more enemies popped up, menacing Clark's parents and his colleagues at the *Daily Planet*. Other villains threatened everyone from Clark's high school football coach to his Metropolis accountant. Superman rounded up everyone he could and told them to take shelter in John Henry Irons' Steelworks complex.

The Master Jailer locked down the Capitol Building. His chains proved strong enough to bring down the Man of Steel.

When Superman's secret ID was revealed, every criminal in Metropolis targeted Clark Kent's friends and family. Superman tried to protect his loved ones while an old enemy emerged as the plot's mastermind.

ENDING BATTLE

RUNNING THE GAUNTLET

With his allies out of harm's way Superman faced a coordinated attack from every enemy at once. The Master Jailer walled off Metropolis to...

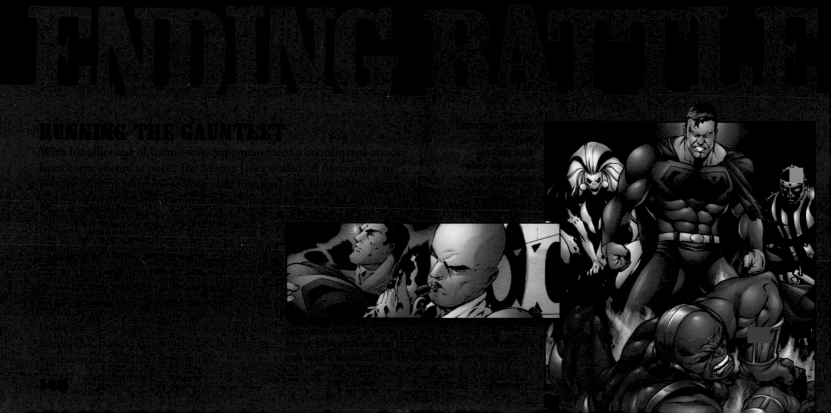

MANCHESTER BLACK

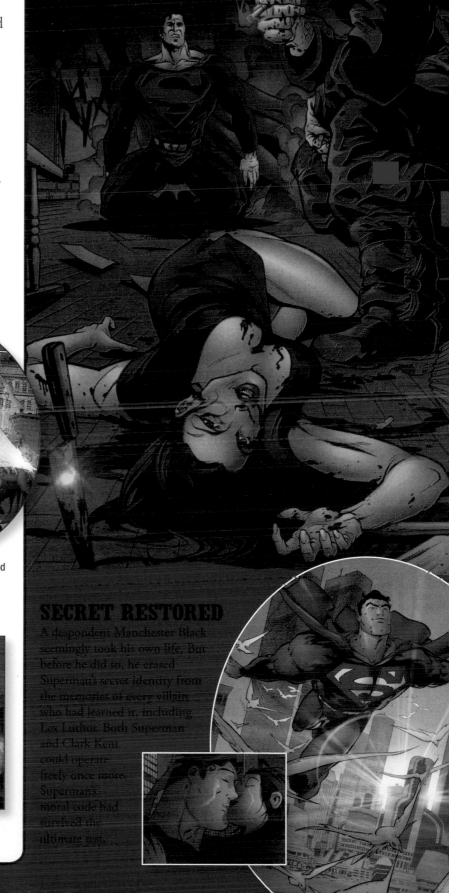

Superman couldn't deny what he saw with his own eyes—his beloved Lois was dead, murdered by Manchester Black.

The world's most powerful telepath, Manchester Black commanded the Elite, a squad of anti-heroes. Black and his teammates rejected the morality of heroes like Superman and killed their opponents in cold blood. Superman had defeated the Elite once before, but a top-secret government agency freed Black on condition that he worked for it. Black hated Superman and what he stood for: fighting for justice in a cruel and unfair world.

Black possessed the power to read minds, create visions, and project telekinetic shields.

Black broke through Superman's mental defenses and discovered that the hero lived as Clark Kent and enjoyed a happy marriage to Lois Lane. Vowing to make Superman snap, Black fed the Man of Steel a telepathic illusion showing Lois' dead body. Superman's hatred for Black burned so intensely that he nearly incinerated him on the spot, but he held back—refusing to take the life of another in the heat of vengeance. Realizing his sadistic psychological experiment had failed, Black revealed the real Lois, alive and well.

Superman longed to kill Black, but stayed true to his principles.

SECRET RESTORED

A despondent Manchester Black seemingly took his own life. But before he did so, he erased Superman's secret identity from the memories of every villain who had learned it, including Lex Luthor. Both Superman and Clark Kent could operate freely once more. Superman's moral code had survived the ultimate test.

Superman's character couldn't be cracked, not even by Black's vilest tricks. Black ended his challenge and the false Lois vanished in Superman's arms.

THE MODERN AGE

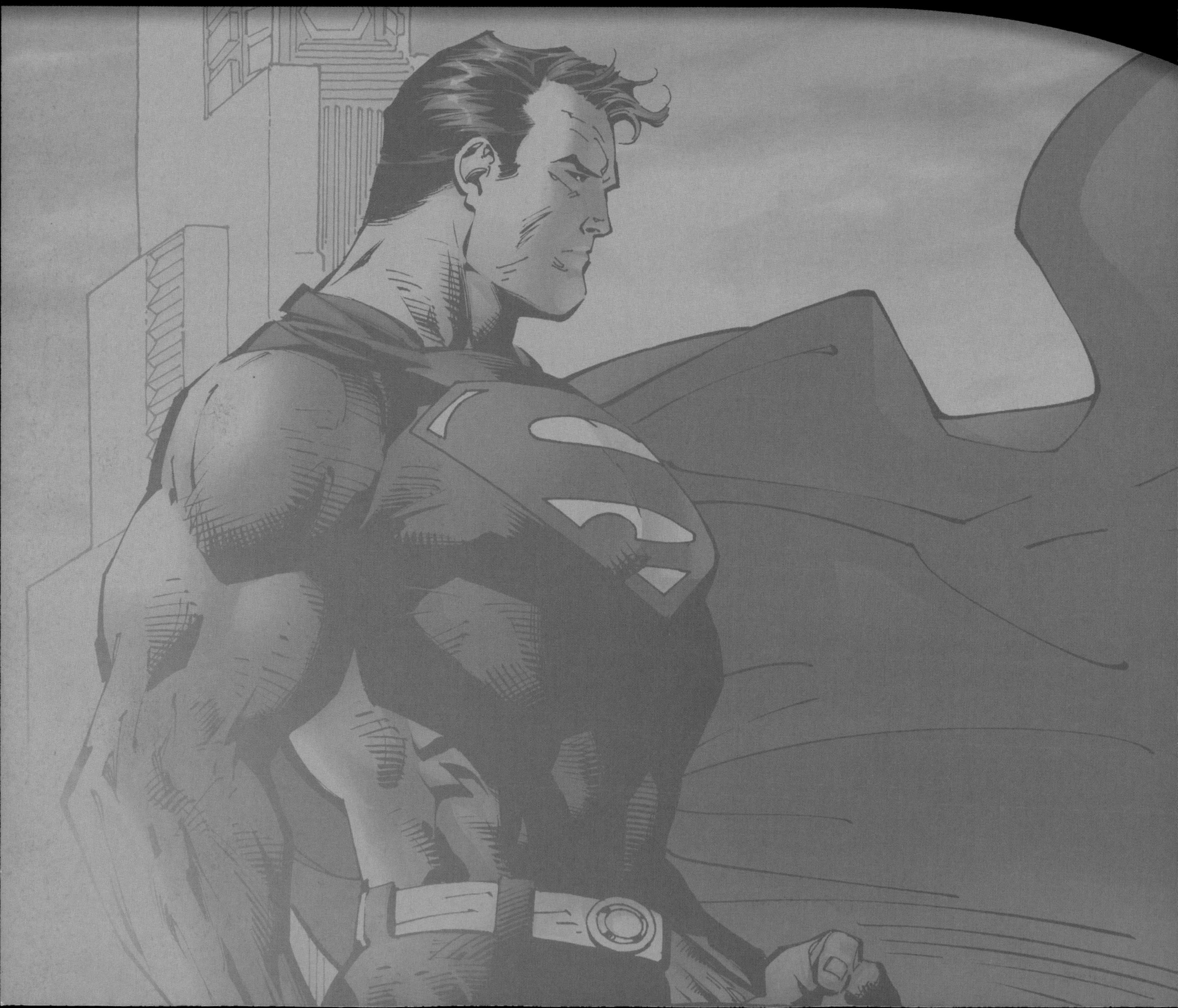

As DC Comics moved into the new millennium, the company restored and updated the most enduring parts of the Superman legend. New audiences got to know the Man of Steel on television and in movie theaters, providing DC with a sounding board to discover which parts of the Superman mythos resonated the most with fans. Down the road, these insights would pay off in a major reboot.

As the decade went on, tweaks to the existing lore made Superman's story more accessible. Supergirl, a Silver Age creation, came back into continuity as Superman's cousin. General Zod and the bottle city of Kandor had also suffered muddled histories; both received fresh incarnations that captured the essences of their appeal. In addition, Superman and Batman, frequent partners during the *World's Finest* era, received a new outlet for their teamup with the launch of the title *Superman/Batman* in October 2003.

In 2011, DC launched the *Flashpoint* series to put its comics universe through a history-altering shakeup. Just as *Crisis on Infinite Earths* had done a quarter-century earlier, *Flashpoint* gave DC the chance to start afresh. Every existing comics title ended its run at the same time. The month after the *Flashpoint,* DC COMICS—The New 52 was launched with the debut of 52 titles, each starting with an all-new #1 issue. At the same time, accompanying this universe revolution, DC made a bold move into digital distribution.

Just as Superman had done in the Golden Age, the Man of Steel once again headlined *Action Comics* #1. But now he was portrayed as a champion of the people who was still exploring the limits of his fantastic powers. *Superman* #1 filled in more details of Superman's life in The New 52 universe. He and Lois weren't married and had no relationship beyond their friendship as co-workers. Martha and Jonathan Kent no longer acted as Superman's mentors—both had died before Clark set out for Metropolis on his hero's journey. The launches of the related titles *Superboy*, *Supergirl*, and *Justice League* gave Superman an interconnected group of books worthy of his legacy.

OVERLEAF *Infinite Crisis* #5: In an image that echoes the cover of the Man of Steel's debut in *Action Comics* #1 (June 1938), different worlds come into conflict as the Superman of Earth-Two confronts the modern day Superman.
Art: Jerry Ordway

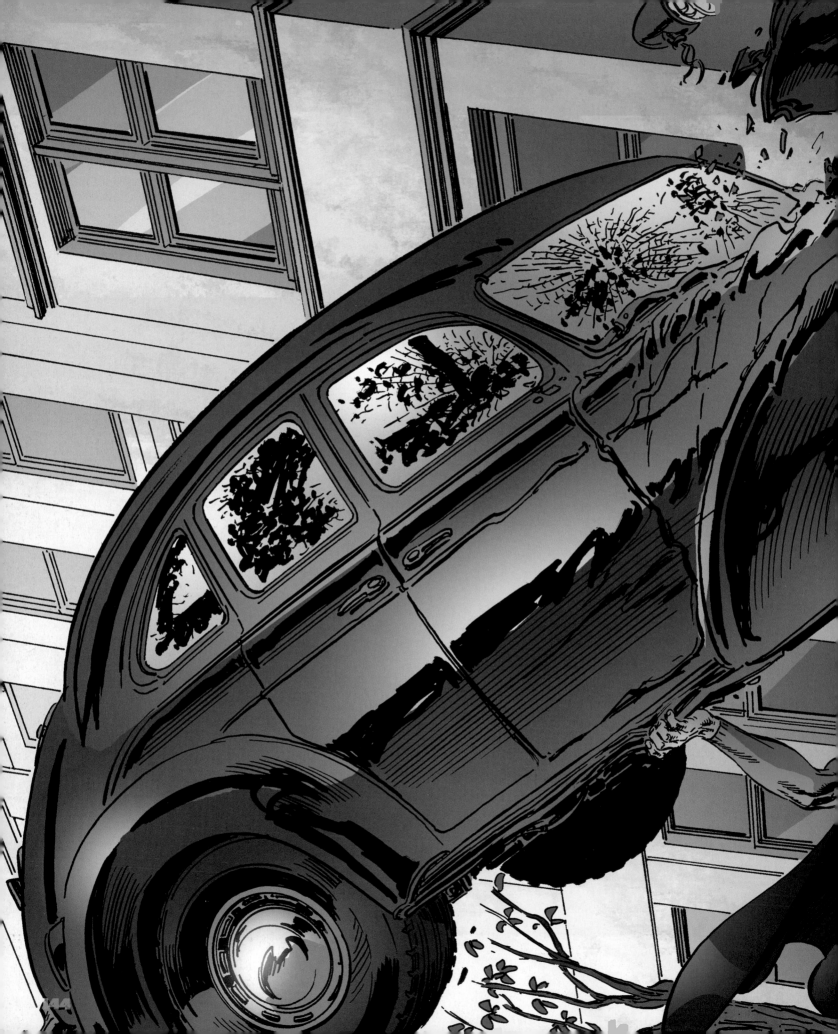

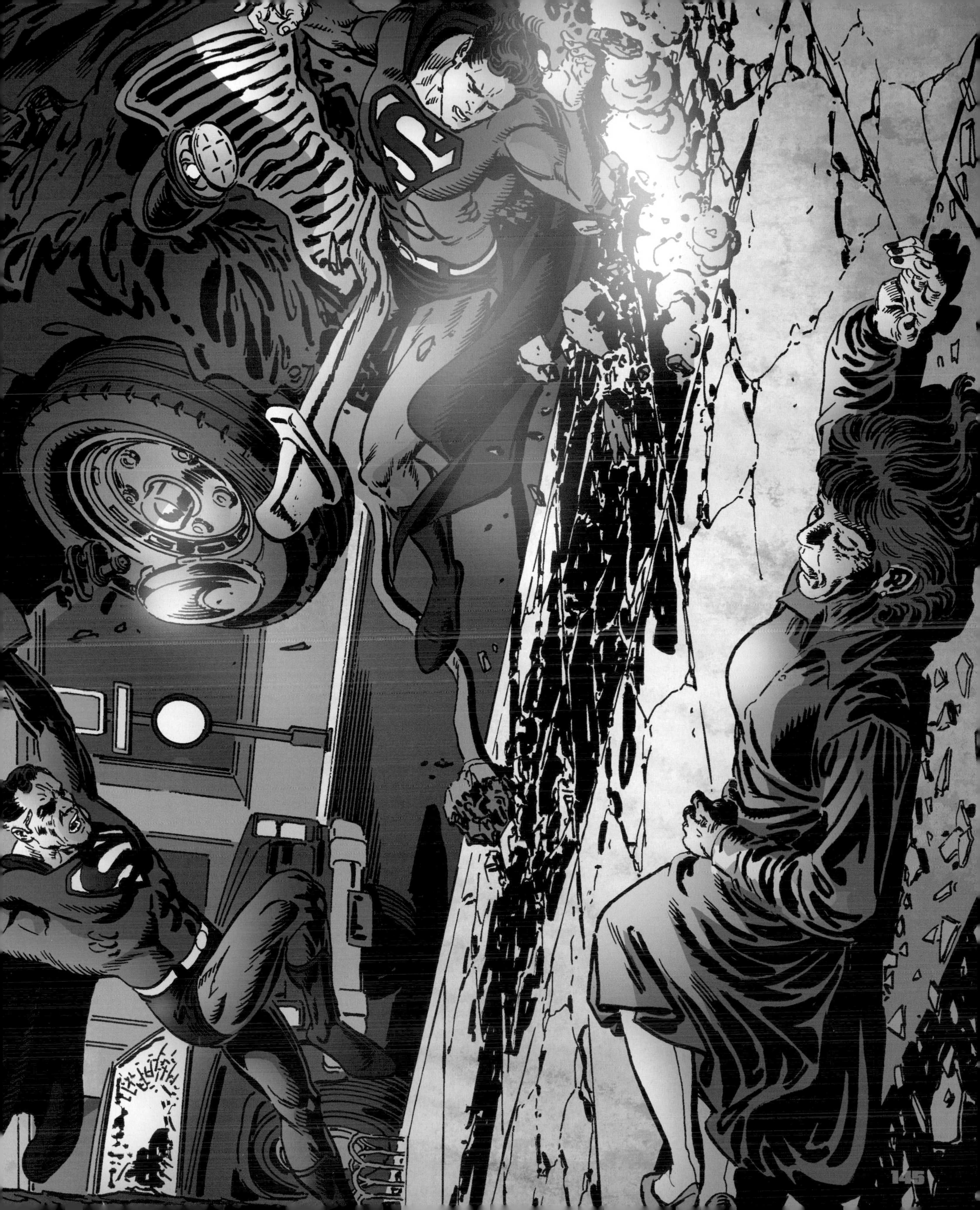

The device that had triggered the Vanishing also had the power to bring back its victims—if Superman could divine its secrets.

FOR TOMORROW

The disappearance of Lois Lane and a million others forced Superman into a spiritual crisis, one that challenged his faith and tested his commitment to humanity.

HIGHER POWER

The mysterious incident called the Vanishing saw the disappearance of a million people from across the planet. Superman, who blamed himself for not preventing the tragedy, visited a priest, Father Daniel Leone, to unburden himself of his guilt. Superman allowed his guard to drop and spoke freely about his fears and frustrations. But while Father Leone enjoyed these confessionals, he had worries of his own—he was dying of cancer. A high-priced mercenary named Mr. Orr offered to cure Leone, but instead handed him over to a secret military project that turned the helpless Leone into a brainwashed soldier.

Mr. Orr claimed to work for unseen figures that held more power than all the world's presidents and prime ministers put together.

EQUUS

The agency that employed Mr. Orr had already created one soldier, codenamed Equus. Equipped with exotic cybernetics, and razor-sharp claws, Equus was sent to aid revolutionary leader General Nox in the Middle East. When Superman fought Equus, the high-tech killer triggered another Vanishing event and blinked out of existence.

METROPIA

Superman followed the trail of the Vanishing and discovered Lois, Equus, and Earth's missing people. They existed in Metropia, an idyllic version of Krypton's Phantom Zone. As his memories came back, Superman realized that he had created Metropia as an "escape hatch" for Earth's people in case they faced an apocalyptic threat similar to the one that had destroyed Krypton.

Metropia was very nearly a perfect world, yet it faced a grim threat from the Phantom Zone's version of General Zod.

PHANTOM ZOD

Within Metropia, a new version of Krypton's General Zod arose. He vowed revenge against Jor-El—in reality, a robotic defender constructed by Superman—and the people Jor-El protected. Superman intervened, and the fury of his battle with Zod reverberated throughout the Metropia's fragile structure.

PILATE

Now a soldier forced to obey the orders of the puppeteers who had created him, Father Leone, under the code name Pilate, murdered innocents. When Superman returned from Metropia to confront him, Leone begged the Man of Steel to end his life.

Cybernetic headgear gave Leone his orders to kill.

His humanity not yet fully extinguished, Father Leone lunged at Equus. Both combatants disappeared in a flash of light.

THE RETURN

The fierce battle between Superman and Zod collapsed the Phantom Zone foundation of Metropia. As this reality crumbled, Superman seized the Vanishing device and reversed its effects, phasing everyone back to their original locations on Earth. He tried to save Zod, too, but his enemy remained defiant to the end.

As Earth recovered from the Vanishing, Superman decided to build a new Fortress of Solitude in the Amazon rainforest, where he would have a stronger connection to living things.

148-149

BIRTHRIGHT

A dramatic shakeup to Superman's origin story reframed his relationship with Lex Luthor and gave Clark Kent a global perspective on humanity's problems.

Jor-El and Lara had no hope of escaping Krypton before it exploded, but they could save their son. Within Kal-El's interstellar cradle, they placed a memory device loaded with the cultural and historical records of their homeworld. Jor-El programmed the spacecraft to seek out a world with a yellow sun, knowing that the solar radiation would endow the boy with powers that would protect him from harm. The rocket crashed in Smallville, Kansas, while glowing green meteorites—chunks of Krypton's radioactive core—pelted the countryside.

Kal-El grew to adulthood as Clark Kent, learning honesty and determination from his adoptive parents, the Kents. He also sought to understand the otherworldly images displayed on the strange device that had accompanied him to Earth.

Krypton exploded, but the craft carrying Kal-El outraced the blast wave. With its life-support systems almost exhausted, the rocket finally reached Earth's atmosphere.

"OUR SON, THE LAST OF THE EL FAMILY. THE LAST SON OF KRYPTON. LET HIM NEVER FORGET."

SEEING THE WORLD

After graduating from Smallville High School at age 18, Clark Kent spent the next seven years as a globetrotting photojournalist. He gained an understanding of different cultures and of the problems facing humanity. He also vowed that he would never take the life of another. In West Africa, his failure to protect a political activist from gunmen made him realize that, even with his incredible powers, he couldn't be everywhere at once. Clark ultimately decided that he would be able to do more good in the world if he finally emerged from obscurity.

Clark had viewed images of traditional Kryptonian clothing in the databanks that were Jor-El's legacy to his son. Embracing his heritage, Clark gave his mother Martha designs that incorporated a chest symbol copied from a Kryptonian family crest. She sewed the blue, yellow, and red costume that would announce her son as a superpowered protector.

LUTHOR IN SMALLVILLE

Teenaged genius Lex Luthor arranged for his family's move to Smallville, so he could be closer to the site that he considered to be ground zero for an extraterrestrial invasion. The locals disliked Lex, but Clark—a fellow outcast— befriended him. While living in Smallville, Lex discovered Kryptonite but didn't suspect that the alien he sought was living right under his nose. Lex moved away after an explosion in his lab burned down the Luthor mansion and killed his father Lionel.

Lex had built a device to generate a spatial wormhole. It overloaded, burned away his hair and set his home ablaze.

METROPOLIS

Clark Kent moved to Metropolis, and Superman was soon headline news. Clark concealed his secret identity by working as a reporter for the *Daily Planet*, but had difficulty fitting in with his co-workers. Lex Luthor, meanwhile, had become an astrobiologist and corporate icon in the years since he'd abandoned Smallville. The appearance of a flying superhuman validated Luthor's longtime suspicions that aliens had plans to take over Earth. Luthor used an armed military drone to test Superman's powers, nearly destroying the *Daily Planet*'s news helicopter in the process. But this was just a warm-up for his true plan—to exploit the public's fear of the unknown and for Lex Luthor to be acclaimed the true hero of Metropolis.

Perry White saw the makings of a solid reporter in Clark Kent, even though the Smallville transplant seemed timid and distracted during his job interview.

Their helicopter badly damaged, reporters Lois Lane and Jimmy Olsen seemed doomed. Luckily, Superman flew to the rescue.

KRYPTON ATTACKS!

Intrigued by ancient Kryptonian transmissions he had intercepted in his laboratory, Lex Luthor constructed facsimiles of Krypton's war machines and hired costumed actors to play the parts of alien shock troopers. Luthor blamed their arrival on Superman, and prepared to deploy his own Earth-First Security Force to save the day. When his deception came to light, Luthor found himself facing criminal charges.

Luthor kept a chunk of Kryptonite from his stay in Smallville and spent years trying to tap its power.

His alien invasion revealed as a fraud, Luthor's grand scheme came crashing down. Superman took him out with one punch and set to work restoring his image among the shell-shocked citizens of Metropolis.

LAST SON

Not only was the alien arrival in Metropolis another Kryptonian, he was the son of General Zod! With Superman's guidance, Christopher Kent proved that anyone can be a hero.

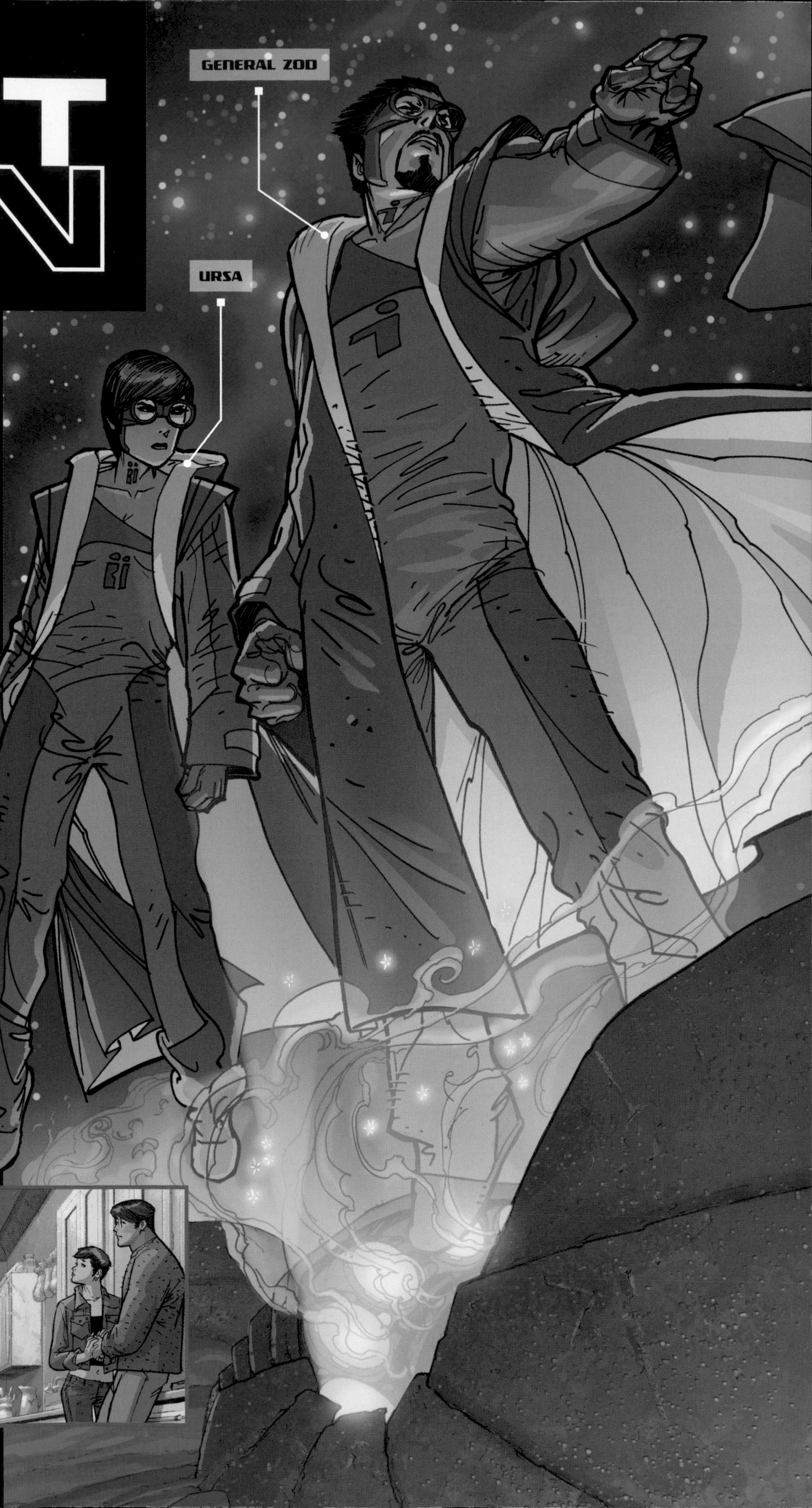
GENERAL ZOD
URSA

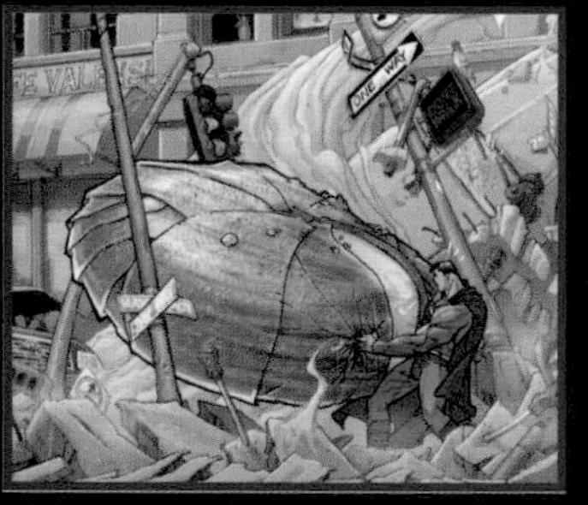

The pod skidded to a landing in downtown Metropolis and revealed its surprising passenger.

KRYPTONIAN BOY

Superman knew the boy posed no threat, but the military wanted him kept under armed guard. Exasperated by government stonewalling, Superman stole the boy out of US custody. Batman created a forged adoption paper trail, and Jonathan and Martha Kent offered parenting advice. Clark and Lois soon welcomed "Christopher Kent" to their Metropolis apartment.

Clark Kent and Lois Lane agreed to adopt the boy as their foster son, giving him a red-sun wristwatch to keep his powers under control.

non

Armed with invulnerability, flight, and heat vision, Christopher Kent could protect the people of Earth from the criminals who shared his powers.

CHRIS KENT OR LOR-ZOD?

The Kryptonian convicts threw Superman into the Phantom Zone, removing their only obstacle to world conquest. Zod threatened Lois Lane, but his son struck back to defend the only mother figure he loved. Superman fought his way free from the Phantom Zone and asked for help from Lex Luthor—one person with experience of stopping Kryptonians.

Metallo, Parasite, and Bizarro made up Lex Luthor's Superman Revenge Squad, assembled to combat the Kryptonian threat.

UP AND AWAY

While his Revenge Squad fought the Kryptonians, Luthor found a way to send them back into the Phantom Zone. Superman nearly suffered the same fate, but Chris Kent took his place to return to the dimension of his birth.

ZOD'S ESCAPE

Other pods followed, each one carrying a Kryptonian arch-criminal who had spent years locked inside the Phantom Zone. General Zod led this mob, aided by his lieutenants: the cruel Ursa and the brutal Non. Zod and Ursa's young son, Lor-Zod had been the first to arrive on Earth. Zod sought to reclaim his son, now renamed Chris Kent, while taking his revenge on the son of Jor-El—whom the people of Earth knew as Superman.

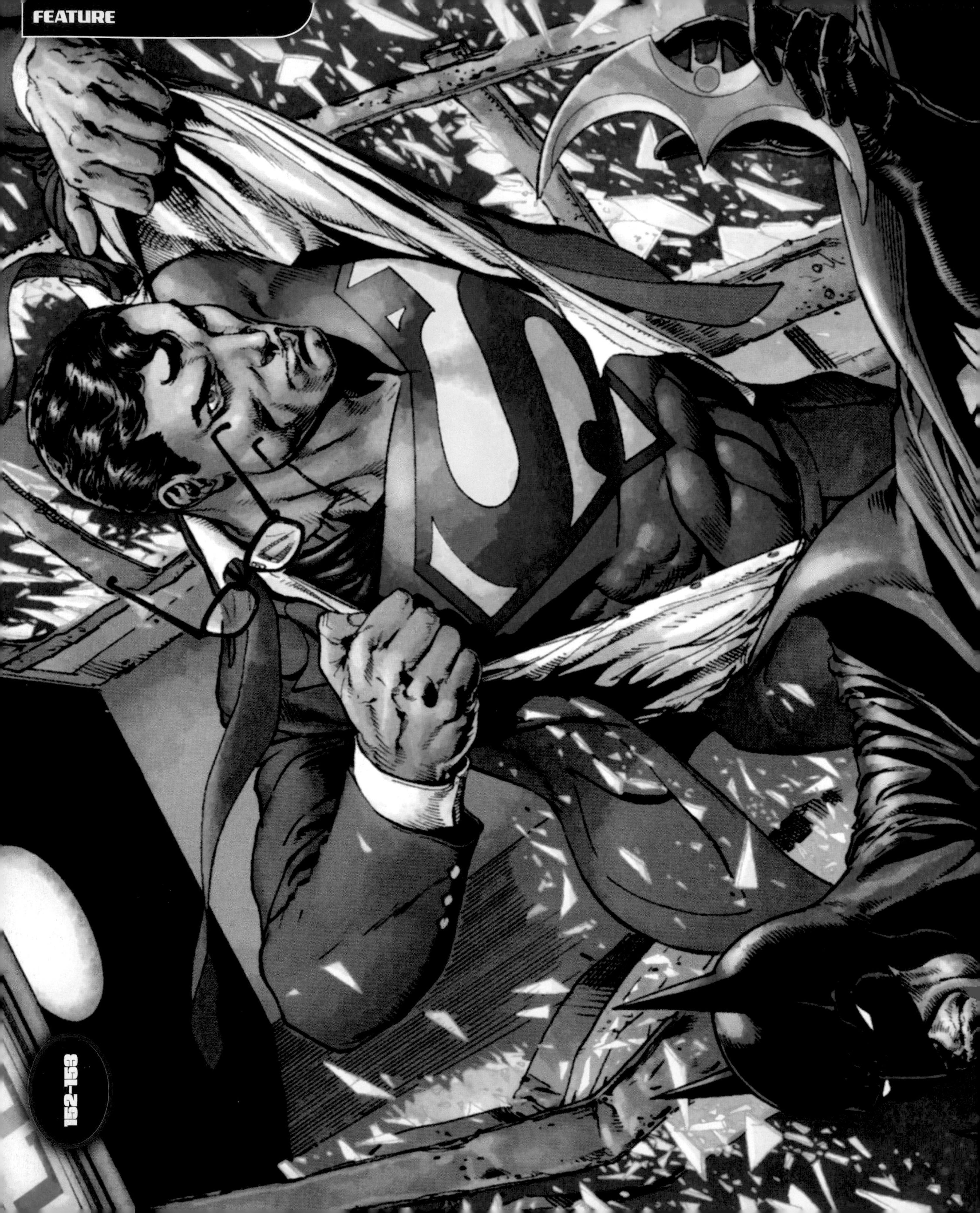

SUPERMAN/BATMAN

They are heroic icons and friends, but their personalities and abilities could not be more different—and that's what makes them such a strong team.

Although Clark Kent came from working-class roots and Bruce Wayne was born a billionaire, the two of them have found common ground as comrades in arms. Superman is open and honest, refusing to wear a mask and available to anyone who needs him in Metropolis. Batman stays in the shadows, but his commitment to Gotham's citizens is no less passionate. Superman can reduce a mountain range to rubble with his fists, while Batman relies on careful observation and the strategic use of gadgets to exploit his foes' weaknesses. Batman is also a supreme tactician, who can order Superman to strike specific targets at super-speed or unleash an aerial bombardment with his heat vision. Finally, Superman supplies the moral conscience that the Dark Knight sometimes skirts in his zeal to bring in the bad guys.

STORYLINES

PUBLIC ENEMIES US President Lex Luthor places a $1 billion bounty on the heads of Superman and Batman, which puts dozens of super-villains on their trail. Luthor ultimately goes after them himself wearing a custom battlesuit.

THE SUPERGIRL FROM KRYPTON Kara Zor-El arrives on Earth. Superman is overjoyed to welcome his cousin, but Darkseid kidnaps Supergirl to force her into service as the commander of his elite Female Furies.

ABSOLUTE POWER Future super-villains Lightning Lord, Saturn Queen, and Cosmic King travel back in time to raise the young Clark Kent and Bruce Wayne as their own children. They create a pair of world-dominating tyrants; but their efforts are undone when the timeline is restored.

WITH A VENGEANCE It's mayhem when Mr. Mxyzptlk battles the Joker, who wields fifth-dimensional, reality-shaping powers stolen from Bat-Mite. Superman's only choice for fighting back is to join forces with Darkseid, but he still faces the threat of the Joker's superpowered pawns.

NANOPOLIS Superman and Batman tackle the ultimate in small-scale problems when they shrink to microscopic size, doing their part to help the inhabitants of an entire miniscule society and undo the damage caused by the Prankster.

LIL' LEAGUERS (ABOVE) Child versions of the Justice League face off against their sinister counterparts, the Lil' Villains. Superman and other heroes do what they can, but the child version of Superman dies at the hands of Lil' Doomsday.

SUPER/BAT During a fight with the Silver Banshee, the powers of Batman and Superman are switched. Superman tries to live an ordinary life, but Batman uses his new abilities to take complete control of Gotham's criminal underworld.

NIGHT AND DAY Gorilla Grodd seeds Earth's atmosphere with Kryptonite. Superman has no choice but to abandon the planet. Grodd believes he now has a clear shot at world domination, but he has overlooked Batman.

STOP ME IF YOU'VE HEARD THIS ONE In a flashback to the first meeting, Clark Kent and Bruce Wayne share a cabin aboard a cruise ship. When the ship is attacked, they have to conceal their secret identities from each other while battling villains from another dimension.

THE SECRET Working on a story for the *Daily Planet*, Clark Kent discovers that a murdered journalist had learned the truth of Bruce Wayne's secret identity as Batman. Further investigation reveals the Joker's involvement and forces both Superman and Batman to question their individual methods.

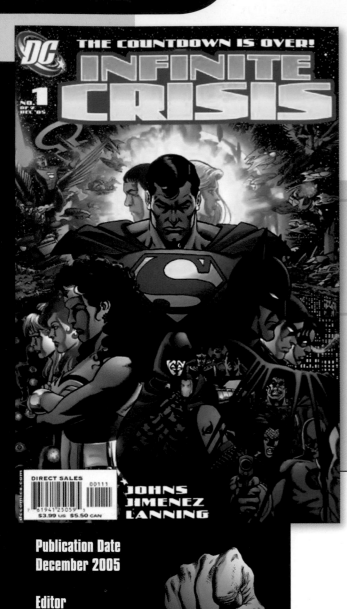

Publication Date
December 2005

Editor
Eddie Berganza

Cover Artist
George Perez

Writer
Geoff Johns

Penciller
Phil Jimenez

Inker
Andy Lanning

Colorists
Jeromy Cox, Guy Major

INFINITE CRISIS
Vol. 1   # 1

"I'm not a god. And I'm not like you, Bruce. I don't need to control everything."

Superman to Batman

Main Characters: Superman, Batman, Wonder Woman
Main Supporting Characters: Superboy, Nightwing, the Spectre, Uncle Sam, the Ray, Mongul, Earth-Two's Superman, Superboy Prime, Alexander Luthor
Main Locations: Justice League Watchtower, Smallville, Blüdhaven, Metropolis, Gotham City, Oa

BACKGROUND

1985's *Crisis on Infinite Earths* ushered in the Dark Age of comics, in which realistic storylines often involved self-doubt, tragedy, and death. 2005's *Infinite Crisis* served as a sequel to its 20-year-old precursor, but this time continuity took a back seat to a meta-commentary on the evolution of comic book storytelling.

Writer Geoff Johns brought back four characters—Alexander Luthor of Earth-Three, Superboy of Earth-Prime, and the Superman and Lois Lane of Earth-Two—all of whom had been granted an honorable retirement in the final issue of *Crisis on Infinite Earths*. Issue #1 of *Infinite Crisis* revealed that these characters from a previous publishing era had been watching the events of the DC universe over the past two decades and become dismayed by what they considered unacceptable levels of violence and a general coarsening of culture. "We've given them a gift they've thrown away," they lamented, and broke out of limbo to try and set things right. The reappearance of the Earth-Two Superman was particularly notable since, in DC continuity, he represented the original, Golden Age version who had debuted in 1938. By the end of the seven-issue *Infinite Crisis*, the first crusader died nobly while fighting for truth, justice, and the American way.

THE STORY

Loose ends from the Crisis on Infinite Earths start to appear during a new, universe-restructuring emergency. While the Earth faces cybernetic OMACs and an out-of-control Spectre, Superman finds himself unable to inspire his fellow heroes to unite in facing the Infinite Crisis.

The world faces a cross-dimensional catastrophe, and the morale of its greatest heroes has never been lower. Superman, Batman, and Wonder Woman gather aboard the Justice League's headquarters to survey the damage from a recent attack **[1]**. Tensions are high; Batman is suspicious of the others following recent memory wipes; Superman blames Wonder Woman for hostility toward super heroes, following her neck-snapping execution of villain Maxwell Lord **[2]**.

In Smallville, Connor Kent gets a pep talk from Martha Kent on why the world needs a Superboy. He considers joining the action **[3]**, but lingering doubts keep him on the sidelines.

Meanwhile, the self-aware OMAC satellite has constructed a legion of cybernetic enforcers, one of which eliminates a third-string villain, the Ratcatcher **[4]**. In the city of Blüdhaven, Nightwing is the first to perceive the massive scale of the OMAC threat, as thousands of units mass in the sky, now tinged with the crimson color that marks a true crisis **[5]**.

The Guardians of the Universe are helpless. They observe that reality is shifting and the planet Earth is acting as the fulcrum **[6]**. In the streets of Gotham, the embodiments of the Seven Deadly Sins have been unleashed from their prison after the death of the wizard Shazam and the destruction of the Rock of Eternity **[7]**. The Spectre—the living manifestation of God's vengeance—is no longer bound to a mortal host and goes on a rampage to stamp out all magic in the universe and execute those who wield it **[8]**.

A few heroes rally against the darkness. Uncle Sam's Freedom Fighters are among those who are overwhelmed by newly-confident villains. The treacherous Doctor Light takes out the Ray **[9]**, and Sam's patriotism is no match for Black Adam's rage **[10]**.

Aboard the Justice League's stronghold, Superman, Batman, and Wonder Woman are ambushed by Mongul. Superman counter-attacks with heat vision and follows up with a jaw-rattling punch **[11]**. He then has to intervene to prevent Wonder Woman from splitting open Mongul's head with her sword. Superman tries to fire Batman and Wonder Woman with the principles of honesty and leadership, but Batman tells his friend that the last time Superman truly inspired anyone was when he was dead—as the martyr who stopped Doomsday. Superman is left alone amid the wreckage **[12]**.

Throughout these events, a group of unseen observers have witnessed the apathy and defeatism of Earth's heroes with dismay. With the whispered suggestion that taking action might save the life of the woman he loves **[13]**, one of the observers shatters the barrier that separates dimensions **[14]**. Four survivors of the original *Crisis on Infinite Earths* stand revealed: Alexander Luthor, Superboy-Prime, and the Superman and Lois Lane of Earth-Two. They are ready to turn back the clock and restore the ideals they once fought for to the universe.

GENERAL ZOD

"You will answer for your father's sins! Do you hear me, son of Jor-El?"

The commander of Krypton's military, General Zod tried to overthrow the government and received a lifetime sentence of imprisonment in the Phantom Zone for his crime. Since then, Zod has sworn revenge on Kal-El, the son of the man who jailed him—the hero known to our world as Superman!

Throughout multiple timelines, Zod has always been a skilled military leader.

ORIGINS

General Dru-Zod's tactical genius led to his rapid rise to the top of Krypton's military and won him the respect of Krypton's leading scientist, Jor-El. When evidence of Krypton's imminent destruction became clear, Jor-El's fellow scientist, Non, tried to rally the public. The Kryptonian Council silenced Non by lobotomizing him, and an outraged Zod tried to unseat the Council. Jor-El saved Zod from death by exiling Zod and his collaborators Non and Ursa to the Phantom Zone.

In exile, General Zod and Ursa bore a son, Lor-Zod. He became the first of the Phantom Zoners to escape to Earth, where Clark Kent and Lois Lane raised him as Christopher Kent. Zod followed, but he and his disciples soon landed back in the Phantom Zone.

Zod reappeared during the events of New Krypton. His attempt to conquer Earth failed when a joint effort between Superman and Lex Luthor returned him to the Phantom Zone once more.

The endless void of the Phantom Zone was perceived by Jor-El as the perfect prison.

Zod and his soldiers have the same powers as Superman but no scruples about killing the innocent.

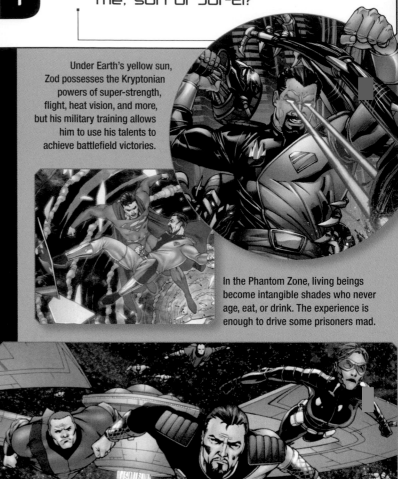

Under Earth's yellow sun, Zod possesses the Kryptonian powers of super-strength, flight, heat vision, and more, but his military training allows him to use his talents to achieve battlefield victories.

In the Phantom Zone, living beings become intangible shades who never age, eat, or drink. The experience is enough to drive some prisoners mad.

Zod's chief lieutenants are Non and Ursa, but he commands many Kryptonian soldiers who have vowed to die for his cause.

Other versions of Zod have existed, including the Kryptonite-mutated ruler of Pokolistan (above). Superman also fought a Phantom Zod (right) who existed only within the artificial reality of Metropia.

FOR KRYPTON

Zod's passion for his homeworld and its people led him to rebel against the Kryptonian Council. Years in the Phantom Zone burned away any tolerance for those who prefer compromise to action. Because both Jor-El and his son Kal-El have acted as his jailers, Zod has vowed to take revenge on the House of El.

Zod often wears goggles, but his Kryptonian eyes are far from vulnerable. Using his heat vision as a high-powered offensive weapon, Zod can blast through the hull of a battleship.

Like Superman, Zod wears a Kryptonian insignia on his chest. It proclaims his allegiance to the militaristic House of Zod.

Many Kryptonians favor elaborate costumes, but Zod prefers practical clothing that maximizes his range of movement.

KEY DATA

REAL/FULL NAME Dru-Zod

FIRST APPEARANCE *Adventure Comics* #283 (April 1961)

OCCUPATION Kryptonian General, super-villain

AFFILIATIONS House of Zod, Kryptonian Military Guild, New Krypton Defense Force

POWERS/WEAPONS A brilliant military tactician. Under a yellow sun Zod possesses flight, super-strength, super-speed, invulnerability, super-breath, heat vision, X-ray vision, and enhanced senses.

BIZARRO

"Me am Bizarro."

A flawed copy of Superman, Bizarro is both a well-meaning blunderer and a terrifying force of nature. With his mirror-image superpowers and his reverse-wired brain, Bizarro represents a special challenge for the Man of Steel.

Lex Luthor hoped his scientists could clone a super-being that would obey his commands.

ORIGINS

In the timeline created after the Crisis on Infinite Earths, Bizarro came to life in the laboratories of LexCorp. Lex Luthor used cloning technology to make his own Man of Steel, but DNA imperfections resulted in a brutish mutation. It collided with Superman and disintegrated, dying a quick death like two subsequent incarnations.

The Joker stole the reality-warping powers of Mr. Mxyzptlk and created a fourth Bizarro to become his Jokerized Earth's Superman. This Bizarro teamed with super-villains during the Infinite Crisis and later joined Lex Luthor's Superman Revenge Squad, assembled to stop General Zod's Kryptonian army.

A Bizarro formed part of Emperor Joker's vision for a world in his own image.

An outsider on Earth, Bizarro crafted a cubical Bizarro World orbiting a blue star. He kidnapped Jonathan Kent to live among the Bizarro duplicates with which he peopled his world. Superman rescued his father, but allowed Bizarro to remain a hero on the world he had made.

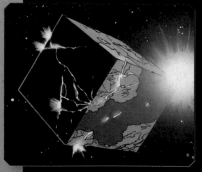

The cube-shaped Bizarro World is also known as Htrae—Earth spelled backward.

Given temporary superpowers, the Joker brought a new Bizarro into existence to be the warped champion of his madcap kingdom. This version of Bizarro often wore a "Bizarro #1" medallion around his neck.

By using the power of "Bizarro Vision," Bizarro can grow duplicate beings out of living tissue. He created Bizarro versions of Lois Lane and Jimmy Olsen in an attempt to make Bizarro World less lonely. Before long he had replicated Bizarro versions of the entire Justice League of America.

Freeze vision and fire breath are just two of the powers exhibited by Bizarro that are the complete opposite of Superman's abilities. Bizarro's version of X-ray vision allows him to see through lead but nothing else.

KEY DATA

REAL/FULL NAME Bizarro

FIRST APPEARANCE *Superboy* #68 (October 1958)

OCCUPATION Misunderstood villain

AFFILIATIONS Superman Revenge Squad

POWERS/WEAPONS Flight, super-strength, super-speed, invulnerability, fire breath, freeze vision, vacuum breath, and the ability to see through lead. Under a blue sun, Bizarro can create other beings like himself.

Not only does Bizarro have a low intellect, he reacts to situations by following a strange reverse logic. He often uses words that convey the opposite of what he means to say, such as greeting newcomers "Goodbye!"

Bizarro can take a beating due to his invulnerable skin and slow reaction time. His deadened nervous system makes it difficult for him to feel pain.

With a strength level that rivals Superman's, Bizarro can crumble a building with one blow. Green Kryptonite has no effect on him, but Blue Kryptonite can kill him.

FRIENDLESS

Bizarro found himself in Gotham City during the Blackest Night event. The people ran from him, terrified. Bizarro tried to make a pet of Man-Bat Kirk Langstrom, resisting the attempts of Langstrom's wife to restore her husband to human form. Bizarro then tried to make friends with Solomon Grundy. The undead villain nearly killed him, before Bizarro "cured" Grundy by flying him into the sun.

MIXED-UP WORLD

Bizarro couldn't understand why he always hurt people when Superman made protecting them look easy. In deep space, Bizarro molded asteroids into the shape of a cubical planetoid and built a replica Metropolis on its surface. Because the rays of a blue sun had given Bizarro the ability to make copies of himself, Bizarro World soon teemed with hundreds of beings created in his image. As a final touch, Bizarro kidnapped Jonathan Kent and imprisoned him in a facsimile of the Fortress of Solitude.

Bizarro shared Superman's memories and recognized Jonathan Kent as his "father." He dragged Pa Kent out of his Smallville home on a journey that spanned light-years.

He was Superman's opposite, but Bizarro's brainlessness didn't make him any less dangerous. A lonely Bizarro created his own mad planet, and then kidnapped Pa Kent.

ESCAPE FROM BIZARRO WORLD

BIZARRO VISION

Bizarro had the power to make clones with his eye-beams, and he wasted no time making imperfect clones of Superman. The Man of Steel battled the inhabitants of Bizarro World, who rejected him as a "bizarro Bizarro." In response, the Bizarro Lex Luthor unleashed the planet's ultimate weapon: Bizarro Doomsday.

Destroying the Bizarro clones wasn't the answer, nor was Bizarro's idea of blowing up the entire planet. Superman had to restore Bizarro as a hero to keep everyone happy.

MUTATED METROPOLIS

Bizarro's backwards parody of Metropolis included a *Daily Planet* for Bizarro Lois and Bizarro Jimmy, and an Arkham Amusement Park where bizarro super-villains served time by riding roller coasters. But after Superman accidentally exposed Bizarro's "Clark Kent" alter-ego, the people of Bizarro World turned on their champion.

"I don't know where this square world came from... but I'm through with this madhouse." Superman

BIZARRO JLA

As well as making duplicates of Lois Lane and other citizens of Metropolis, Bizarro recreated Superman's heroic JLA colleagues, with opposite versions of Batman, the Flash, Wonder Woman, Hawkgirl, and Green Lantern. Bizarro Flash couldn't run more than a few steps without stopping for pizza, and Bizarro Green Lantern had somehow acquired a working yellow power ring that belonged to the Sinestro Corps. This version of the Justice League predictably failed to help Bizarro, but its members never stopped trying to live up to the standards of true heroes.

SUPERMAN VISION

Bizarro World's blue sun enabled Superman to pass his powers on to others. After receiving a jolt of "Superman vision," Jonathan Kent could ignore gravity and punch through solid rock. He helped formulate a plan to put Bizarro back into his people's good graces by having Superman fly around and fix things—a rampage of vandalism on topsy-turvy Bizarro World. Its citizens cheered for Bizarro when he put a stop to Superman.

Bizarro gave Pa Kent a box containing a crude Superman costume. Jonathan Kent wore it on the way back to Smallville. His superpowers vanished on his arrival.

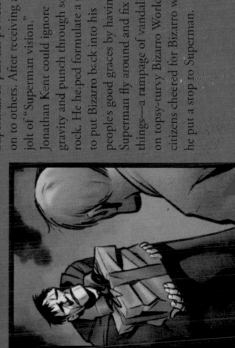

BRAINIAC

"We are the colony of
the Collector of Worlds.
We know everything
there is to know."

Not only is Brainiac one of Superman's greatest foes, he is a harbinger of destruction who takes living specimens from doomed planets and imprisons them against their will. Brainiac has unlimited access to information, enabling him to reinvent himself and stay one step ahead of Superman.

A version of Brainiac originating in the 64th century, Brainiac 13 came to the present day to manipulate the outcome of the war between Earth and Imperiex, hoping to gain unlimited power for himself.

On Colu, computers proved more powerful than their humanoid creators.

The Computer Tyrants of Colu created Brainiac as a computer-spy to reconnoiter worlds governed by "foolish humans."

ORIGINS

In one previous timeline, Brainiac existed as a machine created by the Computer Tyrants who ruled the people of Colu. Brainiac and Lex Luthor teamed up to start their own mission of conquest, until Brainiac double-crossed his partner.

Later revisions to the timeline introduced Milton Fine who became host to Brainiac's consciousness and orchestrated a takeover of Warworld. The final version of Brainiac appeared when he sent robotic drones after Superman and Supergirl, in the process shedding light on how he had captured the Kryptonian city of Kandor prior to the destruction of its planet. When Superman defeated Brainiac he won Kandor's freedom, bringing thousands of Kryptonians to Earth and triggering Brainiac's return and the global unrest of the New Krypton incident.

As a cyborg, Brainiac can transfer his consciousness into many different skeletal bodies. He can also send the bodies into battle as autonomous attack drones.

Brainiac's skull ship is used for interstellar transport and contains a gallery of trophies collected from dead civilizations. It is equipped with a force field generator that can isolate cities prior to miniaturization.

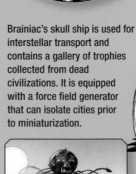

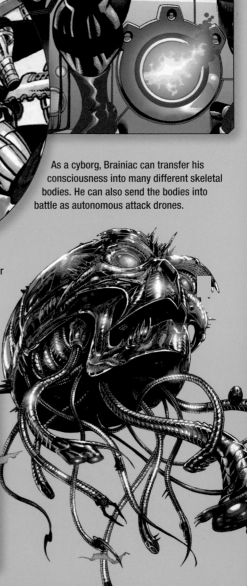

At one time, Brainiac had a companion named Koko with whom to share his predilection for bottling cities.

The diodes on Brainiac's head amplify his mental control of machinery and allow him to plug directly into neural networks.

Brainiac can exist without any physical body at all, but in one of his encounters with Superman he inhabited a muscular form that could easily stand toe-to-toe with the Man of Steel.

KEY DATA

REAL/FULL NAME Not applicable; has been known as C.O.M.P.U.T.O., Brainiac 1.0, and Internet

FIRST APPEARANCE *Action Comics* #242 (July 1958)

OCCUPATION Alien collector and malevolent artificial intelligence

AFFILIATIONS None

POWERS/WEAPONS Incredible intelligence and near-limitless knowledge base. Possesses advanced alien technology, allowing him to project unbreakable force fields and shrink entire cities to bottle size. Brainiac can control machinery and upload his consciousness into any electronic system.

THE NEW 52: BRAINIAC

In the timeline that follows Flashpoint, Brainiac was one of the first aliens to menace Earth. Lex Luthor tried to team up with him, but the Collector of Worlds double-crossed his ally and miniaturized Metropolis. Brainiac forced Superman to choose between saving the city of Metropolis or the city of Kandor. He forgot that Superman always fights to save *everyone*.

The New 52 Brainiac used a centipede-like, cyborg body as a vehicle for his consciousness.

Some of Brainiac's host bodies have super-strength, but if the bodies are destroyed he can move his consciousness into another form and start his attacks all over again.

The environment inside his skull ship is completely sterile, and Brainiac is soon overwhelmed if exposed to the teeming microorganisms of a raw, natural setting like the ecosystem of Earth.

NEW AQUISITIONS

Brainiac traveled the universe absorbing the knowledge of alien civilizations, stealing their greatest works, and annihilating each one in a fiery supernova. Before Krypton's destruction, Brainiac had isolated Kandor inside a force field, miniaturized the city and stored it inside a bottle. Superman was a piece of Krypton Brainiac did not possess, so he sent robotic probes to capture him. After several failures, Superman came to Brainiac! In deep space, the Man of Steel was swept up in the wreckage of another assimilated civilization and found himself a prisoner in Brainiac's laboratories.

Not even the firepower of Krypton's military guild could break through Brainiac's force field.

Superman smashed the robots that tried to collect him, and decided to go looking for Brainiac.

BRAINIAC RETURNS

For Brainiac, knowledge was power. He captured the Kryptonian city of Kandor so no one else could learn its secrets, and longed to finish the job by collecting the last Kryptonians—Superman and Supergirl.

In addition to bottle cities, Brainiac's collection included specimens of unusual alien creatures. Superman had to battle a white-furred ape on his way to locate the ship's master.

RETALIATION

Superman awoke inside Brainiac's skull ship. His enemy intended to study him and download his intellect. Superman tried to turn the tables on Brainiac, but Brainiac miniaturized Metropolis and placed it with Kandor on a display shelf. He also captured Supergirl. Superman eventually defeated Brainiac, returned Metropolis to its proper place on Earth, and found a new home for Kandor near his arctic Fortress of Solitude.

Brainiac made a mistake when he tried to physically restrain Superman.

Supergirl eventually escaped from Brainiac's ship and intercepted a missile he had fired to destroy Earth's sun.

As she watched her husband slipping away, Martha called in vain for Clark.

FAMILY TRAGEDY

Superman defeated Brainiac by knocking him out of his sterile ship and into a swamp teeming with Earth microorganisms. Meanwhile, Brainiac had launched one of his probes toward the Kent farm. Jonathan Kent escaped the impact; however, the shock of the explosion triggered a fatal heart attack. Clark and Martha later laid him to rest in the Smallville cemetery.

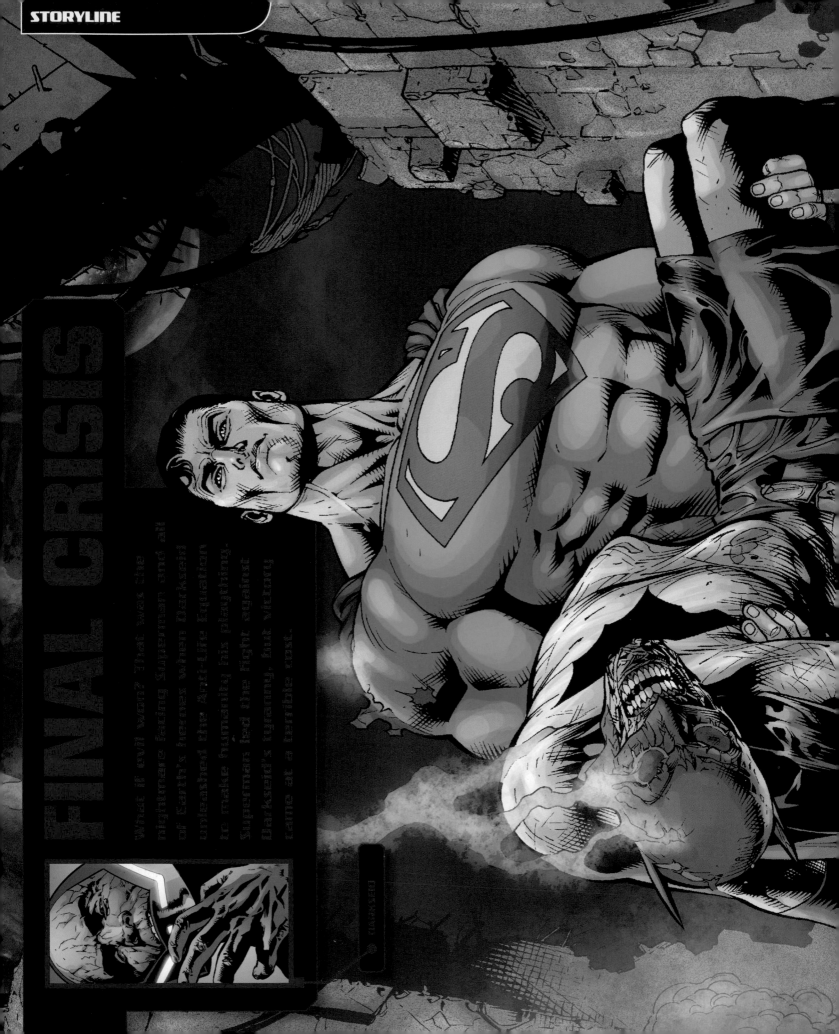

FINAL CRISIS

What if evil won? That was the nightmare facing Superman and all of Earth's heroes when Darkseid unleashed the Anti-Life Equation to make humanity his plaything. Superman led the fight against Darkseid's tyranny, but victory came at a terrible cost.

FACING THE MUSIC

Darkseid, the ruthless dictator of Apokolips, tried to conquer Earth and took on human form. As he gathered his strength he dispatched his agent, Libra, to unite the planet's super-villains. Libra demonstrated his power by executing the Martian Manhunter and most of the super-villains signed up on the spot. Lex Luthor, however, had too much pride to bend his knee to any master. He demanded further proof from Libra, who delivered by laying a bomb in the Daily Planet offices. This act spurred Superman, who took up a vigil beside Lois Lane's hospital bed.

With Lex Luthor now in Libra and Darkseid's camp, the planet's evil was marshaled together under Apokolips. The balloon said super-type to stop Darkseid's Anti-Life Equation learning to a strange Omega-world, where an enemy lived into a multicolored life. There he met one of the Superman, who protected the races beyond imagining.

While Superman pounded his quest, Batman took the fight to the enemy. He fired a radion bullet into the only thing capable of killing a New God directly, a Darkseid in his dying moments. Darkseid blasted his Omega Beam and delivered its attacker. A grieving Superman recovered what Batman believed to be his friend's corpse.

A Lex Luthor switched sides to lead his fellow villains uprising against Libra. Superman used a did century "Miracle Machine" to turn his thoughts into reality. By blowing away the forces of the darkness, Superman called on a world.

The stamping pillar of primal song created a counter-vibration that shattered Darkseid's hold on energy and restored balance to the world.

"YOU DIDN'T GET ALL OF US, DARKSEID. IT'S NOT OVER YET."

KANDOR RESTORED

The intergalactic conqueror Braniac had miniaturized the city of Kandor and added it to his collection of curiosities from doomed worlds. Superman restored Kandor to full size near the Fortress of Solitude in Earth's arctic wastes. The Kryptonians gained Superman's powers, but lacked his appreciation for Earth's moral codes. Militant Kryptonians kidnapped and executed super-villains, forcing Superman to intervene.

General Sam Lane oversaw the interrogation of Brainiac, but only Lex Luthor was capable of understanding the data Brainiac revealed.

NEW KRYPTON

Superman believed he and Supergirl were the last survivors of Krypton. But the restoration of the bottle city of Kandor brought 100,000 Kryptonian immigrants to Earth, each possessing the same powers as the Man of Steel.

THE BEST OF KRYPTON

Seized by Brainiac at the height of its development, Kandor represented the pinnacle of Kryptonian culture. After its citizens absorbed the rays of Earth's yellow sun, many of them flew off to explore every corner of the globe.

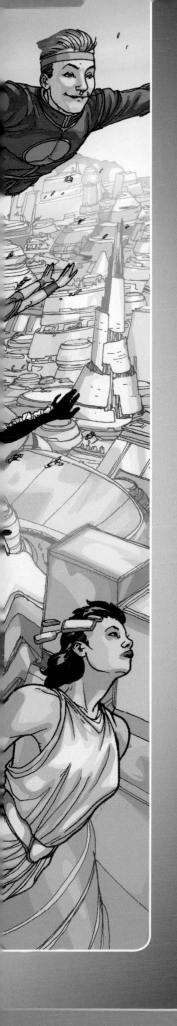

SUPERGIRL'S TRAGIC LOSS

Rocketed to Earth as a teenager, Supergirl thought she would never see her parents again. But her father Zor-El and mother Alura had survived inside Kandor and now ruled the city as joint heads of the Council. The reunited family's joy did not last. Alura insisted on protecting Kandor at all costs and refused to give up the names of Kryptonians who had committed crimes on Earth. Lex Luthor's agents Metallo and Reactron infiltrated Kandor and attacked from the inside. Zor-El died in the crossfire.

ANOTHER WORLD

Alura, grieving and enraged, launched Kandor into space where it became the planetoid New Krypton. She released General Zod from the Phantom Zone to lead her armies, prompting a concerned Superman to live among the people of New Krypton as a commander within Zod's military guild. Internal tensions between Kryptonian castes led to the attempted assassination of Zod. Superman ultimately uncovered a plot within the highest reaches of New Krypton's government to weaken the planetoid's defenses in advance of an attack organized by General Lane and Lex Luthor.

Zod's ruthlessness toward suspected traitors clashed with Kal-El's compassion, forcing Kal to resign his commission in the military guild.

ZOD'S VOW

Brainiac, now freed, teamed up with Luthor to bring ruin to New Krypton. Brainiac tried to put Kandor back into its bottle but Luthor deceived him. He reversed the miniaturization process and expanded Kandor back to full size, destroying Brainiac's skull ship in the process. General Zod tried to execute Brainiac, but Superman stopped him. When Brainiac later escaped, Zod vowed to take revenge on Luthor and the entire population of planet Earth.

To the survivors of New Krypton, Brainiac was an enemy from their worst nightmares.

169

BLACKEST NIGHT

The dead rose from their graves when the Green Lantern Corps fought Nekron, Lord of Death. Superman was caught up in the action when a Black Lantern ring resurrected his counterpart from another world.

UNDEAD SUPERMAN

The Superman and Lois Lane of Earth-Two had perished during the events of the Infinite Crisis. Nekron sent Black Lantern power rings to reanimate the corpses of fallen heroes and villains, and two of the rings traveled to Smallville to call forth Superman and Lois from their place of rest. The undead Kal-L, the Earth-Two Superman, fought the true Superman and Superboy, making them question their will to fight. Earth-Two's Lois Lane pursued and kidnapped Martha Kent.

Meanwhile, Supergirl experienced gruesome Blackest Night troubles of her own on New Krypton, when her dead father, Zor-El, reappeared as a decaying corpse to taunt her and her mother Alura.

Superman did everything he could to contain the threat facing Smallville, but realized that this battlefront was merely one of many pressure points with which Nekron hoped to break the spirits of Earth's defenders and enlist more slaves into his growing legion of Black Lantern warriors.

Superman and Superboy teamed up to face the threat of the Earth-Two Superman, whose powers were superior to their own.

Superboy had recently returned to life; the Superman of Earth-Two tried to convince him that his true place was among the ranks of the undead.

MASK OF THE PSYCHO-PIRATE

In life, the Psycho-Pirate could force others to experience any emotion he wished by projecting mental commands through his Medusa Mask. Killed by Black Adam during the Infinite Crisis, the Psycho-Pirate returned to pseudo-life during the Blackest Night and used his Medusa Mask to control the citizens of Smallville. Superboy seized the Medusa Mask and, using its powers to broadcast his own array of emotions, attracted the Black Lantern rings toward him. The instant the rings left their fingers, the Psycho-Pirate and the Earth-Two Superman became corpses once more.

> "Maybe you don't know me so well after all, Kal-L? I never give up!" **Superman**

The Psycho-Pirate's ability to manipulate emotions let him tap into the emotional spectrum, the same force powering the multicolored rings worn by the members of the Lantern Corps.

KRYPTO'S LOYALTY

The Earth-Two Lois Lane went directly after Martha Kent. However, she underestimated the grit of the Kansas farmer and was also unprepared for the superpowered canine Krypto. Martha Kent torched the corn fields bordering her farm to set the undead Lois ablaze and used the confusion to order Krypto to attack. The dog went straight for Lois' Black Lantern ring, tearing her rotted hand loose and rendering her body completely inert.

Without the malevolent influence of the Black Lantern ring, the Earth-Two Superman returned to his lifeless state. At last, the greatest hero of them all could rest in peace.

REVIVING SMALLVILLE

The population of Superboy's adopted hometown had fallen victim to the whims of the Psycho-Pirate. After Superboy seized the Psycho Pirate's Medusa Mask and eliminated the threat of the Black Lanterns, both he and Superman began putting out fires and rescuing trapped citizens. But the real work of defeating Nekron had just begun. After joining up with members of the Green Lantern Corps, Superman merged with the universal life force of creation to temporarily become a White Lantern and defeat Nekron.

WAR OF THE SUPERMEN

The presence of New Krypton, a planet of super-powered beings, so near to Earth brought conflict. The Kryptonians planned an invasion, while Earth's General Lane plotted devious defence. Whose side would Superman be on?

ZOD'S INVASION FORCE

Since his release from the Phantom Zone, General Zod had made New Krypton's military guild into an elite fighting force. He believed that war with the humans of Earth was inevitable, and that his preparations would save his people from disaster. With their vicious acts of spying and sabotage, General Sam Lane and Lex Luthor confirmed Zod's worst expectations. A call to arms went out to his followers, and Zod launched New Krypton's invasion of Earth.

BATTLE FOR MARS

Earth soldiers belonging to the Human Defense Corps maintained an outpost on Mars, where they watched for extraterrestrial threats. They were no match for General Zod's super-powered Kryptonians. The Mars base fell in minutes.

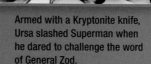

Armed with a Kryptonite knife, Ursa slashed Superman when he dared to challenge the word of General Zod.

DAY OF DOOM

Superman tried to reason with Zod, but the general refused to compromise. But while Zod's soldiers flew toward their targets, Supergirl and her mother Alura interrogated the captured villain Reactron, unaware that Lex Luthor had implanted Reactron with a doomsday device. The blast shattered New Krypton; only Supergirl survived. Zod's forces, their home planet destroyed, vowed to punish those responsible— as well as any human being who refused to surrender.

The explosive radiation released in Reactron's dying moments cracked the core of New Krypton, killing nearly every inhabitant.

General Lane knew that, under a red sun, Kryptonians would lose powers and die in the vacuum of space.

EARTH FIGHTS BACK

General Sam Lane quickly followed up the destruction of New Krypton with the deployment of his secondary weapon. This turned the sun's rays red and deprived all Kryptonians of their powers. Nightwing (Christopher Kent) and Flamebird (Thara Ak-Var) reversed the process to bring back Earth's yellow sun, though Flamebird sacrificed her life in the effort.

THE HUNDRED-MINUTE WAR

The survivors of Zod's army descended from the skies to strike essential sites around the world. Supergirl defeated Ursa on the White House lawn and Superman managed to send Zod back into the Phantom Zone. As Earth recovered from the lightning onslaught, Lois Lane mourned her father General Sam Lane, who had taken his own life in the war's closing moments. Supergirl, who had lost her mother during the death of an entire world, left a memorial flower amid the ruins of New Krypton.

SECRET ORIGIN

A fresh take on the Man of Steel's history placed new importance on his Smallville years, and restored the Legion of Super-Heroes in shaping the destiny of the super hero.

Holograms of Jor-El and Lara sprang to life when Jonathan Kent showed his son Clark the Kryptonian rocket that had brought him to Earth.

Lana Lang knew Clark's secret. Clark had once shielded her from the blades of a farming thresher with his bulletproof body.

When Lana leaned in for a kiss, Clark's heat vision went haywire.

A SMALLVILLE EDUCATION

As Clark grew, his powers appeared. When Clark accidentally broke the arm of his friend Pete Ross during a football game, Jonathan Kent told his son to show restraint and keep his amazing abilities from attracting attention. A pair of glasses kept Clark's heat vision in check and also made him look a little smarter. Hoping that Clark might be a fellow intellectual, Lex Luthor befriended him. Later that same day, Clark whisked Lana out of a tornado's path and flew for the very first time.

> "This can be a great planet, Lois, but making it great starts with each one of us."
> **SUPERMAN**

Lex Luthor schemed to kill his abusive father and ditch Smallville for the bright lights of Metropolis. His discovery of Kryptonite was evidence of his genius.

INSPIRING THE FUTURE

Martha Kent sewed a costume for her son so he could perform acts of heroism around Smallville, but Clark didn't want to be thought of as some kind of "Superboy." He changed his mind when he ran into three 31st-century time-travelers: Cosmic Boy, Lightning Lad, and Saturn Girl. In one thousand years, they explained, Clark's feats would be so famous that they would inspire the creation of their own team, the Legion of Super-Heroes. The three brought him to future Smallville to tour the sights, and he viewed tangible evidence that his life would one day change the world.

Still unsure of his place in life, Clark spurned Lana Lang's romantic advances.

After arriving in the future, Clark helped the Legion stop a gang of human supremacists.

EARLY DAYS IN METROPOLIS

With his genuine heartland friendliness, Clark Kent stood out among the cynical citizens of Metropolis. He hit it off with Lois Lane during his first day at the *Daily Planet* when he helped her sneak into LexCorp to witness the unveiling of an experimental military exoskeleton.

Lois, Jimmy, and Perry White were skeptical of the *Daily Planet*'s new employee.

When the demonstration turned into a disaster, Clark rushed into action as Superman and saved Lois from death. Superman later befriended Jimmy Olsen, who became his first real pal in Metropolis.

Responding to an emergency for the first time since arriving in Metropolis, Clark Kent shed his reporter's clothes to become the Man of Steel.

Superman and Lois Lane got acquainted in mid-air after he halted her multistory plunge.

LEX'S REVENGE

The poor people of Metropolis used to beg Lex Luthor for handouts. Now all they talked about was Superman. Luthor called in favors from General Sam Lane who sent Metallo after Superman and ordered the army to arrest the hero as a national security risk.

The public defended Superman against Lane's soldiers. The Man of Steel told both sides to cool down.

Grounded

Feeling disconnected, the Man of Steel decided to get in touch with ordinary folk with a coast-to-coast journey on foot. After seeing the country's problems from ground-level, Superman gained a new appreciation for his mission.

Wake-Up Call

His experiences with General Zod and the Kryptonians who had escaped Kandor caused Superman to question his place—did he belong with others of his kind or the people of Earth? These doubts were confirmed by the criticisms of a widow, angry that he hadn't used his powers to save her husband from a brain tumor. Superman felt that he had lost perspective on the things that really mattered.

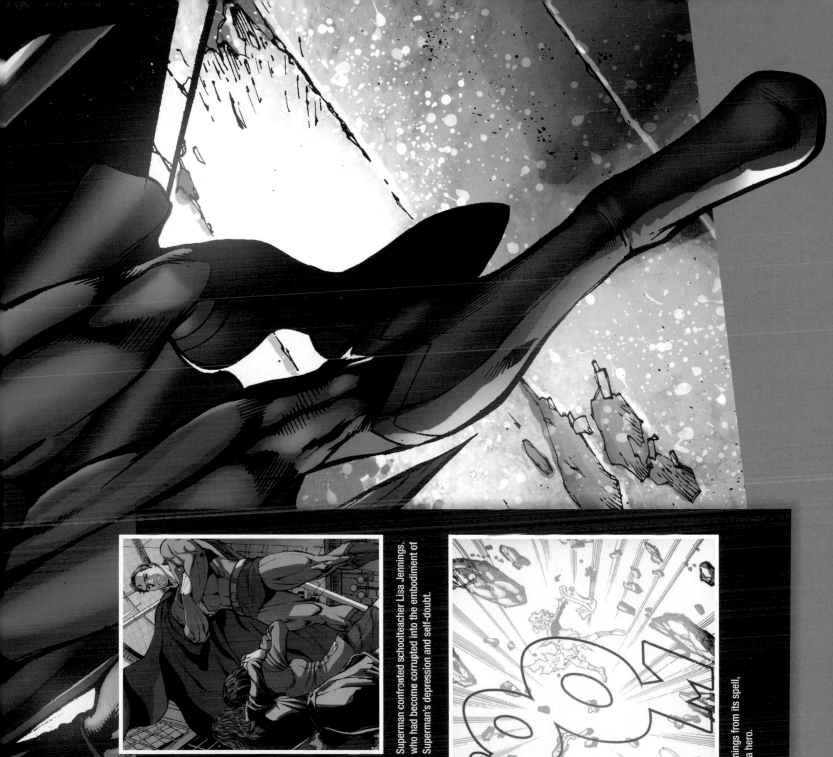

Journey's End

Superman's trek forced him to confront everyday problems. In Illinois, he helped a boy deal with an abusive father. In Detroit, he jump-started the local economy by replacing idle auto factories with medical centers churning out advanced alien technology. By the time he reached Seattle, Superman had discovered hundreds of causes worth fighting for. But one challenge remained. He needed to free a woman who, due to the psychic influence of a Kryptonian sunstone, carried all of Superman's negative emotions.

Superman confronted schoolteacher Lisa Jennings, who had become corrupted into the embodiment of Superman's depression and self-doubt.

The shattering of the sunstone released Lisa Jennings from its spell, freeing her to choose her own path to becoming a hero.

REIGN OF DOOMSDAY

Doomsday had once killed the Man of Steel. Now Doomsday had returned, with backup! The Doomsday clones had new powers including flight, telekinesis, and indestructible armor. They captured everyone who wore Superman's symbol. The Man of Steel, meanwhile, faced an even worse foe: an invincible Lex Luthor.

Luthor asked to see Superman's greatest loss. He was shocked to witness the death of Jonathan Kent.

POWER TO LEX

In his quest for omnipotence, Lex Luthor had absorbed the abilities of the godlike Zone Child. Luthor could now control all of time and space and sent multiple Doomsdays to torment Superman's allies. But in his zeal to make Superman suffer, he discovered that Superman's greatest emotional pain had been the death of Clark Kent's father. Luthor suddenly realized the truth of Superman's dual identity. Enraged that the secret had eluded him for so long, Luthor refused to accomplish anything constructive before his powers faded away.

"Do your worst, Luthor. Do it forever. I won't break."

Supergirl and Earth's other heroes rallied to battle multiple Doomsdays at global hot spots.

DOOMSDAY'S CLONES

Steel, Supergirl, the Eradicator, and Superboy worked alongside the villainous Cyborg Superman to gain control of the space prison where they had been trapped, only for the vessel to lock into a collision course with Earth. The Eradicator transferred his consciousness to the original Doomsday, giving the heroes an unstoppable powerhouse in their fight against the various Doomsday clones.

DOOMSLAYER

The ultimate Doomsday named itself the Doomslayer and tried to trigger planetary extermination through a catastrophic orbital impact. The heroes stopped its plan, and the Eradicator sacrificed himself by casting the Doomslayer into a bottomless singularity from which it could never return.

Superman was prepared to die to prevent the Doomslayer's spacecraft from smashing into the Earth. With help, he slowed its momentum enabling a safe splashdown in Metropolis's harbor.

FLASHPOINT

In the alternate timeline of Flashpoint, Superman was a lab experiment instead of a hero. A rocket carrying an alien baby crashed in downtown Metropolis and the military raised the child as part of Project S.

Scientists spent years torturing their Kryptonian test subject to determine the limits of his solar-based powers.

Lt. Sinclair volunteered for superpowers under Project S, but lost his humanity.

SUBJECT 0

Years before the arrival of the rocket from Krypton, the US government took steps to counter the perceived growing threat of aliens, Atlanteans, and metahumans. Within the top-secret, subterranean bunker of Project S, General Sam Lane oversaw the transformation of Lieutenant Neil Sinclair into an "everyman hero," designated Subject 0. A fusion of human and alien DNA made Sinclair more powerful with every passing year; however General Lane could see that Sinclair was slowly turning into an emotionless killing machine. When Subject 0 tried to escape the facility with the Kryptonian boy designated Subject 1, Lane stopped him by activating a Phantom Zone device. Subject 0 and General Lane disappeared into other-dimensional limbo for 20 years.

Subject 1

The Kryptonian child that crashed to Earth became Project S's top priority. Subject 1, or "Kal" as General Lane called him, couldn't be physically damaged and had power levels that far surpassed Subject 0. When Subject 0 vanished into the Phantom Zone, Kal became more valuable than ever. Project S kept Kal in an underground vault, where Earth's sunlight couldn't supercharge his natural abilities.

Two decades in the Phantom Zone drove Subject 0 insane. DNA strands taken from Doomsday made him almost unstoppable.

The Death of Lois Lane

General Lane's daughter Lois bonded with Kal during Subject 0's breakout attempt. But she and Kal would not see each other again for decades. It wasn't until Aquaman and Wonder Woman's Amazons split the world into warring factions that Kal, helped by Batman, Cyborg, and the Flash, escaped Project S. Lois had infiltrated the Amazons and was supplying intelligence to Cyborg's freedom fighters. When Subject 0 reappeared to take revenge against Kal, the battle between the two titans claimed Lois' life. Kal would never know her love, but he took inspiration from her dying words: "You have to save these people."

THE NEW 52

The first issue of *Action Comics* is set during Superman's first adventures in Metropolis.

Superman created his costume from everyday items. Only his cape was Kryptonian.

THE LAST SON
Jor-El and Lara knew the days of their planet Krypton were numbered. They sent their son Kal-El to Earth inside a self-aware rocket that had the ability to change its shape.

STREET SMARTS
When he first started, Superman couldn't fly. Bulletproof skin, lightning speed, heat vision, superior senses, and super-strength enabled him to do good deeds—and also evade any interfering police.

JIMMY AND LOIS
Despite working for rival Metropolis newspapers the *Daily Planet* and the *Daily Star*, Jimmy Olsen and Clark Kent became friends. Jimmy's colleague Lois Lane grew to respect Clark's skills, and suggested to her editor, Perry White, that he hire Clark.

A SUPER HERO IN METROPOLIS

The public wasn't sure whether to fear or cheer Earth's first ever costumed hero. When Superman targeted corrupt businessmen like Glen Glenmorgan, the police and General Sam Lane of the US military started to pay attention. General Lane enlisted scientific genius and billionaire industrialist Lex Luthor to capture the alien vigilante. To combat Superman's perceived threat, Lane turned Sgt. John Corben into the cyborg soldier Metallo. The super-villain Brainiac miniaturized Metropolis and Superman saved the city and reclaimed artifacts of his Kryptonian heritage. He later staged Clark Kent's death and assumed a new identity as firefighter Johnny Clark. A clash with Captain Comet, the evolved "neo-sapien" Adam Blake, convinced Superman to resume his heroic role.

The relaunched versions of *Action Comics* and *Superman* became twin cornerstones of DC's New 52 universe. *Action Comics* showed an eager hero still learning the ropes; *Superman* starred a Man of Steel with five years of experience as the city's defender.

Other super heroes wear masks, but Superman leaves his face uncovered to show people that they can trust him.

The New 52 *Superman* title features a more experienced Superman, a few years after the events introduced in *Action Comics* #1.

SUPERMAN

The Man of Steel had been Metropolis's guardian for five turbulent years. Morgan Edge, CEO of Galaxy Communications, now owned the *Daily Planet* and Lois Lane was vice president of new media. Clark felt sidelined, especially after Lois found love with someone else. His reputation as Superman took a blow when alien nanites impersonated him. After defeating this threat, Superman soon faced new ones, including the Daemonite warlord Helspont and a creature from another dimension.

His suit is made from a Kryptonian bio-material that can change color and disappear or reappear on command.

KRYPTONIAN SUIT
Aboard Brainiac's collector ship, Superman claimed an authentic suit of Kryptonian clothing. It responded to his touch and displayed the "S" insignia of the House of El.

MA AND PA
Jonathan and Martha Kent had died before Clark Kent arrived in Metropolis. Clark gave the family farm to a neighbor, but frequently visited his adoptive parents' graves in the Smallville cemetery.

LUCY LANE
Lois Lane hoped her sister Lucy would be a good match for Clark, but he stood her up at the rail station when Superman business took priority. A subsequent dinner date was also interrupted by a breaking crisis.

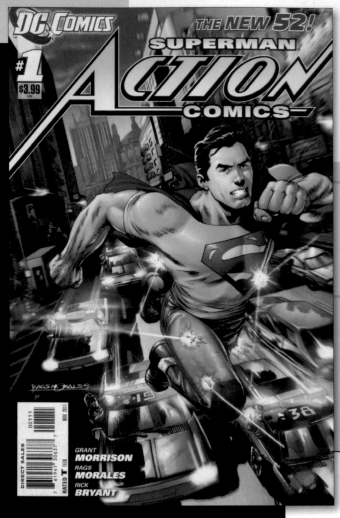

THE NEW 52: ACTION COMICS #1

> "You know the deal, Metropolis. Treat people right or expect a visit from me."
>
> **Superman**

Main Characters: Superman, Lex Luthor, Jimmy Olsen, Lois Lane
Main Supporting Characters: Glen Glenmorgan, Detective Blake, General Sam Lane
Main Locations: Metropolis

Publication Date
November 2011

Editor
Matt Idelson

Cover Artists
Rags Morales &
Brad Anderson

Writer
Grant Morrison

Penciller
Rags Morales

Inker
Rick Bryant

Colorist
Brad Anderson

BACKGROUND

DC had done continuity-rebooting events before, but never in the company's history had it started its entire publishing line over from issue #1. *Action Comics*, in print since 1938, ended its run at #904 before relaunching in 2011. The new *Action* showcased a Superman from early in his career—before he had developed the power of flight, and back when he was known for standing up for the little guy and taking on corrupt plutocrats. In other words, a Superman who shared the same core qualities as his 1938 inspiration. This new Superman hadn't even settled on a costume. He wore the red cape that had swaddled him in his Kryptonian birth rocket, but he rounded out the ensemble with a blue-collar uniform of t-shirt, jeans, and work boots. Readers met a Man of Steel who threw himself into danger with a cocky grin, eager to discover his limits. As Clark Kent, he lived out of a fleabag apartment and pursued another kind of justice as a journalist with a knack for embarrassing the rich and powerful.

Meanwhile, behind the scenes, Lex Luthor pulled the strings, convinced that Superman represented an "invasive species" threatening humanity's dominance of the planet.

THE STORY

Who is Superman? In the months since his debut, the hero has electrified Metropolis with astonishing feats of strength. The poor and the powerless claim Superman fights for them, and General Sam Lane enlists Lex Luthor to stop the newcomer before things get out of hand.

Superman has been on the Metropolis scene for six months and the city is buzzing about the self-proclaimed champion of justice. Corrupt tycoons like Glen Glenmorgan once seemed untouchable, but now a high-rise reception **[1]** is suddenly crashed by a guest who definitely doesn't meet the dress code. Superman announces that he has arrived to shake a confession out of Glenmorgan and warms up his heat vision when security goons pull out firearms **[2]**. By the time the Metropolis police reach the tower's upper floors, Superman has bested his attackers **[3]**.

Detective Blake finds Superman balancing on the balcony's railing, holding a terrified Glenmorgan in one hand **[4]**. Taking a single step backward, he plunges to the pavement, cradling Glenmorgan safely in his arms but rattling the industrialist so badly he admits to his criminal labor practices. The police take a shot at Superman, but he catches the bullet and speeds off with a cheery, "Catch me if you can!"

In a secret US military facility, General Sam Lane and Lex Luthor ponder Superman's latest exploits **[5]**. Time is running out for Luthor to deliver Superman into custody as he'd promised Lane. However, Luthor has constructed a trap. A low-income housing development is scheduled for demolition. The plight of its squatters is the perfect bait for drawing out the city's do-gooder.

Superman comes to the rescue as expected, catching the wrecking ball as it smashes through an apartment complex **[6]**. But Luthor's tanks are waiting and they hit the hero with a rocket-propelled net **[7]**. Superman fights back by swinging the wrecking ball to disable the lead tank **[8]**. More military vehicles roll in to cut off his escape, but the locals step into the line of fire and give Superman the distraction he needs to slip away **[9]**.

Back at his apartment in the impoverished Metropolis district of Hob's Bay, Superman pulls on his baggy Clark Kent attire. He has reason to believe that a commuter train has been sabotaged and phones his friend Jimmy Olsen **[10]** just as he and *Daily Planet* reporter Lois Lane are about to board the train pursuing a scoop. Because Clark works for a rival paper, the *Daily Star*, Lois takes no notice. To save them and avoid a disaster, Clark becomes Superman and forces his way into the pressurized tube that houses the tracks **[11]**. At super-speed he catches up with the train as it hits 200 miles per hour **[12]**, and Jimmy and Lois—aboard the lead car—get told to back off by a gunman they are following **[13]**.

The train is about to crash. Superman does everything he can to slow it down as it hops the rails and skids down a busy Metropolis avenue **[14]**. At last it comes to a rest, crumpling its nose against a skyscraper's foundation – neatly pinning Superman in place, where he can be picked up by General Lane's soldiers **[15]**.

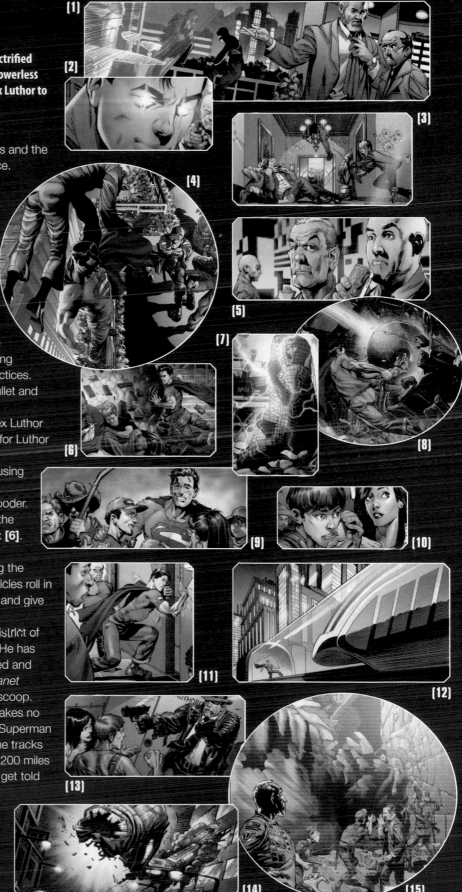

185

DARKSEID

"You will fall.
I am Darkseid."

The ruler of Apokolips is one of the most powerful beings in the universe. Darkseid's pursuit of the Anti-Life Equation, to give him control over all living things, has led him to unleash his Parademon troops on the people of Earth. Only Superman has stood between him and total conquest.

Darkseid's Omega Beams are released from his eyes. The beams channel pure Omega Force, capable of shattering or disintegrating even superhumans who are supposedly invulnerable. During the Final Crisis, Darkseid used his Omega Beams to send Batman backward in time.

The ruthless Uxas tricked his brother Drax into entering the Omega Force chamber in a malfunctioning protective suit.

ORIGINS

The infernal planet Apokolips and the idyllic planet New Genesis are the warring homeworlds of the New Gods. Long ago, Uxas, second in line to Apokolips' throne, seemingly murdered his elder brother Drax to claim the power of the Omega Force. This energy transformed him into the stone-skinned giant Darkseid. He fathered two sons, Kalibak and Orion, murdered his mother, Queen Heggra, and seized power.

Under the terms of a ceasefire with Highfather, ruler of New Genesis, Darkseid sent his son Orion to be raised by his enemies. For his part of the exchange, Darkseid accepted Scott Free, the son of Highfather, to live with him on Apokolips. Both sons later betrayed Darkseid. Orion learned mercy from the peace-loving people of New Genesis; Scott Free became the hero Mister Miracle.

Darkseid launched multiple plans targeting Earth, only to be thwarted by Superman. However the Man of Steel later joined forces with Darkseid to defeat the all-encompassing threat of Imperiex.

Apokolips is covered by a hellish cityscape and gaping firepits. All citizens are slaves for the greater glory of Darkseid. The lowest of the low are known as Hunger Dogs.

One of Darkseid's most powerful minions is Granny Goodness, commander of the elite Female Furies.

Desaad's monkish robes are an ironic disguise, for he is Darkseid's chief torturer. Sadistic, cowardly, and treacherous, Desaad is only loyal to Darkseid out of fear.

Darkseid's sons Orion and the bearded Kalibak are sworn enemies. Kalibak is desperate for his father's approval, but always fails to win Darkseid's heart.

KEY DATA

REAL/FULL NAME Darkseid
(formerly Uxas)

FIRST APPEARANCE *Superman's Pal Jimmy Olsen* #134 (November 1970)

OCCUPATION Cosmic Villain

AFFILIATIONS The New Gods

POWERS/WEAPONS Super-strength, invulnerability, enhanced reaction time, mental powers including telepathy and telekinesis, and a genius-level intellect. Darkseid's Omega Beams can lock onto targets, disintegrate matter, emit a concussive force, send a subject back in time, and produce a variety of other effects.

His armor is largely ceremonial; Darkseid's rocky body is virtually invulnerable. The Omega Force boosted his biology to make him the most powerful of the New Gods.

Darkseid's strength is incalculable, though it is rare that the tyrant actually engages in personal combat. He prefers to work through agents such as Kalibak, Granny Goodness, Kanto, or Grayven.

DARK SCHEMES

Darkseid's invasion of Earth in the post-Flashpoint reality represented a threat so grave that Superman, Batman, Wonder Woman, and other heroes had to pool their talents to battle hundreds of Parademons. The newly-formed Justice League severed Darkseid's Boom Tube teleportation technology and sent his armies back where they'd come from. They also spoiled Darkseid's plans to use Superman as an experimental subject for his chief torturer, Desaad.

SUPERBOY

Born in a laboratory, Superboy established his own identity after escaping from his handlers. The Teen Titans helped him survive the deadly games run by Lord Harvest.

BEGINNINGS

Created by the scientists of the covert agency N.O.W.H.E.R.E., Superboy was supposed to be a living weapon who obeyed Lord Harvest. Instead he found friendship and adventure.

Grunge, an experiment from the same labs that created Superboy, lost the fight when Superboy used his tactile telekinesis to rip out Grunge's cyborg implants.

Wonder Girl Cassie Sandsmark grew close to Superboy on a monster-infested island.

At a nightclub, Superboy encountered a demonic woman called Kiva, who nearly devoured his soul.

Jocelyn Lure, an NYPD detective with a mysterious past, tried to bring in Superboy after he "borrowed" a fortune from a bank.

Warblade fought for Lord Harvest in the Culling. His liquid-metal body is capable of forming itself into swords, knives, or razor-sharp claws.

When Superboy isn't consciously activating his power of invulnerability his suit offers limited protection against injury.

THE CULLING

Lord Harvest collected Superboy and the members of the Teen Titans and forced them to battle for their lives in a high-tech arena. He hoped to eliminate the weak and make the survivors elite servants called the Ravagers. Harvest underestimated Superboy's fighting spirit.

Unlike her cousin Superman, Kara Zor-El didn't grow up on Earth. She didn't even speak the language. Kara had to make tough choices on her journey to become Supergirl.

SUPERGIRL

Reign, commander of the Worldkillers, carries a cleaver and has the powers of flight, super-strength, and invulnerability.

Supergirl wore the costume she received from her father while battling Reign amid the empty ruins of Argo City.

BEGINNINGS

Supergirl grew up on Krypton, caring for her baby cousin Kal-El and undergoing special mental and physical training to pass the Trials and wear her family's crest. When her planet neared its end, her father sent her into space in hopes of a new life.

Supergirl didn't recognize her cousin Kal-El, and lashed out at him in her confusion.

A holographic recording of her father, Zor-El, is the only memento Supergirl has from the world she knew.

Siobhan Smythe, the Silver Banshee, was Supergirl's first friend after she arrived in Metropolis. They teamed up to defeat Siobhan's father, the Black Banshee.

REIGN

Kryptonian genetic experiments created superpowered Worldkillers as living weapons. Their leader, Reign, escaped Krypton's destruction and confronted Supergirl. When Supergirl refused to join Reign's campaign of conquest, the Worldkiller left her there to die while she ▨▨▨▨ed an attack on Earth.

Supergirl built her Fortress of Solitude, named Sanctuary, in the Marianas Trench at the bottom of the Pacific ocean.

Each member of the Justice League has a power or skill that the others can't easily duplicate, making the team capable of any challenge.

THE NEW 52

JUSTICE LEAGUE

They are Earth's greatest champions, the first line of defense against alien invaders and cosmic menaces. Superman is both the JLA's most powerful member and its conscience—inspiring the others and demonstrating what it means to be a hero.

THE TEAM

GREEN LANTERN Hal Jordan is a test pilot selected by the Guardians of the Universe to be the Green Lantern of Earth's sector. His ring is fueled by willpower and creates objects from solid light.

WONDER WOMAN Diana comes from the island nation of Themyscira, home of the Amazon warriors of legend. She can fly, wears bullet-deflecting bracelets, and carries the Lasso of Truth.

CYBORG An accident turned high-school football star Vic Stone into a man/machine hybrid. He can hack into any computer network and can fire blasts of white noise from his arm cannon.

SUPERMAN The Last Son of Krypton lives a double life as reporter Clark Kent. His powers include flight, invulnerability, super-strength, and heat vision.

AQUAMAN Arthur Curry is the king of undersea Atlantis. He can communicate telepathically with aquatic life and is tough enough to survive the pressures of the ocean depths.

BATMAN Orphaned by a mugger, Bruce Wayne became Gotham City's fearsome guardian. Though he lacks superpowers, Batman possesses a brilliant deductive mind and an arsenal of high-tech gadgets.

FLASH Police scientist Barry Allen is the fastest man alive. He can run across the globe in minutes and his quick reflexes make him almost impossible to hit.

During their first meeting, the suspicious heroes fought each other. A shocked Green Lantern learned that Superman could shatter his power ring constructs.

Darkseid's Armies

When strange alien technology popped up in cities around the globe, Batman and Green Lantern ran into each other while following the same clues. Despite a severe personality clash, the two heroes sought out Superman for his advice—and then enlisted the help of the Flash when a misunderstanding led to an all-out brawl. The alien devices suddenly opened interdimensional wormholes and the four heroes agreed to work together to battle Darkseid's invading hordes. Wonder Woman and Aquaman soon joined them. The team beat back the first wave of parademons

Vic Stone's father, a scientist at Detroit's S.T.A.R. Labs, saved his son's life by exposing him to experimental nanotechnology.

with the help of Cyborg, whose prosthetics enabled him to interface with Darkseid's machines. In the end, Cyborg reprogrammed the enemy's teleporter so a coordinated assault by his teammates could send Darkseid back the way he had come.

It was teamwork that sent Darkseid and his parademons back to their own planet, Apokolips. The public cheered, and the superpowered heroes decided to stick together.

ALTERNATE REALITIES

Throughout parallel universes and divergent timelines, the Superman story has been told again and again. Changes to his origin have turned Superman into a different kind of hero, and have even made him the ultimate villain.

TANGENT: SUPERMAN'S REIGN

In the alternate Tangent universe, Superman is an ordinary human being named Harvey Dent until an accident unlocks amazing mental abilities. His evolved intellect allows him to use the powers of telekinesis, telepathy, and universal knowledge, prompting him to assume the title of Superman. Without a moral compass, Dent views humanity not as his equals, but as a problem to be solved, bringing him into conflict with the Superman of our reality.

KINGDOM COME

An aging Superman retires after a new generation of hard-edged heroes arrives on the scene. When violence between metahumans rages out of control, he returns to rein in their excesses. Assembling a league of like-minded heroes, Superman builds a gigantic gulag to house superpowered threats. Batman allies with Lex Luthor to assemble a resistance movement to undermine Superman's efforts as nuclear Armageddon looms.

SUPERMAN: SPEEDING BULLETS

In this merging of the origins of Superman and Batman, baby Kal-El is taken in by Thomas and Martha Wayne and raised in Gotham City under the name of Bruce. After he sees his parents gunned down by a mugger, Bruce uses his heat vision to kill the attacker. He creates the identity of the Batman to wage a ruthless war against crime. He soon faces the madness of Lex Luthor, transformed into a version of the Joker.

SUPERMAN: KAL

The Superman story is transplanted to medieval England when baby Kal is taken in by peasants and raised to become a blacksmith. Kal hides his powers from the wicked Baron Luthor, but lands on Luthor's bad side after entering a tournament to win the heart of the Lady Loisse. Using the alien metal from his Kryptonian spacecraft, Kal forges a suit of armor and an unbreakable sword, which he dubs Excalibur.

SUPERMAN'S METROPOLIS

In an alternate world based upon the visionary 1927 film of the same name, Metropolis is a multileveled urban center in which the laboring class supports the idle lifestyles of the upper class. When Clarc, son of the architect who created the great city, falls in love with the lower-class woman Lois, he is inspired to lead a revolution aimed at overthrowing the cruel scientist Lutor and bringing justice to all of the people of Metropolis.

ELSEWORLD'S FINEST

During the 1920s, Clark Kent and Bruce Wayne become caught up in a pulp-style adventure after Lana Lang puts them on the trail of a mysterious stolen artifact. If they can find the ancient Greek scroll known as the Argos Codex they'll find clues that lead to a legendary lost city, but first Clark and Bruce must face the wrath of Rā's al Ghūl. By the end of their quest, they have claimed the mantles of Superman and Batman.

JLA: AGE OF WONDER

In this version of events Superman's arrival in Kansas occurs in the mid-19th century. Superman makes his first public appearance in Philadelphia in 1876 to celebrate America's centennial. The Man of Steel teams with inventors Thomas Edison and Nikola Tesla to bring about a technological utopia, aided by Kryptonian artifacts found in his birth rocket. The Age of Wonder comes with a dark side as workers find themselves exploited by industry.

JUSTICE LEAGUE OF AMERICA: THE NAIL

A tiny nail blows out a tire on Jonathan and Martha Kent's truck, preventing them from finding Kal-El's space capsule, resulting in a world without Superman. Here, humanity has become hostile toward superhumans. As tensions rise, a genetically-mutated Jimmy Olsen unleashes all-out war against super heroes. At last, the true Superman emerges from the Amish farm where he has been living for decades.

SUPERMAN: RED SON

When a Kryptonian rocket lands in the Soviet Union instead of the United States, Superman becomes a national hero dedicated to truth, justice, and the expansion of Communist rule. The existence of the Soviet hero prompts the US to create heroes of its own, and Lex Luthor grows a Bizarro clone to help reset the global power balance. When Superman becomes ruler of the USSR, a looming nuclear crisis causes the US to fracture into warring states.

SUPERMAN INC.

What would Superman have become without the moral guidance of the Kents? In this tale, a motorist finds a Kryptonian baby and drops him off in a nearby town, where he is raised as Dale Suderman. Using his superpowers to excel at professional sports, Suderman amasses a fortune and invests it into multiple business ventures. An envious Lex Luthor strives to expose Suderman as an alien and bring down his corporate empire.

ALL-STAR SUPERMAN

Given a lethal dose of solar radiation, Superman has less than a year to live. He uses his remaining time to set things right, revealing his secret identity to Lois Lane and writing his last will and testament. His ally, Dr. Leo Quintum, tries to create protectors who will take over in Superman's absence. Meanwhile, Lex Luthor has been sentenced to die in the electric chair but escapes to initiate his revenge.

THE SUPERMAN MONSTER

Set in the late 1800s, this interpretation of the Superman legend features mad scientist Vicktor Luthor, whose attempts to resurrect the dead succeed when he discovers a deceased Kryptonian infant inside a space rocket. Luthor creates a superpowered monster. It escapes and seek shelter with a kindly peasant couple, who name the monster Klaus. The Superman Monster soon faces an angry mob, whipped into a frenzy by Luthor's hatred.

SUPERMAN: BLOOD OF MY ANCESTORS

A battle with a tentacled cyclopean horror triggers the reemergence of long-buried racial memories in Superman's psyche. He suddenly recalls the story of his ancestor El, a muscular barbarian who drew his warrior's strength from the great god Rao. Raised by a poor Kryptonian family, El grew up to fight for freedom against the rule of the tyrant Utor, while finding time to fall in love with the beautiful Laras Lilit.

SUPERMAN: AT EARTH'S END

On a future Earth, a cyborg regime named the Biomech Sevens controls the remaining humans. A bearded Superman lives in exile aboard a hovering city, but returns to action to attack the Biomech Sevens. Superman saves Gotham City from nuclear annihilation and stops the genetic experiments of the mysterious DNA Diktators. Superman uses a gun to kill his enemies and, wounded and morally compromised, chooses to end his life.

SUPERMAN: END OF THE CENTURY

As Metropolis approaches the turn of the century, Lex Luthor has been targeted by an unseen assailant. The immortal Contessa del Portenza soon emerges, demanding that Luthor surrender his daughter Lena to her. The Contessa's son proves to be the true threat. He shares his mother's immortality and has vowed to wipe out all lesser forms of life. Superman and Lois Lane launch an investigation to stop the Contessa's murderous offspring.

SUPERMAN: SECRET IDENTITY

In a world that closely mirrors our own, Superman exists only as a character in comic books and movies. Teenager Clark Kent is tired of getting teased for his famous name, then one day he discovers that he has started to develop the same powers as the fictional Clark. As the years pass, Clark learns how to become a real-world Superman, keeping one step ahead of the government agents who want to draft him into service.

SUPERMAN: THE LAST GOD OF KRYPTON

When Krypton exploded, its pantheon of gods vanished with it—all except one. Cythonna, Goddess of Ice, emerges from the planet's fragments to continue her age-old battle against the gods of light by extinguishing the last remaining relic of her homeworld—Superman. The Man of Steel takes their battle into the heart of Earth's sun. With his superpowers, he leaves Cythonna imprisoned within a star for eternity.

SUPERMAN AND BATMAN: GENERATIONS

Starting with the first appearances of Superman and Batman in the late 1930s, this story follows the heroes as they raise their own sons and daughters to follow in their footsteps. As the decades pass, they face real-world challenges like the Vietnam War, and see their friends fall in battle as Lex Luthor implements the final stages of a revenge plot. Both heroes survive into the far future to witness the progress of humanity.

SUPERMAN: THE DARK SIDE

In a twist on Superman's origins, Kal-El's birth rocket is thrown off course once it leaves Krypton, landing on Apokolips instead. The brutal, authoritarian planet is under the rule of Darkseid, and the Kryptonian infant is brought up to prize cruelty and conquest. After he becomes an adult, the armor-clad Superman is a true New God who leads the Parademon armies of Apokolips against their hated enemies on peaceful New Genesis.

SUPERMAN: LAST SON OF EARTH

In an inversion of the familiar tale, brilliant scientist Jonathan Kent sends his only son into space just prior to an asteroid impact that looks as if it will doom Earth. The boy lands on Krypton, where he is adopted by Jor-El and eventually becomes the chosen bearer of a Green Lantern power ring. His time on high-gravity Krypton gives him natural superpowers, which make him a true superhuman when he eventually returns to the world of his birth.

SUPERMAN: STRENGTH

A master thief develops a near-foolproof plan to steal the world's riches when he gets his hands on a pair of gloves that allows him to teleport. Desperate to live up to the expectations of his cruel father—who supposedly once broke Superman's arm—he tangles with the Man of Steel in a global chase that takes them to the pyramids of Egypt. In the end, he learns that strength means more than just muscle power.

SUPERMAN BEYOND

In the future, an aging Superman returns to New Metropolis to find that its citizens are protected by a squad of superpowered police officers. Superman questions his role in this changed world, but is soon targeted by Lucinda Luthor, daughter of the late Lex Luthor, who seeks to carry out her father's beyond-the-grave plan for revenge.

SUPERMAN: TRUE BRIT

In a humorous tale of cultural stereotypes, the consequences of Superman's rocket landing in England instead of Kansas are explored in detail. Named Colin Clark by the couple who takes him in, Superman keeps his powers under wraps under the guiding principle of "What would the neighbors think?" Super-strong Colin accidentally injures a fellow player during a cricket match, but finds success as a British tabloid journalist.

INDEX

ACKNOWLEDGMENTS

Warner Bros. Consumer Products and the publishers would like to thank the following for their help: Benjamin Harper, Josh Anderson, Adam Schlagman, Patrick Flaherty, Kevin Kiniry, John Wells, Scott Wilson, Kathryn Hill, and Hilary Bird.

The following DC writers and artists have contributed to this book: Art Adams, Greg Adams, Neal Adams, Christian Alamy, Gerry Alanguilan, Oclair Albert, Edemilson Alexandre, Marlo Alquiza, Aluir Amancio, Brad Anderson, Brent Anderson, Murphy Anderson, Kalman Andrasofszky, Ross Andru, Mahmud Asrar, Terry Austin, Derec Aucoin, Tony Avina, Brandon Badeaux, Mark Bagley, Michael Bair, Matt Banning, Carlo Barberi, David Baron, Eduardo Barreto, Eddy Barrows, Hilary Barta, Eric Basaldua, Moose Baumann, Chris Beckett, Ed Benes, Mariah Benes, Joe Bennett, Eddie Berganza, BIT, Patrick Blaine, Alex Bleyaert, Blond, Jon Bogdanove, Wayne Boring, Doug Braithwaite, Brett Breeding, Mark Bright, Rick Bryant, Brian Buccellato, Rick Burchett, Jack Burnley, Sal Buscema, John Buscema, John Byrne, CAFU, Don Cameron, Marc Campos, Greg Capullo, John Cebollero, Keith Champagne, Bernard Chang, Sean Chen, Cliff Chiang, Tom Chu, Chris Chuckry, Ian Churchill, Howard Chaykin, ChrisCross, Barbara Ciardo, Matthew Clark, Ronan Cliquet, Sam Citron, Iban Coello, Vince Colletta, Paul Cornell, John Costanza, Jeromy Cox, David Curiel, Fernando Dagnino, Gene D'Angelo, Tony S. Daniel, Alan Davis, Shane Davis, Mike DeCarlo, Marc Deering, Tom DeFalco, Edgar Delgado, John Dell, Jesse Delperdang, Wellington Dias, Digital Chameleon, Richard Donner, Armando Durruthy, Kieron Dwyer, Dale Eaglesham, Gabe Eltaeb, Randy Emberlin, Nathan Eyring, Rich Faber, Mark Farmer, Wayne Faucher, Carla Feeney, Raul Fernandez, Julio Ferreira, Pascal Ferry, David Finch, Bill Finger, Max Fiumara, Sebastian Fiumara, Travel Foreman, Gary Frank, Ron Frenz, Derek Fridolfs, Richard Friend, Denis Frietas, Carl Gafford, Kerry Gammill, German Garcia, José Luis Garcia-Lopez, Alex Garner, Sterling Gates, Drew Geraci, Sunny Gho, Noelle Giddings, Joe Giella, Keith Giffen, Axel Giménez, Dick Giordano, Jonathan Glapion, Alan Goldman, Frank Gomez, Rafael Grampa, Jamie Grant, Dan Green, Michael Green, Sanford Greene, Tom Grummett, Renato Guedes, Jackson Guice, Mike Gustovich, Gene Ha, Matt Haley, Edmond Hamilton, Bjarne Hansen, Tony Harris, Doug Hazlewood, Hi-Fi, Greg Hildebrandt, Tim Hildebrandt, Dave Hooper, Sandra Hope, Richard Horie, Tanya Horie, Adam Hughes, Rob Hunter, Jamal Igle, Stuart Immonen, Mark Irwin, Jack Jadson, Klaus Janson, Geoff Johns, Dave Johnson, Mike Johnson, J. G. Jones, Ruy José, Dan Jurgens, Gil Kane, Kano, Stan Kaye, Barbara Kesel, Karl Kesel, Karl Kerschl, Joe Kelly, Jack Kirby, George Klein, Scott Kolins, Adam Kubert, Andy Kubert, Andy Lanning, Bob Layton, Rob Lean, Jim Lee, Jay Leisten, Steve Little, Scott Lobdell, Aaron Lopresti, Lee Loughridge, Art Lyon, Dave McCaig, Ray McCarthy, Tom McCraw, Scott McDaniel, Ed McGuinness, Ted McKeever, Angus McKie, Mike McKone, Bob McLeod, Mike Machlan, José Wilson Magalhaes, Elliot S! Maggin, Rick Magyar, Doug Mahnke, Marcelo Maiolo, Guy Major, Francis Manapul, Tom Mandrake, José Marzan Jr., Nathan Massengill, Jeff Matsuda, J. P. Mayer, Jesus Merino, Danny Miki, Brian Miller, Frank Miller, Mark Morales, Rags Morales, David Moran, Grant Morrison, Win Mortimer, Paul Mounts, Patricia Mulvihill, Ted Naifeh, Todd Nauck, Tom Nguyen, Fabian Nicieza, Phil Noto, Kevin Nowlan, Sonia Oback, Patrick Olliffe, Ariel Olivetti, Glen Orbik, Jerry Ordway, Bob Oksner, Andy Owens, Carlos Pacheco, Tom Palmer, Jimmy Palmiotti, Eduardo Pansica, Pete Pantazis, George Papp, Ande Parks, Sean Parsons, Paul Pelletier, George Pérez, Sean Phillips, José Luis Soares Pinto, Al Plastino, Kilian Plunkett, Joe Prado, Frank Quitely, Jay David Ramos, Rodney Ramos, Ron Randall, Norm Rapmund, John Rauch, Fred Ray, Ivan Reis, Rod Reis, Robin Riggs, Chris Roberson, Andrew Robinson, James Robinson, Kenneth Rocafort, Robson Rocha, Denis Rodier, Duncan Rouleau, Alex Ross, Stéphane Roux, Adrienne Roy, Joe Rubinstein, Greg Rucka, Marco Rudy, Nei Ruffino, P. Craig Russell, Matt Ryan, Paul Ryan, Tim Sale, Kurt Schaffenberger, Rob Schwager, Nicola Scott, Trevor Scott, Miguel Sepulveda, Jerry Serpe, Galen Showman, Joe Shuster, Jon Sibal, Jerry Siegel, John Sikela, R. B. Silva, Walter Simonson, Alex Sinclair, Bob Smith, Brett Smith, Cam Smith, Sno-Cone, Ray Snyder, Alex Solazzo, Ryan Sook, Jim Starlin, Pete Steigerwald, Dave Stewart, J. Michael Straczynski, Lary Stucker, Rob Stull, Curt Swan, Ardian Syaf, Philip Tan, Romeo Tanghal, Art Thibert, Anthony Tollin, Tim Townsend, Sal Trapani, Tim Truman, Chris Truog, Michael Turner, Carlos Urbano, Peter Vale, Ethan van Sciver, Wade von Grawbadger, Lynn Varley, Rick Veitch, José Villarrubia, Dexter Vines, Mark Waid, Joe Weems, Doug Wheatley, Glenn Whitmore, Bob Wiacek, WildStorm FX, Mike Wieringo, J. H. Williams III, Anthony Williams, Scott Williams, Chuck Wojtkiewicz, Walden Wong, Pete Woods, Greg Wright, Leinil Francis Yu, Tom Ziuko, Zylonol Studios.

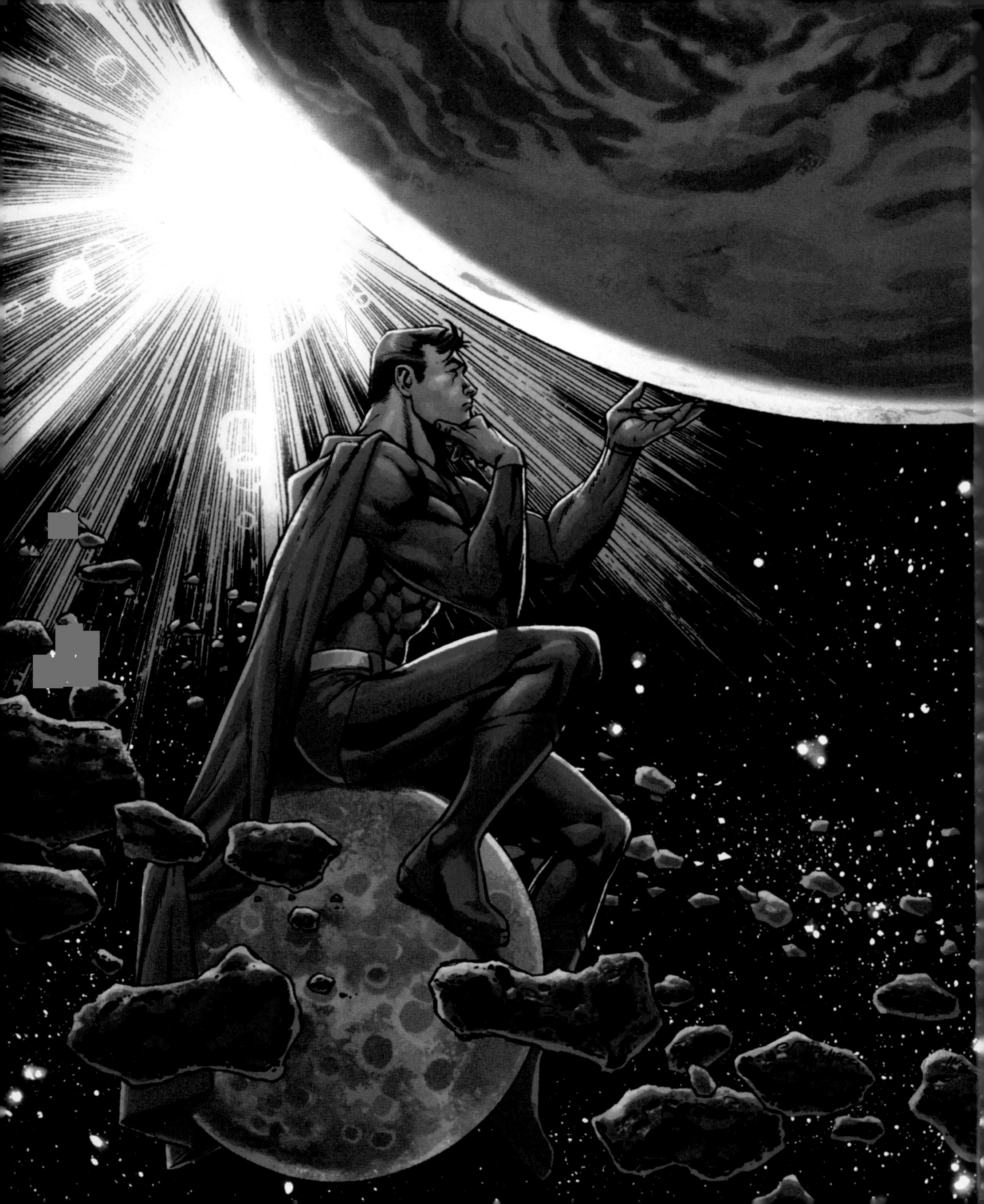